ASK
THE
BIBLE

ASK THE BIBLE

*The 400 Most Commonly
Asked Questions about
the Old Testament*

Morry Sofer

Schreiber Publishing
Rockville, Maryland

Schreiber Publishing
Post Office Box 4193
Rockville, MD 20849 U.S.A.

This book is based on the book *Questioning the Bible* by the same author

All illustrations are by Gustave Doré

Library of Congress Cataloging-in-Publication Data

Sofer, Morry.
 Ask the Bible : the 400 most commonly asked questions about the Old Testament / Morry Sofer.— 1st ed.
     p. cm.
 "This book is based on the book Questioning the Bible by the same author."
 Includes bibliographical references and index.
 ISBN 1-887563-87-3
 1. Bible. O.T.—Miscellanea. I. Title.
 BS1195.S64 2004
 221.6—dc22

                                                    2004007177

Printed in the United States of America

This book is dedicated to all those whose lives have been or will be touched by the Bible, past, present, and future, regardless of race, religion, or nationality.

Were it not for Your Torah, my delight,
I would surely perish in my affliction.

Psalms 119:92

ACKNOWLEDGMENTS

First, I would like to give thanks to the One Who Spoke and the World Was, without whom I would have nothing to say. Next, to my parents, who taught me how to speak Hebrew, the language of the Bible, my mother tongue. Then, to my teachers at Hugim and Hareali Schools in Haifa, Israel, all of whom instilled in me a life-long love for the Bible, without any dogmatism or coercion.

During my graduate work at the Hebrew Union College-Jewish Institute of Religion in Cincinnati, Ohio and in New York City, I was very fortunate to catch a ride on the last train taken by some world-famous biblical scholars. I studied with Nelson Glueck, the biblical archeologist; with Samuel Sandmel, author of scholarly books on both the Jewish and the Christian Bibles; and with Harry M. Orlinsky, editor in chief of the new Jewish translation of the Pentateuch (Jewish Publication Society), and the only Jew on the editorial board of the Protestant Revised Standard Version of the Old Testament. Here again I studied without any dogmatism or coercion.

Other biblical scholars whose work greatly influenced my thinking are Yehezkel Kaufmann and Abraham Joshua Heschel.

I would like to thank all those who went over the manuscript and gave me valuable constructive criticism, particularly Stanley and Naomi Block.

Finally, I would like to thank my wife, Hanita, my "woman of valor," for always being there for me, and my beloved children Joel, Rachel and Marla, for their support.

CONTENTS

Part Three: Writings

THE MOST QUESTIONED BOOK IN THE WORLD

For centuries people have been questioning the Bible. No other book has given rise to more questions or has been interpreted and reinterpreted more often than the Bible. This is not surprising, since the Bible has affected the lives of more people around the globe than any other book. Many of those questions reach deeply into human existence, ranging from the origins of the universe to the problem of good and evil. But just as many are less critical, dealing with such matters as: Was Noah's ark ever discovered? Or: Was Moses a Jewish slave or an Egyptian prince?

Just because some questions appear less important than others, it does not mean they are trivial. Rather, they all seem to rise from the general fascination people have always felt when confronting the biblical narrative. Whether one considers the Bible the basis of one's belief, or whether one approaches it strictly as a human document, it never fails to arouse discussion, speculation, and varying views when any question related to it comes up.

The purpose of this book is to look at the questions that have been most often asked by all sorts of people, from biblical scholars to people with very little knowledge of the Bible, and through an honest discussion, based on general and unbiased knowledge and the opinions of many scholars throughout the ages, offer sensible answers which hopefully will help the reader form his or her own view, and thereby gain a better understanding of the Bible.

The first question this book addresses is "What is the Bible?" The reason for this is that the word "Bible" means different things to different people. This volume will focus on what Jews call the Bible, and what Christians call the Old Testament, or the Hebrew Scriptures. The Jewish Bible, particularly its early parts, has been the object of intense questioning not only by Jews but also by other people in every land and in every age, perhaps more so than the rest of the Scriptures. Dealing with these questions, therefore, should be of interest to everyone.

It is humanly impossible to exhaust all the questions the Bible seems to generate. Therefore, this book does not in any way pretend to be exhaustive. One can only hope that it will shed light on some of the most frequently asked questions, and provide some plausible and informative answers and some healthy food for thought.

THE BIBLE: AN OVERVIEW

What is the Bible?

The word "bible" is derived from the Greek word "biblia," which means "a collection of writings." Actually, there are three such collections: the Old Testament, also known as the Hebrew Scriptures, or, by its Hebrew acronym, the Tanakh (39 books); the Apocrypha, or the "outside"* writings of the Old Testament (14 books); and the New Testament (27 books). Thus, the Bible represents in effect an entire library. Most commonly, however, the Bible is printed as a single volume on thin paper and in small print, so it can be carried around and be easily accessible for individual reading, study, and reflection. This applies both to the Jewish Bible, which contains only the first collection, and to Christian Bibles, which contain either the Old and the New Testaments, or all three.** The Christian versions usually use thinner paper and smaller print, since they need to hold much more text.

The purpose of the present volume is to address only the first collection, so that each time the term "Bible" is used alone, it will refer to what Jews call the Tanakh, and non-Jews the "Old Testament."

* * *

The following tables and maps provide easy reference when you read through this book and look for a quick orientation as to the contents of a particular book or a place mentioned in the Bible.

----

* So named in Hebrew, because they were excluded from the canon of the Hebrew Holy Scriptures.
** The Catholic Church accepts 11 Apocrypha books, while Protestant Bibles exclude them, since they are not part of the Hebrew Bible.

Books of the Bible

The Torah

Genesis:

Stories of creation and the early ages of humankind; stories of the Hebrew patriarchs and matriarchs; Jacob's sons go down to Egypt.

Exodus:

The Hebrew tribes are enslaved in Egypt; Moses frees the slaves and leads them through the desert where they receive the commandments.

Leviticus:

The tribes continue their nomadic existence in the desert, where they are taught the priestly laws.

Numbers:

The tribes are forged into one people under the priestly laws as they end their wandering in the Sinai desert and prepare to enter the Promised Land.

Deuteronomy:

Moses reviews the commandments taught during the exodus and prepares the people for entering the Promised Land.

The Prophets

Early Prophets

Joshua:

Moses' heir, Joshua, leads the conquest of the Promised Land. The land on both sides of the Jordan River is divided among the twelve tribes of Israel.

Judges:

After the death of Joshua, the tribes remain separated from one another, and are led by judges, some of the best known being Deborah, Gideon, Samson, and Jephthah.

Samuel:

At the time of the prophet and judge Samuel, the people ask this leader to crown a king who would unite all the tribes. The prophet selects Saul, who fails him, and subsequently David, who becomes Israel's greatest king.

Kings:

The period of the Kings of Israel and Judea lasts for about five centuries, with many ups and downs in the fortunes of Israel. The Kingdom, after the time of Solomon, David's son, divides in two, and eventually both kingdoms are destroyed, along with the Holy Temple in Jerusalem. The people are exiled to Babylonia.

Later Prophets

Isaiah:

Isaiah chastises Jerusalem after the fall of the Northern Kingdom, and predicts world peace at the "end of days." The book also includes Second Isaiah, a later prophet who proclaims the return to Zion and the renewal of the covenant.

Jeremiah:

Living during the fall of Jerusalem, Jeremiah is not able to persuade his people to repent and be saved. He predicts the return to Zion in 70 years, which happens almost to the day.

Prophets (continued)

Ezekiel:

Exiled to Babylonia before the fall of Jerusalem, Ezekiel foresees the fall of the city, and sees the return of the exiles in his dry bones vision.

Hosea:

Hosea lives before the fall of the two kingdoms. He affirms God's love for Israel, and urges his people to return to God.

Joel:

Joel predicts destruction, using the example of a plague of locust, and ends with a promise of redemption.

Amos:

Amos is the first great champion of social justice among the later prophets, although he claims he is not a prophet.

Obadiah:

Obadiah prophesies judgment on Edom and rescue for Israel.

Jonah:

Jonah, refusing to prophesy, runs away from God, drowns, and is swallowed by a big fish, but is subsequently rescued.

Micah:

A contemporary of Isaiah, Micah asks his people to "do justice, love mercy, and walk humbly with Adonai your God."

Nahum:

After the fall of Assyria in 612 B.C.E., Nahum predicts salvation for the Kingdom of Judah.

Habakkuk:

Habakkuk raises the question of the power of evil in the world, but affirms his faith in God.

Zephaniah:

Zephaniah predicts world destruction and the redemption of Israel.

Haggai:

Haggai lives during the return to Zion from Babylonian exile. He encourages the returning exiles to rebuild the Holy Temple.

Prophets (continued)

Zechariah:

Zechariah works with Haggai on motivating the returning exiles to rebuild the Temple. He provides spiritual guidance.

Malachi:

Malachi ends the prophetic era, reaffirming ethical principles for the renewed community in the province of Judah.

Writings

Psalms:

Poems, prayers, meditations, words of wisdom, arranged in 150 chapters, and attributed primarily to King David.

Proverbs:

Moral instruction based on folk widsom, attributed to King Solomon in his mid-life.

Job:

A parable about a righteous man tested by God, who has to cope with undeserved calamities and who, after various discussions with friends about divine justice, vindicates himself.

Song of Songs:

A love poem in which the young King Solomon is in love with a young shepherdess, believed to be an allegory about the love between God and Israel.

Ruth:

The story of Ruth the Moabite who, loyal to her Judean mother-in-law, follows her back to Judea after the death of her own husband, and becomes the ancestor of King David.

Lamentations:

Poems lamenting the destruction of Jerusalem and the First Holy Temple, attributed to the prophet Jeremiah.

Ecclesiastes:

Observations on the meaning of life, striking a skeptical note and advocating moderation. Attributed to King Solomon in his old age.

Writings (continued)

Esther:

A story about the rescue of the Jews in Persia during the second exile through the good offices of the king's Jewish wife, Queen Esther.

Daniel:

The story of a Jew during the Babylonian Exile who is saved from the lions' den and is granted divine visions.

Ezra:

The return of the Jews from exile under the leadership of the scribe Ezra.

Nehemiah:

The rebuilding of the walls of the Jerusalem under Nehemiah.

Chronicles:

A summary of biblical history from Adam and Eve to the time of Ezra and Nehemiah, focusing on the history of the Holy Temple in Jerusalem.

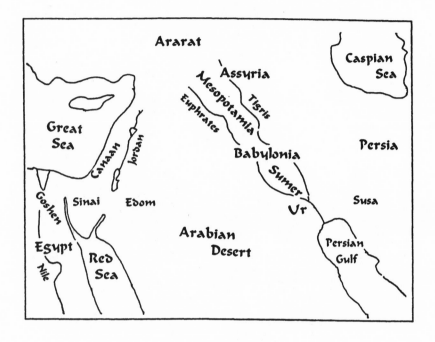

The Biblical World

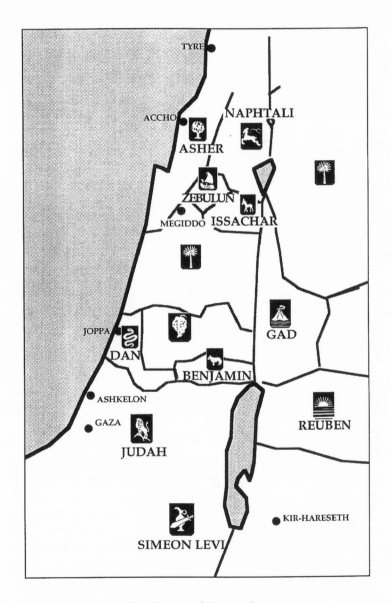

The Time of the Judges

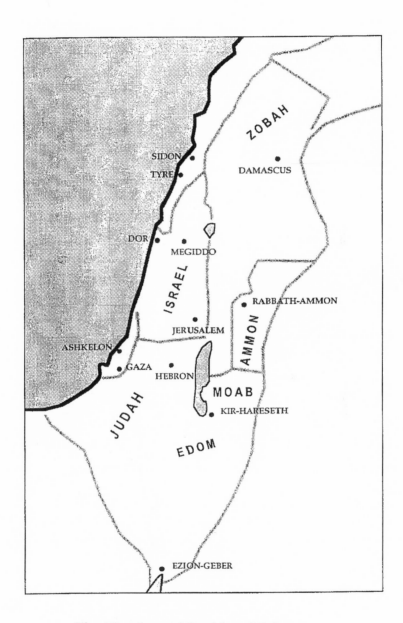

The Kingdom of David and Solomon

GENERAL QUESTIONS

Do we know the exact dates of biblical events?

Chronologies in antiquity were not accurate. Events from the time of the creation of the world to the time of Abraham have no verifiable dates, and are best regarded as biblical prehistory. From Abraham to the time of the kings of Israel dates are approximate. Thereafter, the dates become more precise. The following is a snapshot of biblical dates.

Prehistory (dates unclear)

Creation of the world
Adam and Eve
Cain and Abel
Noah and the flood
Tower of Babel

History (B.C.E.)*

1850 - Abraham leaves Ur
1700 - Jacob and his sons go down to Egypt
1280 - Exodus from Egypt led by Moses
1240 - Joshua's conquest of Canaan
1150 - 1050 - Period of the Judges
1020 - Samuel crowns Saul
1000 - David consolidates the kingdom
960 - Solomon builds the Temple
920 - Kingdom splits
870 - King Ahab and the prophet Elijah
840 - The prophet Elisha
780 - Prophets Amos and Hosea
760 - King Uzziah and the prophet Isaiah
722 - Fall of the Northern Kingdom

---

* Before the Common Era, commonly called B.C.

1

620 - King Josiah's reform
586 - Fall of Jerusalem; Babylonian Exile;
   The prophet Jeremiah exiled to
   Egypt; the prophet Ezekiel prophesies
   in Babylonia
550 - Second Isaiah
539 - Cyrus the Great conquers Babylon
516 - Return from exile; Temple rebuilt
450 - Ezra and Nehemiah; end of biblical
   era
333 - Alexander the Great defeats the
   Persian Emperor Darius III
300 - Hellenistic civilization; Ptolemy of
   Egypt rules Israel
165 - Maccabean victory against
   Antiochus; Temple rededicated

What makes the Bible a holy book?

Three world religions—Judaism, Christianity, and Islam—embrace the Bible as a holy book, or a book containing a divine message. To Jews, this message appears in the first collection of books, called Tanakh, a Hebrew acronym derived from the words Torah, Nevi'im, and Ketuvim, or Law, Prophets, and Writings. To Christians, the divine message reaches its apex in the New Testament. Finally, Muslims look upon both the Jewish and the Christian Bibles as a prelude to a separate sacred text which embodies their own divine message, namely, the Qur'an, a book of later origin than the Jewish and the Christian Bibles.

Which is the "true" Bible?

To each religion, its own Bible is the true Bible. Human experience shows that there are many ways to God. The general consensus among all three religions, however, is that there is one supreme God in the universe, no matter which sacred text one follows. By accepting the so-called Old Testament as the basis for their sacred history and religion, both Christians and Muslims accept the Jewish Bible as the original source of what they consider to be God's word.

In what way is the Bible holy to Jews?

The first five books of the Bible are called the Torah, or divine teaching. This is the holiest part of the Bible for Jews, since it contains what Jews believe to be God's law. Because of its sanctity, the text of the Torah is preserved not only in book form, but also as a handwritten scroll made of parchment, transcribed by a Torah scribe who has faithfully copied the sacred text the same way it has been done since early biblical times (there are several references in the Bible itself to the process of producing such scrolls). Every Jewish house of worship has at least one such scroll. It symbolizes the continuous link between the Jews and God since Moses first brought the Torah down from Mount Sinai.

Is the Torah the only part of the Bible holy to Jews?

The rest of the Tanakh is also holy to Jews, but does not share the same level of holiness as the Torah. Second in holiness is the middle section, known as Prophets, containing messages and teachings which interpret and expand the divine teachings contained in the Torah. Here God speaks to the people through special messengers, known as prophets, who reinforce and seek to implement the teachings of the Torah, with a strong emphasis on the ethical, rather than ritual laws of the Torah.

Finally, the third section of the Tanakh, known as Writings, shares the overall holiness of the Bible, but at a lesser level. It contains words of wisdom, inspiration, and narratives which further reinforce the words of the Torah and of the Prophets. This section does not have the supreme sanctity of the Torah itself, or even the complementary sanctity of the prophetic writings, but it is part of the aggregate of books known as the Tanakh, the text holy to Jews as well as to Christians and Muslims.

Is the Bible a book of history?

The Bible is above all a book of faith. As such, it transcends history. The events described in the Bible, however, are rooted in human history. Only the first ten chapters in the first book of the Bible deal with the question of the beginnings of the universe and the human species, which may be defined as prehistory. In Chapter Eleven the scene shifts to Babylonia, known to be the place of some of history's early civilizations, and to the ancestors of the People of Israel who originated in that part of the Ancient World. The rest of the Bible covers the history of Israel, from enslavement in ancient Egypt to the conquest of the land of Canaan, which becomes the Land of Israel, to exile in Babylonia, and the second return to the Land of Israel.

The overall framework of the biblical narrative is rooted in history. Specific individuals and specific events cannot be readily authenticated, although archeology and such major discoveries as the Dead Sea Scrolls have done much to confirm a great deal of biblical data. Thus, there are no precise records of the physical existence of an individual named Jeremiah, for example. But the prophetic message attributed to Jeremiah is clearly established as the product of the time of the fall of Jerusalem in the sixth century B.C.E.

Who wrote the Bible?

Jews differ in their views on who wrote the Bible. To some, it is the word of God, transmitted directly by God to chosen human messengers, beginning with Moses. To others, the Bible, its great moral and literary stature notwithstanding, is a human document, written through a human understanding of events, both real and imagined. According to a more recent view, the Bible was written by *divinely inspired* human authors. The first view is the traditional Jewish view. The second is the non-traditional, or secular view. The third is a modern religious view.

The divine authorship of the Bible is a matter of personal belief, not historical record, since God transcends human history. It is best left to each person's view.

Did Moses receive the Torah on Mount Sinai?

In the Book of Exodus, the second book of the Bible, there is a detailed description of how Moses went up to Mount Sinai during the wanderings of the Israelites through the desert, and was instructed by God to fashion two stone tablets, upon which he wrote the Ten Commandments. This is the first and only—and subsequently the most important—biblical text which is specifically described in the Bible as being submitted *in writing* from God to the Jewish people. During the rest of the exodus, Moses continues to impart divine spoken messages to his people, which apparently are initially committed to memory.

The first five books of the Bible, known as the Torah, are attributed directly to Moses. In the last chapter of the fifth book of the Torah, or Deuteronomy, an account is given of Moses' death. It is unlikely that Moses wrote that chapter as well.

Traditionally, the entire Bible and, for that matter, all of subsequent Jewish learning and belief, are seen as implied in the teachings of Moses. But historically speaking, Moses is only one of the authors and transmitters of the Bible, albeit the greatest one.

Who, then, wrote the Bible?

According to Jewish tradition (Pirke Avot, Chapter One), Moses received the Torah at Mount Sinai, and gave it to Joshua, who gave it to the elders, who gave it to the prophets, who gave it to members of the Great Assembly. This process covers a period of some one thousand years, during which time the biblical texts were transmitted from generation to generation. Here the word "Torah" is used in the broader sense of divine teaching, and is applied to the entire Hebrew Bible, which includes books written by prophets, scribes, kings, priests, and folk writers. Thus, the Bible is a composite work of some forty generations of a people whom the Muslims have called "the people of the Book," namely, the Jews.

Again, whether one believes the Bible to be the word of God, or merely the words of human beings, whether divinely inspired or not, most agree that it is the composite work of many people.

Who is the main character in the Bible?

God.

Who is God?

When Moses asks the mysterious voice he keeps hearing in the desert "Who are you?"—the answer is: "I Am Who I Am" (Exodus 3:14). In other words, God cannot be explained in human language or in human terms. God simply "is." The "is-ness" of God is something one has to experience, rather than be taught. To wish to know more specifics about God, such as physical features, gender, etc., is to miss the point about God as a reality transcending all human form and understanding. Differently put, how does one explain the reality of such concepts as infinity, or eternity? As finite and temporal beings, we cannot grasp a reality opposite to ours.

According to a Midrash (Jewish lore), a Roman emperor once asked a rabbi why it is that Jews can see the Roman God, namely, Jupiter, by looking at his statue, while Romans have never seen the Jewish God. The rabbi asked the emperor to look at the sun. The emperor raised his head and squinted at the sun. After a few seconds he shut his eyes in pain and said he could not keep looking.

You see, said the rabbi, the radiance of God is infinitely brighter than the radiance of the sun, which is one of God's small creations. If you can only look at the sun for a few seconds, you cannot even begin to see God with your vulnerable human eyes.

What is the biblical name of God?

There are many names for God in the Bible, and yet, God has no name at all. When Moses asks God, who are you? God responds, I am who I am. No name given. Throughout the Bible, while God is referred to as El, Elohim, Shaddai, and so on, the most common designation is YHWH. In other words, four vowels, which do not produce a recognizable sound. In Hebrew, it is read as Adonai, the Master of the Universe. St. Jerome, who translated the Bible into Latin, the common language of Christians in his day, rendered it as Jehovah. Biblical scholars today usually translate it as Yahweh. However, all of these are guesses. Jewish tradition tells us that only the high priest in the Holy Temple in Jerusalem during biblical times knew how to pronounce the ineffable (or unpronounceable) name, and only uttered it once each year, during Yom Kippur, while alone inside the Holy of Holies in the Temple.

As for all other names of God in the Bible, those are mainly descriptive terms, such as The Merciful One, God of Hosts, and so on, while El or Elohim means deity, rather than the direct name of God.

How is the God of the Bible different from all other gods?

Aside from the familiar theological and philosophical differences between the one God of the Bible and all other deities, there is one that is not often emphasized, yet seems to be of critical importance to human existence. The God of Israel stands for the rejection of human tyrants and for the assertion of human self-determination and freedom. Long before the Magna Carta, the Bill of Rights, and the French Revolution, there was the faith of Abraham, Moses, and Jeremiah. Throughout all of their stories, a common theme emerges: The Jew only accepts one ultimate authority—the biblical God who stands in direct relationship to each individual. All human authority is fallible. Even the greatest biblical leaders, Moses and David, had human failings.

The Pharaohs and the caesars of antiquity were deified. Even in our time, kings and tyrants have been called infallible. In some religions, the religious leader cannot be questioned. Not so in historical Judaism. The Jew is only accountable to God which, put differently, means to one's own conscience. The Jew prays: Our God, we have no ruler but You. And the great Rabbi Akiva said: "Happy are you, O Israel, for before whom do you cleanse yourselves, and who purifies you? Your Heavenly Father" (Talmud, Yoma 55b).

If God has no human aspects, why does the Bible use expressions like "God spoke," or "God saw?"

Maimonides, the greatest of Jewish philosophers, explains that the Bible purposely uses human terms in talking about God, so that all people, even the least sophisticated, may understand its message. God does not have a human voice, nor does God see through human eyes. However, when God chooses to send a message to someone like Moses, God conveys it through a mode of communication which a mortal like Moses can grasp.

Did God create man, or did man create God?

The French philosopher Voltaire once said: "If God did not exist, we would have to invent God." In other words, we humans have a need for God, whether or not God exists. Hence one could readily argue that God is a human invention. Nevertheless, the objective existence of God does not depend on what we do or do not believe. We humans may have created our own understanding of or belief in God, but God may still exist beyond anything we understand or believe. By accepting the notion that God is beyond our understanding, we are in effect giving up the idea of a God created by us, and accept a reality beyond ours to which our own reality is subordinated.

Can we talk "rationally" about the existence of God?

Pascal, the French philosopher and mathematician, offered a way to approach the question of the existence of God rationally. In his famous "wager," he proposed the following: Mathematically speaking, God either exists or does not exist. Hence, God's existence is a fifty-fifty proposition. He, Pascal, decides to wager on the first fifty percent, namely, that God indeed exists. If he is right, he would spend his life following the right path and gain salvation. If he is wrong, he would still be following the right path and lose nothing. Interestingly, the Talmud confirms Pascal's (a devout Roman Catholic) thinking. It states that one can keep God's commandments, or mitzvot, and live a godly life, without necessarily believing in God. In Judaism, what matters is not so much what one believes, but what one does.

Is God a male or a female?

Spinoza, the great Dutch Jewish philosopher, once said that if triangles had a God, that God would look like a triangle. Men traditionally have thought of God as male, while a growing number of women today think of God as female. The God of the Bible is neither male nor female. Gender differentiation has to do with procreation. God is not born, does not marry, and does not procreate. God has neither beginning nor end. Hence dwelling on the gender aspect of God is missing the entire point of the nature of God.

Could God make a stone so heavy even God couldn't lift?

This is clearly a trick question. If God is all-powerful, then once God made that unliftable stone, God would cease to be all-powerful. On the other hand, if God is all-powerful, God can do anything, including create such a stone. How does one wiggle out of such a seeming contradiction?

The answer is found in Jewish mysticism, or Kabbalah. According to the Kabbalah, in order to create the universe God had to "shrink," so to speak (a concept called *tzimtzum* in Hebrew), because the unlimited power of God cannot create a universe with physical limitations and limited power. This does not mean that God ceased to be all-powerful, but rather that God, endowed with all-powerfulness, could, and can, at any given moment, choose to limit the unlimited power of God, to make room for the creation of the universe.

Does the Bible believe in life after death and in heaven and hell?

The belief that after death one goes on to another form of life, or, for that matter, that one finds oneself either in a place called para- dise, or a place called hell, or in some transition place between those two, is not biblical. It evolved in post-biblical times, at which time it was adopted by Jews, and served as a key concept during the birth of Christianity.

The first human couple, Adam and Eve, was originally sup- posed to live forever in a place called Garden of Eden, which is the Hebrew term for paradise. After the two disobeyed God by tasting of the fruit of the Garden, they were banished from the Garden, and became mortal. Thereafter, the Bible makes it clear that indi- vidual life is finite. However, one's life continues through one's children and children's children.

Not unlike the ancient Greeks, who believed in Hades, the place of the shadows of the dead, the ancient Hebrews believed in Sheol, where the spirits of the dead dwelled. This was a folk belief which is not given official sanction in the Bible, as can be seen in the story of King Saul, who called on the witch of En-Dor to conjure up the spirit of the prophet Samuel from Sheol.

What does the Bible have to say about the soul?

The Hebrew Bible does not have a distinctive word for soul. In some places it refers to it as *nefesh,* which primarily means a living person, and in other places it calls it *neshamah,* which means breath. It appears, therefore, that the distinction between body and soul is not a biblical concept, but a later one.

What does the Bible have to say about the resurrection of the dead?

The resurrection of the dead is a belief which appears in Judaism around the end of the biblical period (see Daniel, p. 299). Ancient Israel believed in life here and now, and did not look to a future time when the dead would be resurrected. The prophet Ezekiel describes a vision in which he sees a multitude of dry bones scat- tered in a valley, suddenly rising and coming back to life. But he makes it clear that it is an allegorical vision, dramatizing the national rather than personal resurrection of the people of Israel who return to their land after the Babylonian Exile.

What does the Bible say about the messiah?

The word "messiah" in Hebrew is a noun derived from the verb "to anoint," hence it means "the anointed one." The kings of biblical Israel were anointed with oil by the priest, a custom preserved to this day with some present-day kings. The term "messiah" in the Bible refers to a leader who saves the nation in time of trouble, not to a divine being who revives the dead and redeems the world. Nor is the idea of a messiah central in the biblical belief system. It is not until post-biblical times that Jews begin to believe in a messiah as the future savior of the Jews and of humanity.

What about a messianic age?

The Bible does offer a vision of a future age when peace and harmony will reign throughout the world. One example of such a vision is found in the Book of Isaiah, where the prophet describes a scene at the end of days, when all nations will assemble in Jerusalem to establish a universal peace, "and shall learn war no more." The Bible, however, seems to put more emphasis on another future time, called "The Day of Adonai," akin to the later concept of "judgment day," during which time universal justice will be done. Presumably, such a time will precede the messianic era, which will signal the "end of time."

What does the Bible say about reward for good and punishment for evil?

That the world is ruled by justice is perhaps the Bible's most important concept. In ways not always readily grasped by human understanding, evil is punished and good is rewarded. However, all throughout the Bible, the question is raised as to why good people suffer so often, and evil seems to go unpunished. The Book of Job is dedicated to this question. Job, a good man, is tested, as calamities are heaped upon him for no obvious reason. When he questions God, he is told that divine will is beyond human understanding. In the end, Job is rewarded and vindicated, although his children whom he lost cannot be brought back.

What are angels?

The word "angel" in the Bible means "messenger." A biblical angel is a messenger from God, who appears to humans in human form. What are we to make today of this belief in angels, for which we have no direct proof and of which we have no direct experience? This question is best left to each person's imagination and belief. (See also the stories of the patriarchs.)

What is the biblical golden rule?

"You shall love your fellow person as yourself." According to some of the Talmudic sages, this is the main teaching of the Bible.

The story is told of a Gentile who came to Rabbi Shamai and asked to be taught the entire Torah while standing on one foot. Shamai rebuked him for his insolence, and sent him away. He then went to see Rabbi Hillel with the same question. Hillel replied: "What is hateful to you, do not do to others. This is the entire Torah. The rest is commentary. Now you are ready to start studying the Torah."

Does the Bible talk about "Chosen People?"

The term "chosen people" is probably one of the most misunderstood ideas in the Bible. For centuries, it has been taken by non-Jews to mean that Jews see themselves as God's chosen, or God's favorites, superior to other people. Nothing could be further from the truth. Nowhere in the Bible are the Jews shown to be better than other people. On the contrary, more often than not the Jews fail the trust God places in them.

According to the Torah, the tribes of Israel were called upon to commit themselves to God's commandments, and live by God's high moral standards. This did not make them superior to others in any way, but rather challenged them to live by a demanding code of conduct, so as to serve as witnesses of God's law to others.

In the post-Holocaust world, many Jews seem to feel that this "chosenness" has exacted a terrible price.

Can the Bible be understood on different levels, such as literal, allegorical, or mystical?

In the Book of Deuteronomy we are told that while "the hidden things are only known to God, the revealed things are known to us and to our children" (Deut. 29:28).

The sages of the Talmud believed that the Torah can be read on four different levels: literal (*pshat*), suggestive (*remez*), allegorical (*drash*), and mystical (*sod*). The acronym of these four words is PaRDeS, Hebrew for orchard. The Torah, then, is like an orchard where one enters and finds different kinds of meaning. Thus, for example, they took the love story in the Song of Songs to mean an allegory of God's love for Israel. They looked upon some of the writings of the prophet Ezekiel as mystical revelations, which later figure prominently in the Kabbalah. As for the story of Job, some of them argued that Job never existed, but was only an allegory.

The Bible is meant to be read on many levels, and questioned without fear of detracting from it in any way. By asking, for example, whether angels really exist, nothing is detracted from such a story as Jacob's struggle with the angel. One could argue that Jacob was struggling on the night he was awaiting the fateful meeting with his estranged brother Esau not with a supernatural being but with his own conscience. He becomes a changed person, and his name is changed from Jacob to Israel. Whether the angel was real or imagined, the nocturnal struggle resulted in a new Jacob who originated a nation called Israel.

What is the problem of reading the Bible in translation?

The words of the Bible were first uttered and transmitted over 3000 years ago in Hebrew. At that time, languages like English or Spanish did not even exist. While modern Hebrew is remarkably similar to biblical Hebrew, the meaning of many words has changed. Moreover, for a book covering an enormous amount of ground, the entire biblical vocabulary consists of slightly over 5000 words. Compare this to modern English, which consists of *over half a million words!*

Inevitably, many biblical words have more than one meaning, sometimes even five or more. The word "day" in the Bible means, besides the common meaning of a 24-hour period, also a stage, a time, an era, a destiny, and more. Moreover, there are words in the Bible that appear only once or twice, and their meaning has been lost. Then there are many words of which we only have an approximate idea.

Since people have and continue to draw their faith from the Bible, the language problem here is rather serious, as one mistranslation can change everything. One should keep all this in mind when reading the Bible in a language other than Hebrew. In the following questions, the language aspect of specific questions will be carefully considered.

What is the best English translation of the Bible?

Here opinions may vary, but in the opinion of this writer and many others, the four-hundred-year-old King James Version is still the best. The countless English translations that have and continue to appear almost every year have not improved on this early work of English literature. The King James does, however, have its drawbacks. Primarily, it is written in outmoded English, dominated by "thee"s and "thou"s. It translates the name of God, or YHWH, as "Lord," which does not convey the full meaning of the ineffable Hebrew original. And it does what all biblical translations do; namely, it guesses at the meaning of obscure words or phrases.

For the purposes of this book, the author has offered his own translation. Based directly on the Hebrew original, it does away with archaic English, as well as any gender references to God. It renders God's name as Adonai, the way it is commonly said in Hebrew, to avoid using the inaccurate English terms (Lord, Yahweh, Jehovah, etc.) Where the meaning of a word or a phrase is unclear, it is rendered in the spirit of the context in which it appears.

TORAH,
PROPHETS,
WRITINGS

PART ONE: TORAH

"Let there be light."

GENESIS:
THE BEGINNING

Did God create the universe?

The Bible's point of departure is the creation of the universe. The first sentence of the Bible reads: "In the beginning God created the heaven and the earth." Why should we believe those words? On whose authority?

The easiest answer would be, we don't know how the universe started. We have some scientific theories, but we are in the dark when it comes to the so-called ultimate questions, and may always be. On the other hand, there are many points of agreement between the biblical narrative and modern science.

In his book *God Exists*, the former Soviet physicist Joseph Davydov argues that science in our time fully corroborates the biblical account of creation. He refers to our current understanding of matter, according to which something physical can be created out of nothing. He points out to the existence of light before such luminaries as the sun existed (as suggested by Genesis). And he makes the case that, scientifically speaking, everything created must have a creator. He calls this creator the "absolute God" who created our "relative universe."

What do words like "heaven, earth, day" mean in the story of creation?

"In the beginning God created *the heaven and the earth*." Actually, the exact translation of the Hebrew is: ". . . the sky and the land." Are we to believe this statement? If so, on whose authority? Moreover, what is meant here by "heaven, sky, earth, land?"

19

Let's start with the last question. A careful reading of the entire narrative of creation reveals that two colossal events—the creation of the entire universe and of life on earth—are covered here in very few words and told in the simplest way possible. We have to ask ourselves, who is this story told to? Clearly, it is not told to space-age people like us, but to bow-and-arrow people in the early stages of human civilization. It communicates huge concepts in a language that reminds us of nursery rhymes. This is why the rabbis, centuries ago, realized that the Bible had to be understood on different levels.

The word *shamayim*, translated as either heaven or sky, is derived from the Hebrew words *sham–mayim*, meaning, "there–water." Water is the source of life.

Eretz, earth or land, means matter, or the physical universe.

Yom, or day, does not mean here a 24-hour period. Rather, it means an era, a stage of creation, which could have lasted any length of time, even billions of years. This would conform with today's cosmogony, cosmology, astronomy, and physics.

Taking the Bible strictly in its literal sense is not within the mainstream of Jewish thinking. Nor is it the predominant approach in other religions. But there are always people in every faith who prefer to be literalists.

Why does the Bible start with the story of creation?

If the Bible is a book of law and faith, why does it start with stories about the formation of the natural universe, instead of concentrating on issues of law and faith?

Most likely, because the Bible is, primarily, the history of the God of the universe, and only secondarily the story of a certain small people in antiquity called Israel to whom God turned to transmit the knowledge of the absolute universal God, which they in turn were to impart to the rest of the world.

On the face of it, the biblical story of creation is a folk myth, like so many other folk myths around the world. People have always wondered where they came from, and how it all started. Many stories about the origins of the universe and of human life have come down to us from civilizations as old or even older than the

Bible. Some of the best known are the Babylonian Myth of Gilgamesh, the stories of Greek mythology, and the Popol Vu text of the ancient Maya. In all of those stories, some superhuman being or beings create the physical universe in which we live, and fashion human beings out of the elements of this physical creation, such as earth, water, and so on.

In this context, the story of creation in the Book of Genesis in the Hebrew Bible is another myth of creation among many. But there is an essential difference between the biblical account and all others.

Most importantly, the biblical creator, unlike the one or ones in other cultures, is not superhuman, but rather meta-human, or beyond human. In other words, The nature of the creator is beyond any human experience or understanding. One can never hope to reach direct and concrete knowledge of this metahuman reality. One can only experience its creation, but not the creator per se. In this sense, the Bible puts forth the idea of a God who created the universe, but whose existence transcends the universe.

Why did God create the universe?

Unlike other stories of creation, in which the world and human beings are created for no obvious reason, or, in some cases, for the gods to amuse themselves, the story in Genesis makes it clear that creation has a purpose and a reason. This idea is conveyed in the words, repeated on each day of creation (twice on the third day): "And God saw that it was good." In other words, the universe was created in such a way that it has what one may call a moral purpose, reflecting the will of a creator who is not merely an aimless cosmic force, but one that created the universe for a reason. That purpose can be seen in the words, "Let us create a human being in our own likeness." The likeness here is not physical, since God has no physical likeness (as it is made clear in the Ten Commandments, "You shall make no graven image of what is in heaven above"). Rather, it is the likeness of God's attributes of justice and mercy, which human beings must live by.

How were man and woman created?

There are three versions of the creation of human life in Genesis. In chapter 1, Adam, meaning "person," is created as male and female. In chapter 2, Adam is first created alone from the *adamah* ("earth" in Hebrew). Finally, in the third version, God decides Adam needs a "helpmate," and takes a rib out of Adam's body from which Eve, meaning "companion," is created.

The first version, then, makes no distinction between male and female creation. Both are created at the same time. The second and third, taken together, seem more allegorical than factual. Some may look upon this version as sexist, suggesting male superiority, while others may point out to Adam's words after Eve is created from his rib: "She is now bone of my bones and flesh of my flesh," and take it as an expression of man and woman being equal.

Are all people descendants of the "first human couple?"

Human life as we know it started somewhere, at some point in time. One could also argue that it started simultaneously at different places and times. Witness the existence of different races whose cultures developed separately from each other all over the globe. Recently, genetic studies have shown remarkable similarities among human groups as far apart as China and Africa, Russia and South America. It appears that if we go far enough back in time, the entire human race is interrelated.

There is also a moral lesson implied in the biblical version of the appearance of human life on earth. There are no superior or inferior races. There are no superior or inferior people. All people stem from a common ancestor, and all have a common purpose.

Furthermore, as the Talmud teaches, each person has the right to say, "For my sake the world was created." Each person is as important before the universal law of justice as the next one, whether prince of pauper, great genius or common laborer.

Finally, destroying one human life is equal to destroying the entire universe, for each person embodies the entire work of creation.

How are we to understand the story of Adam and Eve and the snake?

> *And the snake was more cunning than any*
> *other beast of the field whom Adonai God*
> *had made. And he said to the woman:*
> *Even though God has said that you may not*
> *eat from any tree in the garden. . .*
> *So the woman told the snake: We can eat*
> *from the trees of the garden. But from the*
> *trees inside the garden God said do not eat it,*
> *and do not touch it, for you may die.*
> *And the snake told the woman: You shall*
> *not die. For God knows that on the day*
> *you eat from it your eyes will open and you*
> *will become like God in knowing good from*
> *evil.*
> *So the woman saw that the tree was fit for eating,*
> *and that it was a delight to the eyes, and it made*
> *one knowledgeable. She took some of its fruit*
> *and ate and gave some to her husband, and*
> *he did eat. And so their eyes opened and they*
> *realized they were naked, and they sewed*
> *fig-leaves together and made themselves girdles.*
> (Genesis 3:1-7)

A talking snake is not an everyday occurrence. Disobeying God, on the other hand, is. The outcome of this famous story is punishment, whereby man is to toil and earn his daily bread by the sweat of his brow, and woman is to experience physical pain at childbirth, as both become mortal. In other words, this story addresses the question of why people must toil to survive, why women must suffer giving birth, and why all human beings must die.

In short, the talking snake is not the main point of the story, and can be looked upon as allegorical. The main point is the failure of the first human couple to take responsibility for its actions. Endowed with free will, they both make the wrong choice. Paradise is lost. Human life as we know it begins.

Why a snake?

The Bible reads: "The snake was more cunning than any other animal of the field." This, then, is the reason given for why the snake is the one who succeeded in bringing about the fall of the human race. But why an animal? For one thing, because there were no other human beings around at that time. What kind of a snake was it? This is not clear, except that it had four legs which, as a result of its deceptiveness, it lost. In Medieval lore, the four-legged snake becomes Satan, the symbol of evil in the world, who constantly tempts human beings. In ancient mythologies, the snake is a powerful animal endowed with both natural and supernatural powers, as seen in ancient Egypt, in the stories of Moses and Pharaoh. A walking snake also may evoke the collective memory of ancient cultures regarding the age of large walking reptiles, or dinosaurs.

Did Adam and Eve eat a forbidden apple?

This may seem an insignificant question, but it has to do with a misreading of the Bible, which ought to be corrected. The Hebrew text does not use the word apple. Instead, it refers to "the fruit of the tree of the knowledge of good and evil." We are never told what kind of fruit it was. This is an example of an interpretation, rather than an accurate rendition of the biblical text.

Why was man given free will?

God could have created an obedient creature, who would do God's bidding at all times and never stray from the straight and narrow path. But this is not what God chose to do. God created a being in God's likeness, namely, one endowed with free will. This has been the source of both human greatness and human trouble. After Eve talks Adam into tasting of the forbidden fruit, God asks Adam why he did it. Adam shifts the blame to Eve, who in turn shifts it to the serpent. It is then that God realizes man must be taught to take responsibility for his actions, which can only be done through hardship and struggle. This may well be the main lesson of the Bible.

After World War Two and the Holocaust, many have asked:

Adam and Eve expelled from the Garden of Eden

How could God have allowed this to happen? Even now, after centuries of human experience, people still fail to realize that human actions, no matter how horrendous, are the result of human choice, not divine will.

Why is so much human history compressed into the first ten chapters of the Book of Genesis?

As was seen previously, the Bible is not primarily a book of history. It is not the intention of the author of Genesis to narrate in detail the history of the human race. Instead, the first ten chapters of Genesis set the stage for the rest of the Bible, providing us with a brief summary of the origins of humankind, seen through the perspective of God's ethical plan for the world.

Because of the brevity of this account, it seems to raise more questions than provide answers. Despite its brevity, it manages to present a large number of details which are puzzling and open to many different interpretations, as can be seen in the following questions.

Cain and Abel—the beginning of civilization?

> And Abel was a shepherd, while Cain was a
> tiller of the soil. Some time later, Cain brought
> of the fruit of the land as an offering to God.
> And Abel also brought from the firstlings of
> his flock and their fat. And God acknowledged
> Abel's offering, but not Cain's. And Cain was
> exceedingly angry. . .
> And when they were in the field, Cain stood
> over his brother and slew him. And God
> said to Cain: Where is Abel your brother?
> And he said: I do not know. Am I my brother's
> keeper?
>
> (Genesis 4:1-9)

This story regarding Adam and Eve's two sons is not so much about the actual two children of the first human couple, but rather

Cain and Abel

a morality tale about the early stages of human civilization. Abel is a shepherd, while Cain is a farmer. Here we have the beginnings of civilization, when man learns how to domesticate animals and cultivate the soil. The two activities are in conflict with each other, as one's flocks infringe upon the other's fields. Conflict results in violence which leads to murder, or the destruction of God's handiwork, created "in the likeness of the divine image." Once again, as in the story of the temptation of Adam and Eve, the one who breaks God's law fails to take responsibility for his actions. When God asks Cain, "Where is your brother Abel?" Cain replies, "Am I my brother's keeper?"

Thus, human progress does not result in moral progress. Once again the biblical text makes it clear that rivalry and conflict are at the heart of the human condition.

Who lived 900 years?

The familiar answer is Methuselah who, according to Genesis, chapter 5, actually lived 969 years. Others in this chapter, including Adam, also lived over 900 years. The chapter provides a capsule genealogy of the human race, from Adam to Noah's sons, Shem, Ham, and Japheth (Shem being the ancestor of the Semitic people; Ham of the black people; and Japheth of the Caucasian people).

The practice of assigning centuries of life to an individual of great importance is common in ancient Middle East inscriptions and tablets. One Babylonian king is said to have ruled for over 250,000 years. There is a clear intent here to aggrandize. One might wonder if the individual in question, such as Methuselah, does not in effect represent an entire dynasty, rather than one person.

Noah and the flood: history or fable?

The story of the flood (Genesis, chapter 6) points to a time of a global natural calamity, when life on earth was destroyed. The Bible looks upon natural calamities as an act of God meant to punish evil. Stories of great floods are found elsewhere in Near East mythology, and in other parts of the world. They may allude to earlier prehistorical times of great natural cataclysms. It is quite possible that the story was borrowed from Babylonian mythology and adapted by the biblical author.

To what extend this story contains any historical facts is hard to say. That a particular individual saw a great flood coming and built an ark, or an enclosed vessel, in which he rescued his family as well as species of animals and plants and started life again is quite possible.

Was Noah's ark ever found?

During the 1950s, archeologists explored the peak of Mount Ararat, where, according to the biblical account, Noah's ark landed. Embedded in the ice they found wood fragments dating back 5000 years. This gave rise to speculation that pieces of the biblical ark were recovered. There is no way of ascertaining this view, but the discovery does give some merit to this possibility.

Is there a message of hope in the story of the flood?

As human life spreads across the earth, we are told that "the inclination of man's heart is evil from an early age." The flood that destroys all human life except for Noah and his family is attributed to the prevalence of evil among people. Even after the flood, evil remains prevalent.

At first blush, one feels a sense of despair in the story. Is there really any hope for the human race? And yet we find here a message of hope as well. God makes a solemn vow never again to destroy all human life on this earth. The vow is made in the form of a covenant between God and Noah. The sign of this covenant is the rainbow that appears in the sky after the flood. This is a physical covenant of survival. It will be followed later on by a spiritual covenant between God and Abraham.

The Tower of Babel: Who was at fault?

In the story of the Tower of Babel (Genesis, chapter 11), the entire human race is concentrated in one place, presumably Babylonia (today's Iraq). All people speak the same language. Civilization makes great progress. Tall towers are built, presumably the ziggurats of ancient Babylonia. All seems well, until we hear people, who are given no specific identity, say:

> *Let us build ourselves a city and a*
> *tower reaching into the sky, and*
> *make a name for ourselves, lest we*
> *be scattered over all the earth.*
>
> (Genesis 11:4)

God decides to punish the builders by confusing their language, so that they are not able to communicate easily with one another, and as a result they stop the construction and are scattered over the earth.

Of all the biblical stories about man's origins, this seems to be the least readily understandable. Are we to take it to mean that unity and a common language lead to a folly such as building a tower reaching into the sky? Did the builders seek to become like God? Did they fail to follow God's command to spread and fill the earth? Commentaries of this story have abounded over the ages. Whatever the case may be, this story represents the culmination of the first ten chapters of Genesis, as the human race, incapable of living in harmony and unity, is scattered over the face of the earth.

What do the stories of the beginnings of human history teach us about the human condition?

The picture that emerges from the biblical stories about the early origins of humankind is not very complimentary. Quite to the contrary. "The inclination of man's heart is evil from an early age," we are told early in the book of Genesis (8:21). This is confirmed by the fratricide committed by Cain against his brother Abel (and his refusal to take responsibility); by God's decision to bring on a flood and put an end to a generation in which only one person, Noah, is found to be righteous; and by the arrogant act of building a tower reaching into heaven.

The Bible seems to suggest that, left to its own devices, humanity fails time after time. It is for this reason that God decides to turn to one specific person, namely, Abraham, to start a historical pro-

Tower of Babel

cess involving Abraham's descendants, that would lead to a re-affirmation of God's plan for humanity, namely, the pursuit of a world of justice and righteousness.

Who is Abraham?

> *And Adonai said to Abraham: Go forth*
> *from your country, from your native land, and*
> *from you father's house, to the land that*
> *I will show you. And I will make of you a great*
> *nation, and I will bless your name and*
> *make it great, and you shall become a blessing.*
> (Genesis 12:1-2)

With the stories of Abraham, starting in Genesis, chapter 11, we emerge from biblical prehistory and enter history. This is not to say that we have historical records to support the existence of a specific person named Abraham. However, the stories of Abraham, as all subsequent biblical stories, are rooted in historical fact.

Abraham is a native of the Babylonian culture that dominates much of the early stories of the Bible. According to the Midrash, when Abraham was little, he realized that the idols worshiped by the Babylonians were powerless, and grasped the existence of the one invisible God who ruled the universe. So that when, years later, he hears God telling him to leave his native land and go to a strange land where his descendants would become a great nation, he does not hesitate, and embarks on the journey to the land of Canaan.

Abraham, then, is an ordinary person with an extraordinary mission. He is a nomad who owns flocks, and who seeks grazing land and water. As will be seen in subsequent stories, he is a man of great integrity, faith, courage, and compassion. His name in Hebrew means father of a multitude (*av* = father; *ham*[*on*] = multitude).

Abraham and God: Why does God form a special relationship with one particular person?

When God created human life, God started with one man, Adam. When God orders Abraham to go to the "land that I will show you," it appears that now God is repeating the act of creation, this time not physically but spiritually. Abraham is the first man who is spiritually ready to accept God. While God speaks to Adam, to Cain, and to Noah, it is a one-way relationship. None of them is ready to accept God. Abraham is the first who not only listens to God, but also seeks to carry out God's will on his own initiative. The stories of Abraham are a series of tests of faith, culminating in his willingness to sacrifice his son Isaac. Thus, Abraham chooses God, even as God chooses Abraham.

Why does Abraham, and why do his descendants, go down to Egypt during a time of famine?

The Middle East has always suffered from water shortage. Most of the land is arid, and rainfall is scant. Crossing the Sinai Peninsula, which could be done by camel in a few days, one reaches the land of Egypt, watered by one of the world's greatest rivers, the Nile. Here water was always available, and grain was stored for future use and could be bought for money. As can be seen in the story of Abraham's and Sarah's journey to Egypt (Genesis, chapter 12), there were dangers associated with this trip, and one had to be crafty if one were to go there and come back intact.

What is God's covenant with Abraham?

In Genesis, chapter 15, God makes a covenant (*berit* in Hebrew) with Abraham, whereby God assures Abraham he would give birth to a "large nation, and his descendants will possess the Promised Land." The act of entering into a covenant is central throughout the Bible. The first covenant is made with Noah and his children, and through them with the entire human race. The gist of this covenant is God's promise not to bring on another flood, and not to destroy the human race again. The sign of this covenant is the rainbow that appears after the flood.

The covenant with Abraham is the first in a series of covenants between God and Israel. The most dramatic and central covenant in the Bible is the bringing down of the two tablets of the covenant from Mount Sinai, upon which the Ten Commandments are inscribed. Here the Israelites pledge to obey God's law. Seven centuries later, the covenant is renewed during the time of King Josiah, when a scroll of the Book of the Torah (probably Deuteronomy) is found in the Holy Temple in Jerusalem. The Jews, some of whom have become idolatrous, pledge to rededicate themselves to the Law. After the Babylonian Exile, towards the end of the biblical period, the covenant is renewed again under Ezra when the Jews return to Jerusalem from Babylonia.

Why is the covenant with Abraham repeated through circumcision?

In the first covenant with Abraham, sacrificial animals—a calf, a goat, a ram, a turtledove, and a chick—are offered. Throughout biblical times, animal sacrifices are the common form of worship. In Genesis, chapter 17, Abraham, now in his late nineties, enters into a second covenant with God. This time the sign of covenant is circumcision. Abraham has himself circumcised, and pledges to circumcise all males in his household.

Presumably, the first covenant with Abraham sufficed in terms of Abraham's own relationship with God. But a second covenant was needed to perpetuate the covenant with Abraham's descendants. The term for circumcision in Hebrew is *berit milah*, the covenant of circumcision.

Has the covenant changed? Does it still hold?

In reaffirming the covenant through the ritual of circumcision, God refers to it as "an eternal covenant." Both covenant stories make it very clear that the pact between God and Israel is immutable. Despite Israel's frequent failure to live up to the covenant, God will never revoke it. Every Jew, by undergoing circumcision, reaffirms the covenant, and then further reaffirms it by following the Torah, or the Book of the Covenant, especially the law of observing the Sabbath, which is a symbol of the covenant ("It [the Sabbath] is a sign between Me and the People of Israel forever").

Is the covenant only made with Israel?

In Genesis 17:4, God says to Abraham: "My covenant is with you, and you shall become the father of many nations." The implication here is that through the merit of Abraham, the covenant, in different variations, will be shared by other nations. This becomes a reality through both Christianity and Islam. Abraham has a son from his second wife, Hagar, named Ishmael, who is considered the progenitor of the Arab people. Islam, the predominant religion among the Arabs, looks upon Abraham as the common ancestor of both Arabs and Jews.

As for Christianity, the first chapter of the first book of the New Testament (or "New Covenant" in Hebrew), traces the ancestry of Jesus to Abraham. Christians look upon Jesus as the culmination of the covenantal relationship between God and Abraham. In their zeal to spread Christianity, Christian advocates often argued that the new Christian covenant replaced the old Jewish one. This, however, is no longer the common Christian view. Pope John Paul II made it clear in a recent address to Jews and Christians that the Catholic Church believes the covenant between God and Israel continues alongside the Christian one.

The conflicts of Abraham's household—what is the biblical writer trying to tell us?

Abraham and Sarah represent a turning point in the biblical narrative of the origins and evolution of the human race. If the Bible is a book of faith, they are the first human couple to embrace that faith and bequeath it to future generations. This makes us think of them as giants of virtue and morality.

And yet, the domestic life of this first family of faith is far from idyllic. When Sarah, well past the child-bearing age, fails to conceive, she arranges for her maid, Hagar, to serve as a surrogate. This does not go well since, once Hagar conceives, she starts slighting her mistress. Sarah deals harshly with Hagar, forcing her to flee the household, only to return once she is given divine assurance of her destiny to become the mother of a large nation. Later on, Sarah gives birth to Isaac, who is raised along with Hagar's

Hagar and Ishmael

son, Ishmael. The older Ishmael mistreats Isaac. Sarah fears Ishmael will take her son's place as Abraham's heir, and decides to send mother and son away. God tells Abraham to do as Sarah requests, and Abraham, the kindest of men, sends away his own son and his son's mother into the wilderness, where they nearly die.

What is the biblical writer trying to tell us in presenting this picture of what today we may refer to as a dysfunctional family?

Here as in all subsequent biblical stories concerning the Bible's great personalities, such as the patriarchs, kings, prophets and others, we are reminded time and again that they are mere mortals, like all the rest of us. They all have their human failings, no matter how great their faith may be or how great their achievements.

Who are the "three angels" who visit Abraham?

In Genesis, chapter 18, Abraham is visited by three men. In the following chapter we are told of two angels who go down to the city of Sodom to find out about the wickedness of the Sodomites. Since the two stories are interrelated, the three men in the first part have been taken to be three angels.

There seems to be an ambiguity in the Bible as to the nature of angels. In both Greek and Hebrew, the word "angel" is derived from the word "messenger." Thus, an angel is often an intermediary between man and God. In this story, the messengers are sent to investigate the evil deeds of men, which may result in divine punishment.

In post-biblical Judaism and in post-biblical religion in general, angels seem to occupy a much more prominent position than in the Bible itself, where their appearance is infrequent and often vague. There is a whole branch of Christian theology called "angelology," which deals with the study of angels. In Judaism, on the other hand, angels are mostly seen in the realm of allegory, rather than objective reality.

Did Abraham serve milk and meat to the "angels?"

In the story of the three messengers, Abraham serves the three strangers milk and meat, which they eat. This seems to contradict the dietary law, and has raised questions among traditional Jew-

The three angels appear before Abraham

ish commentators. Some of them have suggested that the two were not served at the same time, although the text makes it clear that they were.

The separation of milk and meat as practiced today by observant Jews is post-biblical. It is based on the biblical verse, "You shall not see the a kid in its mother's milk." The original intent of this prohibition might have been not to commit an act of cruelty. Another reason may have to do with a pagan ritual of biblical times which involved an offering of a kid seethed in its mother's milk, practiced by some of Israel's northern neighbors.

Sodom and Gomorrah—Why did Abraham question God?

In sharp contrast to Abraham's hospitality in the story of the three messengers, the people of Sodom and Gomorrah, who lived near what is today's Dead Sea, treat the two angels who go down to Sodom, and their host, Abraham's nephew Lot, with extreme cruelty. God lets Abraham know that the wicked cities of Sodom and Gomorrah are facing total destruction.

Abraham is taken aback by the thought of collective punishment. Apologizing for his audacity, he questions God. Would God destroy those cities if there were 50 righteous persons living there? What about 45, 30, 20, 10? To each figure, God responds: If such a number is found, the cities will be spared. In the end, the only righteous person found in both cities is Lot.

Questioning God's actions is not an uncommon phenomenon in the Bible. Biblical faith is not blind obedience. Since the ways of God are often unknown to mortals, questioning seems necessary. It is not questioning for the sake of rejecting divine authority or justice, rather for coming to terms with what one does not readily understand.

Did Lot's wife turn into a pillar of salt?

Fire and brimstone are showered from heaven, and the two cities of the plain go up in smoke and disappear from the face of the earth. This story may well refer to a major earthquake in antiquity, which created the volcanic valley stretching from the sources of the Jordan River in the north, to the Red Sea in the south. Today

Lot's wife becomes a pillar of salt

the site is the lowest spot on earth, with a salt lake called the Dead Sea.

Lot and his family flee Sodom while there is still time. They are commanded not to look back, lest they turn into a pillar of salt. Lot's wife ignores the order, looks back, and turns into a pillar of salt. To this day the local Arabs point to a pillar of salt overlooking the Dead Sea and call it Lot's Wife. It is possible that when she looked back she fell behind, and was overtaken by the earthquake.

The would-be sacrifice of Isaac: Why did God test Abraham?

In Genesis, chapter 22, we are told:

> *And God tested Abraham. . . and said:*
> *Take your son, your only son, the one*
> *you love, and go to the land of Moriah*
> *and sacrifice him as a burnt offering*
> *on one of the mountains which I will*
> *show you."*
>
> (Genesis 22:1-2)

Abraham does as he is told, and at the last minute God stops him from doing it.

No story in the Bible is more vividly engraved in the collective memory of the Jewish people than this one. Not only Jews, but also Christians and Moslems have puzzled over it throughout the ages. The Danish philosopher Soren Kierkegaard found it to be the great ethical puzzle of the Bible. What exactly was the purpose of such a brutal human sacrifice?

The Bible does not answer this question. It is left to us to ponder it. A common view has it that Abraham was living at a time and place where human sacrifice was common, and therefore did not question such a divine command. The purpose of the story is to show us that human sacrifice is not part of the Jewish faith.

But questions still linger. Why subject a mere flesh and blood to such a horrendous ordeal? Actually, one could ask the same question about the central story of Christianity, namely, the crucifixion.

Over the ages, Jews have felt that the many misfortunes that befell them—the persecutions and the massacres of the past 2000 years—are repetitions of Isaac's sacrifice.

The sacrifice of Isaac

We only know one thing: Abraham was put to the supreme test by a God we cannot question, and prevailed. He thus became worthy of transmitting the faith to future generations.

Why does God send an angel to stop Abraham rather than do it directly?

God (Elohim) tests Abraham's faith by ordering Abraham to slaughter his own son. Abraham obeys, and at the critical moment, we are told, "an angel of Adonai" calls out to him and tells him not to harm his son.

According to rabbinic tradition, the name Elohim represents God's attribute of justice, while Adonai represents mercy. Here, God's mercy overcomes God's justice. As for the role of the angel in all of this, one could argue that once the decree was lifted, there was no longer any need for God to intervene directly in this matter.

Why did the patriarchs marry strictly within their own extended family?

Abraham sends his servant back to Babylonia to find a wife for his son, Isaac, from among his relatives in the "old country." Isaac's son, Jacob, also goes back to Babylonia to find a wife. What was the reason for this? Why didn't the patriarchs look for wives among the local people in Canaan, where they spent their days?

The answer may be simple. In the tribal system in antiquity, as the case is even today in tribal societies around the world, one married within one's own tribe. One, however, could go a step further and refer to God's promise to Abraham: "To you and to your descendants will I give this land." The implication here is that Abraham's descendants, rather than become part of the nations around them, had to maintain their own identity in order to fulfill their mission, later on defined in the Bible as one of becoming "a light unto the nations."

What is the role of Isaac in the stories of the patriarchs?

The Bible sandwiches Isaac between two towering giants: his father, Abraham, and his younger son, Jacob. Isaac himself is dis-

missed with a few short episodes, which portray him as a passive—certainly not impressive—personality. He first appears as
the willing victim in the sacrifice story. A marriage is arranged for
him with his cousin, Rebecca. They beget twins—Esau and Jacob.
Although Jacob grows up to be a righteous person, while Esau is a
wild and unruly hunter, Isaac prefers his firstborn, for he brings
him back venison from the hunt to feast on. When Isaac lies on his
deathbed, and it is time to confer the blessing upon his successor,
Rebecca manages to fool her husband, who has gone blind, and
makes him believe Jacob is Esau, so that the blessing is given to the
younger brother without Isaac realizing what he is doing.

Interestingly, his name, Isaac, is derived from the Hebrew word
for laughter (his mother, Sarah, gave him this name because she
claimed God was making fun of her, enabling her to become preg-
nant in her nineties). One almost hears the author of the Isaac stories chuckle as he tells them.

What are we to make of all of this? Once again, as in the stories
of Abraham's and Sarah's domestic life, the Bible makes it very
clear that the patriarchs and matriarchs, when all is said and done,
are flesh and blood like everyone else. One of them, namely, Isaac,
is not even particularly impressive. He happens to be Abraham's
son and Jacob's father. Thus he links between the founding father
and the nation-builder. This may be his entire claim to fame.

If Jacob was destined to have the birthright, why was Esau born first?

When Rebecca conceives and is about to give birth to twins, she
can tell the two are struggling in her womb. When she asks God
for the reason, she is told:

> *There are two nations in your womb,*
> *And two people will separate from*
> *your bowels.*
> *One shall be stronger than the other,*
> *And the elder shall serve the younger.*
> (Genesis 25:23)

The younger turns out to be Jacob, who is born second. And
yet Jacob is destined to give rise to the Jewish people, so that

Rebecca at the well

God's promise to Abraham may be fulfilled, and therefore he needs the birthright. Why, then, wasn't Jacob born first, so as to carry out God's promise? Why did his mother, Rebecca, have to cheat his father, Isaac, to secure the birthright for him?

Jacob's life, both in this instance and in subsequent stories, seems to be a great object lesson regarding human life and God's ways. Just because God has made a promise, it does not mean man can sit back and let God do all the work, so to speak. As was explained earlier on, God gave man and woman free will, or the ability to think and make decisions. That makes them partners with God. Nothing in life is easy. While Jacob was destined to become Abraham's heir, the birthright was not handed to him outright. He had to earn it. And earn it he did.

Why does Jacob see a ladder in his dream?

When Isaac sends his son, Jacob, to find a wife among his relatives in Babylonia, Jacob, who, we are told, had chosen a sedentary, non-nomadic life ("dwells in tents"), is facing a very hazardous journey. In a state of high anxiety, he dreams and sees a ladder leading up to heaven, with angels of God going up and down. God then appears to him as the God of his forebears, Abraham and Isaac, and proceeds to renew the ancestral promise.

The vision of the ladder is one of the most intriguing scenes in the Bible. It is rife with symbolism. Here Jacob meets God for the first time, albeit in a dream. Jacob is not yet ready to meet God directly. A ladderful of angels provides contact between his earthly place and heaven. God has let down that ladder. Now Jacob is ready for his mission. The ladder is the symbol of human-divine contact. In time, it will become a ladder of prayers, through which Jacob's descendants will seek to reach God.

Jacob's struggle with the angel: Can man defeat God?

After years of absence from Canaan, Jacob returns with his wives and children to his native land. Once again, Jacob is experiencing great fear. His brother Esau is seeking revenge. Rumor has it he is about to attack Jacob. The younger brother fears for his life

Jacob's struggle with the angel

and for the welfare of his family. Once again, he is having a most unusual nocturnal experience:

> *And Jacob was alone, and he wrestled*
> *with a man until dawn. And he saw he*
> *could not prevail, so he touched the*
> *socket of his thigh, and the socket of*
> *Jacob's thigh was out of joint, as he*
> *wrestled with him. And he said: Let me*
> *go, for it is dawn. And he said: I won't let*
> *you go unless you bless me. And he said:*
> *Let me go, for it is dawn. And he said:*
> *What is your name? And he said: Jacob.*
> *And he said: No longer will your name be*
> *Jacob, but Israel. For you have struggled*
> *with God and with men and you have*
> *prevailed.*
>
>   (Genesis 32:24-28)

This short biblical episode bears a profound message. God does not expect us to simply worship God, but rather to wrestle with our belief in God. There is nothing easy about truly believing in God. It is, rather, a constant struggle. Jacob's faith on the night prior to his encounter with his estranged brother was shaken. After all the bad experiences he has had since his youth, could he still trust God to keep the ancestral promise? The mysterious stranger can be understood in various ways. One way is—Jacob actually struggled with his own faith.

Why are the Jacob stories so full of deception?

The name Jacob in Hebrew means, among other things, to follow someone stealthily, connoting deviousness. Jacob's entire career seems to be a crooked road, full of twists and turns. His mother has to cheat his father to secure the birthright for her son. He himself exploits his brother's hunger to buy the birthright from him. His father-in-law-to-be, Laban, cheats him and gives him his older daughter, Leah, for a wife on his wedding night, instead of

Rachel, his beloved. His sons lie to him when they sell his favorite son, Joseph, as slave to the Medianites, and tell old Jacob the boy was devoured by a wild beast. And on and on.

Why would the author of the Bible, who surely did not wish to put his (or her) own people in a bad light, present us with such a series of uncomplimentary stories about his (or her) own ancestors? Why not at least soften them a bit, make them sound better?

One could speculate about this at great length. But whatever one's answer may be, it is clear that the author is holding up a mirror to Jacob's life and shows us what the human experience is all about. As adults, we know that we do not live, nor have people ever lived in a fairytale world. Life is not an easy road free of pitfalls.

Other cultures may have embellished the history of their founders and ancestors. But the Bible is always brutally honest. Domestic strife, sibling rivalry, human conflict, all are part of life. Jacob is not an angel. He is a man whom destiny yanks by the scruff of his neck, and tosses across the ancient world, all the way to Babylonia, back to Canaan, and later to Egypt, putting him through many trials and tribulations. He marries two sisters and two of their maidens, and begets twelve sons and one daughter, whose lives are far from calm and uneventful. Out of the turmoil of his and his large family's life a people is born who will go through centuries of great glory and even greater tragedies, leaving their mark upon the human race unlike any other people in the world. The mirror held up to Jacob's life is the same mirror held up to the history of the entire human race, and, to repeat, it is told with brutal honesty, which is the hallmark of the biblical narrative.

What is Jacob's place in biblical history?

Of all the three patriarchs, Jacob's name appears most often during the one thousand years of biblical history. This is because Jacob, particularly under his new name, Israel, embodies the Jewish people. The trials and tribulations of Jacob's life and the trials and tribulations of the Jews from the time of Moses to the end of the biblical period and beyond, are the same. Like Jacob, the Jews have often found themselves wrestling with their belief in God.

Like Jacob, they have wandered from land to land. Like Jacob, they have dreamed great dreams, found great fulfilment, and suffered great adversity. When God says to Jacob: "Fear not, O my servant Jacob, for I am with you," every Jew can hear God talking to the entire Jewish people.

While Jacob is one of three patriarchs, or fathers, of the Jewish people, there is something personal about his fatherhood. He remains in the collective memory of the people as the one everyone can identify with on a personal level, not as a remote patriarch, but as an immediate parent.

The matriarchs and other women in the Bible: What do we learn here about the role of women in ancient Israel?

It is a mistake to talk about the Bible as a sexist book. Rather, the Bible is an honest book, which reflects a sexist time in history (which certainly did not end with the biblical period). But one thing can be said about the four matriarchs of Israel—Sarah, Rebecca, Leah, and Rachel. They were certainly not passive women who simply did their husbands' bidding. They all played decisive roles in promoting their own children according to what they believed was God's plan. They all stand tall alongside their husbands not merely as helpmates, but as leaders in their own right, who played a critical role in the formation of what became the people of Israel.

While Jacob became the symbol of the Jewish people, his beloved Rachel became the archetypal mother of Israel. When the Jews go into Babylonian Exile, the prophet Jeremiah evokes Rachel with these words: "A voice is heard on the high hill, wailing and bitter crying, Rachel is crying for her children, refusing to be consoled. Refrain from crying, and wipe the tears from your eyes, for your children will yet return to their land."

Are the ancestors relevant to our life today?

The ancestors are relevant to believing Jews, Christians, and Muslims alike. Each of the three faiths looks upon them as the founders of their faith, and they are equally revered by all three. In Jewish liturgy, the patriarchs and the matriarchs are invoked in the

Rachel and Jacob

Amidah, the main prayer of Jewish liturgy. In asking God's mercy and favor, Jews do not mention their own merits, for they find themselves falling short of being worthy of divine grace. Rather, they remind God of the merits of the ancestors, which have the power to elicit such grace.

But even for the secular, non-believing Jew, the ancestors are role models par excellence. They are certainly relevant to our life today, and will always be. Their contribution is timeless, and their example will always shine bright as the ones who put humanity in contact with the one absolute God of the universe. Their stature can never diminish.

Jacob's Children: A rowdy bunch or worthy nation builders?

Actually, both. The stories of Jacob's twelve sons and one daughter cover the entire gamut of human behavior, from the best to the worst. Sometimes they band together. Sometimes they betray one of their number because of sibling rivalry. Sometimes they disobey their father, Jacob, and sometime they go to great length to protect him.

When Jacob is about to die, he gives a blessing to each of his sons. Each blessing, or prediction, is different. To some he promises great victories, and to others defeats. Some are put in a favorable light and some in a bad light. In typical biblical fashion, old Jacob does not mince any words.

In the following questions we will find out more about the behavior of the founders of the tribes of Israel.

Did Joseph have a coat of many colors?

Joseph was Jacob's favorite son, born to his favorite wife, Rachel. Jacob, we are told, makes a special garment for Joseph, commonly known as "the coat of many colors." The Hebrew text, however, makes no mention of colors, but refers to it as a "striped shirt." Here again, as in many other instances in biblical translation, we have a mistranslation. The meaning of the words literally translated as "striped shirt" was never clear. Some thought it was a "sleeved garment" (both the Midrash and the Catholic *Jerusalem Bible*). Others, a garment with more than one color (Rashi). And the King James translation (1611) gives us "coat of many colors."

This is a perfect example of the many linguistic problems associated with the Hebrew text of the Bible. Even in early post-biblical times many words were not clear, and had to be interpreted. In the course of time, the problem became further complicated because of the multitude of interpretations. Anyone who claims to know exactly what Joseph's garment looked like, is simply overreaching.

Joseph and his dreams: What is the point of these stories?

Few stories in the Bible are more intriguing, more exciting, richer in meaning, than Joseph's dreams. The other thing that can be said about those dreams is that there is a certain strangeness, or "otherness," about them. They take us away from the main thread of the stories of Genesis.

Beginning with his early dreams, in which he sees his brothers as sheaves of wheat standing in the field and bowing to him, and as the sun and the moon representing his father and mother, and eleven stars representing his brothers, bowing to him, to his later dreams in which he sees the seven lean cows devouring seven fat cows, and so on, there is a common element running through them: Joseph has his father's gift of predicting the future, a gift which his brothers do not seem to have.

Joseph successfully puts this gift to practical use. After his brothers gang up on him and sell him as a slave to a passing caravan of Ishmaelites (and here we have poetic justice, for Ishmael was sent away by Joseph's great-grandfather, Abraham, and now the beloved son of Abraham's grandson becomes a slave of Ishmael's descendants), he finds himself in Egypt, where his gift of dream interpretation (which even Freud greatly appreciated) gets him out of jail and into Pharaoh's court, where he becomes second to the king.

What manner of man is Joseph?

Joseph is destined to save his family from famine. While he is serving the Pharaoh as chief economic advisor, there is famine in the land of Canaan, and Jacob's sons go down to Egypt to look for bread. Joseph sees them, but they do not recognize him. He does not repay them for what they had done to him, and instead becomes their patron.

Thus, Joseph, who started out as Jacob's spoiled child, has becomes Joseph the savior. Later tradition refers to him as Joseph the Righteous. He is undoubtedly one of the most engaging personalities in the Bible.

Joseph is the first prototype in history of a Jew who gains a prominent position in a foreign land, and directly or indirectly benefits his people. In the Bible the next great example is Queen Esther, who saves the Jews of Persia. In more recent times one could point to Disraeli, Queen Victoria's prime minister, who wrote about Jewish rebirth in the Land of Israel; or to Kissinger, Nixon's secretary of state, whose mediation after the Yom Kippur War started the process that ended the state of war between Israel and Egypt.

Jacob's family in Egypt: Who were those Hebrews who went down to Egypt?

While we have many historical records of Egyptian history during the time of Jacob, we do not have records of Joseph, Jacob or any Hebrew or Israelite people living in Egypt, later enslaved, and finally liberated by a Moses. This raises the question: Are these stories historically true? And if so, who were those Hebrews?

It shouldn't surprise us that we do not have records of those foreigners who came to Egypt at that time, driven by hunger. Egyptian history during that period was very turbulent, with foreign invaders conquering the land, and later defeated and expelled. The records preserved by subsequent Pharaohs were the ones they cared to preserve, while all other records most likely were destroyed.

But we do have documentation of two ancient people coinciding with the time of both Abraham and Jacob. The first were called Habiru, a name very close to Hebrew, who wandered through Babylonia and Canaan. The second were called Hyksos, who invaded Egypt at the time of the Patriarchs and among whom the name Jacob in various combinations (Jacob-Baal, Jacob-El, Jacob-Har) appears several times. As in many other biblical narratives, the overall historical background can be authenticated. The specific individuals and events, on the other hand, are yet to be substantiated.

Joseph sold to the Ishmaelites

Jacob's last words to his sons: What is the message?

On his death bed, Jacob assembles his children and foretells their future. He settles scores with Reuven, Levi, and Simeon, who failed him. The last two, Jacob predicts, will be scattered among the other tribes. He promises the most glorious future to Judah, whose tribe will give birth to King David and will lend its name to historical Jewry and to Judaism. He sings the praises of the remaining sons, some of whom would become warlike and others sedentary. And he gives a special blessing to Joseph, his favorite.

Jacob's words to his sons seem to be a mixture of retribution, accurate prediction of the future (particularly in the case of Judah), and, once again, a show of favoritism to his beloved Joseph. In time, the twelve tribes will establish the united kingdom of Israel, and later split between Judah in the south and the ten tribes of Israel in the north. The ten northern tribes will be taken into exile and disappear forever. Judah will remain, become the Jewish people, and return to its land and its capital, Jerusalem, first from Babylonian Exile in the sixth century B.C.E., and then a second time in our time, in the twentieth century.*

Why is Jacob's last wish to be buried in the Land of Canaan?

The Book of Genesis ends with Jacob's children taking their father's body to be buried in the family burial cave in the Land of Canaan, and with Joseph exacting a promise from his brothers that he too will be buried there. While the brothers continue to live in Egypt, and while Joseph continues to serve as Pharaoh's high official, the message here is clear: All of Jacob's sons look upon their sojourn in Egypt as temporary. In time, their descendants will return to the land which God had promised to their ancestor, Abraham.

When the Israelites are finally liberated from Egypt by Moses some 400 years later, they take Joseph's bones with them to be buried in the Promised Land. This example which the patriarchs

---

* When the State of Israel was first being formed in late 1947, the first name chosen for the new state was "Judah." By May 1948, when the Declaration of Independence was signed, the name had officially been changed to "Israel."

Jacob and his progeny go down to Egypt

offer of their attachment to the Land of Canaan establishes the bond between the land and the people, whereby this land is perceived not only as a geographical location, but also as the spiritual home of their descendants for all time.

Exodus:
Bondage and Redemption

What is meant by "the Pharaoh who did not know Joseph?"

The Book of Exodus begins with a brief paragraph according to which the generation of Joseph and his brothers was now gone, while their descendants who remained in Egypt grew so numerous they filled the entire land. The second paragraph begins with the words: "A new Pharaoh arose in Egypt who did not know Joseph." Who was that Pharaoh? Is it possible that he had no knowledge of such an important personality in recent Egyptian history as Joseph, the second to the king?

According to Rashi, the leading biblical commentator, this new Pharaoh pretended not to have heard of Joseph. In the time of Joseph, the seventy members of Joseph's family who came down to Egypt did not pose any threat to the throne. But a few generations later, the Israelites grew into a large community that was perceived as a danger to a new ruler, as foreign groups that settled in the Land of the Nile often came to be looked upon.

What is it about the words "who did not know Joseph" that provides a portent regarding future events in Jewish history?

What makes events and concepts in the Bible so powerful and archetypical is the fact that they repeat themselves throughout history. Jews have a 3600-year history of living in countries where they greatly contribute to the welfare of the land, until one day a new ruler comes along who chooses to forget all the

Joseph reveals himself to his brothers

good they had done, and turns on them with disastrous results. Some of history's best examples start in the Bible itself, first here and later in the Book of Esther, and continue under both Christianity and Islam, the most notorious being the Crusades, The Spanish Inquisition, the expulsion from Spain, the Chmielnicki massacres in Eastern Europe, and most recently the Holocaust in Nazi-occupied Europe.

What did the Hebrew slaves build in Egypt?

The new Pharaoh says: "Let us outsmart them, lest they multiply and, in case of war, join our enemies and fight us and go away." The Hebrews become enslaved, and they begin to do slave labor, building Pharaoh the towns of Pithom and Ramses.

Popular imagination has associated this statement with the building of the pyramids, which is not what the Bible says. In fact, the three great pyramids near Cairo had already been in place for centuries when Jacob's descendants came to Egypt, and other pyramids long predate Abraham. The two towns that are actually mentioned here are modified by the word *miskenot*, translated by Onkelos (Aramaic) as treasure houses, by the King James Version as treasure cities, and by contemporary Jewish and Christian English versions as either store-cities, or garrison cities.

The name Ramses in this context refers to Ramses II (called the "Great"), the enslaving king of that time, who left us great monuments to admire, testimony to his great power and achievements.

Was Ramses a great king or history's first Hitler?

Depends on who you talk to. When he orders all newly-born Hebrew males to be cast into the Nile, he acquired the distinction of being the first in a long line of tyrants who sought to commit genocide against the Jewish people. What is amazing about Jewish history, is the fact that each tyrant, from Pharaoh to Hitler, who turned on the Jews, found his doom in one way or another.

Who was Moses, a Hebrew child or an Egyptian prince?

Some of those who sought to demythologize the Bible, have

argued that the infant who was raised in Pharaoh's court was actually an Egyptian prince who later became the Hebrew liberator. There is no way of proving or refuting this idea. According to the Bible, Moses was born to a Hebrew couple who belonged to the tribe of Levi. We can leave it at that, or we can look for more seemingly sophisticated theories. None of this would change the fact that, to quote the modern Hebrew philosopher Ahad Haam, what matters is that Moses has had an impact on every generation of Jews to this day. Whatever his origin, this fact cannot be altered.

What are the elements of historical authenticity in the baby Moses story?

First, the name Moses, given to him by Pharaoh's daughter who found him after his mother and sister, rather than drown him as decreed by the Pharaoh, deposited him in a papyrus basket and sent him afloat on the Nile. The name Moshe, Hebrew for Moses, is akin to the Egyptian name Mashu. Second, the physical elements of the story, such as the description of the banks of the Nile, the basket and the materials it was made of, and the general atmosphere of the story, all are clearly Egyptian.

Was Moses a terrorist or a freedom fighter?

When Moses grows up, he goes to see his enslaved people. He sees an Egyptian striking a Hebrew slave. This becomes the defining moment of his life. He strikes the offender, presumably a taskmaster, who drops dead. Seeing that there are no Egyptians around, he hides the body in the sand. The next day he sees a Hebrew striking another Hebrew. He turns to the evil Hebrew and asks him why he is doing it. To his surprise, the man replies, Are you going to kill me as you have killed the Egyptian? Moses realizes the word has spread concerning his action. It is his first exposure to the sad fact that the Hebrew slaves are not animated by the spirit of freedom, but rather accept their oppression. He runs to the Sinai desert to hide, and his role as liberator begins.

Was the killing of the Egyptian an act of terrorism or the first strike for freedom? The cynical reply of our time is that one

Baby Moses is found by the daughter of Pharaoh

person's terrorist is another person's freedom fighter. Moses was acting purely on his natural instinct to help the weak and to protect his people. What the Bible doesn't tell us is whether the man died accidently (by falling off a scaffold, for example), or whether Moses struck him with an intent to kill. In either case, what the story points to is that the liberation from Egypt did not happen peacefully. It took a series of plagues culminating in the death of Egypt's firstborn males to pry the Hebrews out of slavery.

Moses in the desert: What do we make of this story?

Moses starts a new life in the desert. He marries the daughter of the priest of a desert tribe called Medianites, and becomes a shepherd. Quite a transformation for someone who grew up in Pharaoh's court. Also, by doing so he becomes a nomad like his ancestors Abraham, Isaac, and Jacob. Additionally, he becomes acquainted with that part of the ancient world where he will later on lead his people during the exodus. It is in this desert that God will first speak to him, then later on give him the Ten Commandments. It is in this desert that he will turn a mob of slaves into a covenanted nation, ready to enter the Promised Land.

The burning bush: fact or fiction?

> And Moses was tending the flock of his
> father-in-law Jethro, the Medianite priest,
> and he took it to the back side of the
> desert, to the Mountain of God, in Horeb.
> And the angel of God appeared to him inside
> the fire in the bush, and he saw that the
> bush was burning but was not consumed.
> (Exodus 3:1-2)

A burning bush not consumed—fact or fiction? Most people's first reaction will be: fiction. Not so quick. Let us examine the situation on the ground.

Moses grew up in Egypt, also a desert land. But there is a vast difference between nature alongside the Nile and nature in an inland arid desert. Moses is now discovering new desert phenomena he had never seen before, including a burning bush that is not consumed. Not so strange as it may seem, if we consider the fact that there is an oily bush growing in the Sinai desert that is known on hot summer days to catch fire, which feeds on the outer layer of oil without burning the leaves and the branches.

Later, during the exodus, Moses will be told by God to strike a rock with his cane to perform the miracle of the water gushing out of the rock. Here again we have a very simple explanation from the life of the Bedouins in the Sinai desert. They are known to search for water by tapping rocks with their canes. When they hear a hollow sound they know there is a rainwater deposit inside the rock. By hitting it harder they make a hole out of which the water comes gushing forth.

What is the deeper meaning of the burning bush?

The burning bush is the great turning point in the Bible, as well as in world history. God's original pledge to the ancestors was a promise for the distant future. It had to be taken on faith. Now, as the young and inexperienced Moses is confronting God for the first time, it is no longer a matter of a future dream, but rather present reality. Back in Egypt there is an oppressed Israelite nation. Liberating it from slavery is mission impossible. Moses is a fugitive from Egyptian justice. He has neither a military force nor any skills to become a liberator. Yet God says to him: "Go, I send you to Pharaoh, the most powerful ruler in the world. Bring my people Israel forth from Egypt."

Moses replies: "Who am I that I may go to Pharaoh and take the Israelites out of Egypt?"

God reassures him: "For I will be with you."

Moses asks God for his name, so he may tell the people who has sent him. God responds: "I am who I am. Tell the Israelites, 'I am who I am' sent me to you."

Does God really expect slaves who are surrounded by huge monuments of the Egyptian gods to believe Moses and his nameless God?

Freedom is not easy to come by. One must pay a price. But once the idea of freedom is tossed into the world, it cannot be stopped.

What do we make of Moses' refusal to go?

Moses is looking for all sorts of excuses to get out of performing this mission. God endows him with magic powers to help him gain self confidence. He tells him to throw his cane on the ground, which then turns into a snake. He tells him to pick up the snake, which then turns back into a cane. But Moses is not convinced. He finally tells God he is a stutterer, and cannot be a spokesperson for his people. Losing patience, God tells Moses to appoint his brother Aaron as his spokesperson, while he, Moses, will continue to receive God's word.

How did Moses become a stutterer?

We now learn that Moses was a stutterer. According to Jewish legend, when baby Moses was brought into Pharaoh's court, the king suspected he was no ordinary baby, and that he would bring about the king's downfall. He decided to put the infant to the test, and placed before him two bowls—one filled with gold and jewels, and the other with glowing coals. The foundling extended his hand to the first bowl, but the angel of God moved his hand to the one with the coals, to show that he was an ordinary baby, more attracted by the glow of fire than by the cold glint of gold. As he burned his fingers, Moses put them in his mouth and burned his tongue, thus becoming a stutterer.

Why does God harden Pharaoh's heart?

God tells Moses: "I will harden Pharaoh's heart so he will refuse to let the people go." This statement raises two questions: First, if one is created with free will, why would God interfere with one's attitudes and decisions? Second, why is God making Moses' job more difficult than necessary?

The most likely answer is that God has allowed Pharaoh to behave in any way he chose. But at a certain moment God decides Pharaoh has gone far enough in oppressing the Israelites, and it is time for retribution. God knows Pharaoh will not repent, and therefore decides to make the monarch's heart even harder than it is, so that the punishment may be even greater. Not only would such punishment—the Ten Plagues—result in Pharaoh finally letting the Israelites go, but the meaning of it will sustain their faith in God for all time.

Why does God seek to kill Moses?

Moses takes his family and begins the journey back to Egypt. On the way, we are told, he meets God, who seeks to kill him. Consequently, Moses' wife, Zipporah, circumcises her son, and calls him "bridegroom of blood." Only then does God relent.

What is the point of this rather strange story? As happened with the patriarchs before him, it appears that Moses' faith is being tested. There is an interesting parallel here between the would-be sacrifice of Isaac and the spontaneous act of Moses' son being circumcised by his mother. Now that God was revealed to Moses, it is Moses' turn to affirm his own faith in God by the act of circumcision. In other words, Moses must earn the right to carry out God's will, rather than passively serve as God's messenger.

Is Moses' God the same as the God of Abraham, Isaac, and Jacob?

Once Moses begins his mission of asking Pharaoh to let the Israelites go, God appears to him and assures him God will live up to the covenant made with the patriarchs. God proceeds to tell Moses that the patriarchs only knew God as El Shaddai, but did not know the ineffable, ultimate name of God, YHWH.

Was, then, the God that appeared to Moses the same as the God who appeared to the patriarchs? According to Jewish tradition, each person has a different personal view of and relationship with God. While God remains one and the same, the way each person and each generation grasp God is different. Also, the relationship between God and successive generations and individuals evolves, never remaining the same. While God's relationship with Abraham, Isaac, and Jacob was an individual, one-on-one relationship, in the case of Moses it is a collective relationship, meant to encompass all Israelites. As such, it is not an "El Shaddai" relationship, but rather a YHWH one, a name which represents the ultimate reality of God.

The Ten Plagues: Random punishment or poetic justice?

Moses and his brother Aaron go to see the Pharaoh, and ask him to let the Israelites go so that they may worship their own God. Pharaoh refuses, and Moses inflicts the first plague on the land of

Egypt. This scene is repeated ten times, starting with turning the water of the Nile into blood, continuing with covering the land with frogs, then lice, flies, cattle pestilence, boils, crop-destroying hail, vegetation-destroying locust, darkness, and finally culminating in the killing of all Egyptian firstborn males. Only this last plague, which also kills Pharaoh's firstborn son, finally prompts the king to release the Hebrew slaves.

On the face of it, this seems to be random collective punishment. But if seen in the context of Israel's sojourn in Egypt it begins to make sense. First, the turning of the water of the Nile into blood. Pharaoh's decree to cast the Hebrew newborn male children into the Nile had stained that river with their innocent blood. Now God reminds Pharaoh of this atrocity by causing the water of the mighty river, the source of life for Pharaoh's kingdom, turn into blood. The plagues that destroy crops and cattle remind us that Joseph, the ancestor of the Israelites, had saved Egypt from famine by predicting the seven lean years which would have depleted Egypt of wheat and livestock. Instead of showing gratitude to his descendants, "A new king arose in Egypt who did not know Joseph." Finally, the killing of the Egyptian firstborn males was in retribution for the killing of the newly-born Hebrew male children. Now, with the punitive measures commensurate with the crimes the Egyptians committed against the Israelites having come full circle, the road to freedom is open.

Why did the Israelites leave Egypt at night?

Egypt finally reaches the breaking point, and the Hebrew slaves are told to leave the country immediately, before there is nothing left of Egypt. The Israelites do exactly as they are told. They do not even wait for their bread to rise in preparation for the long journey, but rather take along flat bread (hence the custom of eating matzo on Passover). They stay awake and leave during the night.

Why such haste? As we shall see later, Pharaoh will soon have a change of heart, and pursue them into the desert. They realize they have a small window of opportunity to become free, and they are not about to miss it.

Moses and Aaron before Pharaoh

Is the exodus from Egypt the key event in Jewish history and the Jewish faith?

The answer is yes to both. That night 3300 years ago marks the birth of the Hebrew nation. It also marks the birth of a community of faith that will have an unparalleled impact on civilization. Every major Jewish prayer, every Jewish holiday, and particularly the Sabbath, all mention and commemorate this event. To every Jew to this day, the celebration of the going out of Egypt, known as the Passover Seder, is the most important celebration of the Jewish year. Jews who have given up nearly every other Jewish observance, are still drawn to the Seder table, as, for that matter, are many non-Jews as well.

The splitting of the Red Sea: natural or supernatural event?

As was mentioned before, Pharaoh has a change of heart. He gathers his chariots and pursues the Israelites into the desert. The Israelites, standing on the bank of the Red Sea, are not able to cross, and find themselves in mortal danger. God intervenes, instructing Moses to lift his hand over the sea, whereby a strong desert wind starts blowing and does not stop until the sea is split in half, enabling the Israelites to walk through.

Few events in the Bible have given rise to more speculation and theories than the splitting of the Red Sea. It is entirely possible that the so-called Red Sea, which is a narrow finger of water separating Egypt from the Sinai, was at the time on the verge of drying up at the spot where the Israelites stood, and that a strong desert wind accelerating the drying-up process. As in the stories of the burning bush and the drawing of water from the rock, here too we may have a natural desert phenomenon rather than the monumental and supernatural event people throughout the ages have imagined it to be.

Was the Red Sea actually red?

The name Red Sea is another example of a mistranslation of the Hebrew original, in this case *yam suf*, or Sea of Reeds. Since no one has bothered to correct this mistake, the name Red Sea has

Death of the Firstborn of Egypt

stuck to this body of water surrounding the Sinai Peninsula and stretching south between Saudi Arabia and the African coast.

The Song of the Sea—praise to God while ignoring the destruction of human life?

After the Israelites cross the Red Sea, Pharaoh's chariots reach the shore and begin to come across, when the water returns and drowns them. Moses and the Israelites burst into song, and praise God for destroying their enemies and granting them salvation:

> *Then Moses and the children of Israel*
> *sang this song to Adonai saying:*
> *I will sing to Adonai who became greatly exalted,*
> *Horse and rider were cast in the sea.*
> *God is my strength and my song,*
> *And God became my salvation.*
>   (Exodus 15:1-2)

The rabbis, who later on coined the expression "When your enemy falls do not rejoice," made the following comment: When God heard the Song of the Sea, God reminded the Israelites (or actually the angels in heaven, who also joined in the singing) that the Egyptians are also God's children, and therefore rejoicing in their death was inappropriate.

Slave mentality and the slave experience: what is the Bible trying to teach us?

Having just witnessed one of the greatest miracles of all time, which resulted in their rescue, the Israelites nonetheless begin their desert wandering by bitterly complaining to Moses about their dire condition. They will continue to complain every day for forty years, to the day Moses dies and the exodus comes to an end. In fact, the reason for such long wandering is the realization that the generation that came out of Egypt was not prepared to possess the Promised Land, and became the "desert generation" that would die in the wilderness before the new generation, born in freedom, was ready to start the conquest of Canaan under the leadership of Joshua.

Pharaoh's army drowning in the Red Sea

Clearly, the generation that came out of Egypt could not shake off its slave mentality, no matter how hard Moses tried. But there seems to be a profound reason why Israel's descendants underwent a long period of bondage during their 400-year stay in Egypt. Before God was ready to give the Israelites the law of justice and mercy, they had to experience oppression on their own flesh, so as to understand the plight of the weak, the downtrodden, the enslaved. Several times in the Bible Jews are reminded to pursue justice and mercy, "for you were slaves in the land of Egypt." Slavery was not a badge of shame for the enslaved, but rather for the enslaver.

What do the words "Kingdom of priests and a holy nation" mean?

The time has come for the Israelites to receive God's law. Now God begins to address the entire people through Moses. God tells Moses to tell the Israelites the following:

> *If indeed you obey Me and keep My*
> *covenant, you will become My own*
> *treasure from among all the nations, for*
> *the entire earth is Mine. And you shall*
> *become a kingdom of priests and a holy*
> *nation."*   (Exodus 19:5)

God is about to give the Israelites the Ten Commandments, the cornerstone of monotheistic morality. By accepting these commandments, each and every Israelite becomes a priest, or a servant of God, and the entire community of Israel becomes a nation consecrated to observing God's law, hence a "holy nation." To this day, this is the Jewish understanding of Israel's mission in the world.

What is the meaning of the Ten Commandments?

The Ten Commandments read as follows:

1. *I am Adonai your God who brought you out of the Land of Egypt, from the house of bondage.*

2. *You shall have no other gods before Me.You shall make
   no graven image or likeness of what is in the heaven above
   or on the earth below or in the water under the earth. . .*
3. *You shall not take the name of Adonai your God in vain. . .*
4. *Remember the Sabbath day to keep it holy. . .*
5. *Honor your father and your mother. . .*
6. *Do not commit murder.*
7. *Do not commit adultery.*
8. *Do not steal.*
9. *Do not bear false witness against your neighbor.*
10. *Do not covet your neighbor's wife, slave, maid, ox, ass,
    or anything that belongs to your neighbor.*

(Exodus 20:2-14)

The first striking thing about the Ten Commandment is their brevity. Ten brief statements that encompass the entire ethical code, the relationship between the human and the divine, and one's relationship with oneself as well as with others.

The first commandment defines monotheism, the belief in one God. For Jews, this God is the one who took them out of the house of bondage in Egypt.

The second inveighs against making false gods, and warns about the repercussions of such backsliding.

The third teaches reverence for God.

The fourth refers to the cornerstone of Jewish belief and observance, namely, the Holy Sabbath, the sign of the covenant between God and Israel, and one of the oldest pieces of social legislation in the world (at a time when other nations have not yet learned the meaning of a weekly day of rest, and worked its slaves and working class to death).

The fifth teaches respect for and devotion to one's parents, who next to God are one's most sacred beings.

The sixth forbids committing murder.

The seventh forbids adultery.

The eighth forbids stealing.

The ninth forbids perjury.

The tenth forbids coveting.

The law of the Hebrew slave—what is the intent?

Of the 613 commandments in the Bible, it is interesting to note that the first that follows the Ten Commandments has to do with slavery. Here as in all subsequent biblical laws, we must keep in mind that these laws date back over 3000 years, long before the Magna Carta, the French Revolution, and the Bill of Rights. Seen against their place and time, they appear in a totally different light than if we were to hold them up to today's democratic standards. In fact, many laws which, at first blush, appear to be backward and restrictive, in effect are quite advanced for their time and only restrict excessive punishment, rather than promote it.

In the case of the Hebrew slave, the Bible sets a time limit on keeping such a slave, namely, six years, to be freed on the seventh year. The underlying idea here is that a Jew is not meant to be a perpetual slave. If, however, a Hebrew slave refuses to go free on the seventh year, he undergoes the ritual of having his ear pierced against the doorpost of the house, and is kept for good.

"An eye for an eye and a tooth for a tooth"—what is the intent of this law?

This law can be seen in two different ways. Either as a primitive law of blind retribution, or a sophisticated law restricting the extent of the retribution exacted from the offender, such as going so far as killing him for blinding the victim in one eye. Seen against the typical behavior of that time, the second possibility in more likely. It is worth noting that Rabbi Hillel, living two centuries after the biblical period, modified this law to mean that "an eye for an eye" means paying the monetary value of that lost eye rather than blinding the offender in one eye.

Animal sacrifices: pagan rites or legitimate manifestation of biblical monotheism?

Among the first laws given to the Israelites at this early stage of their national history, laws related to the ritual sacrificing of animals figure prominently. We have seen references to animal sacrifices as far back in history as the time of Cain and Abel, and according to Jewish legend, Adam was the first to offer a sacrifice to God. We know from historical records that animal sacrifices were common in all ancient civilizations, including ancient Greece and Rome. Some old cultures, such as the Maya in Central America, still practice animal sacrifices to this day.

This raises the question of whether the ancient Hebrews simply copied animal sacrifices from their neighbors, or whether in ancient Israel animal sacrifices took on a different character. Two leading Jewish philosophers, namely Yehudah Halevi and Maimonides, disagree on this issue. According to Halevi, animal sacrifices were and remain an integral part of the Jewish religion, and should be restored when the Holy Temple in Jerusalem is rebuilt (a view upheld to this day by many Orthodox and even Conservative Jews, but rejected by Reform Jews). Maimonides, on the other hand, sees them as a compromise with paganism, having served their purpose in their day. Maimonides and other scholars, such as Abrabanel, point to the fact that while at first the Israelites sacrificed everywhere, once they were settled in their land and had their Temple in Jerusalem, the Temple became the only place where sacrifices were allowed, so as to restrict this practice. It should be pointed out that besides providing a spiritual outlet for the person offering the sacrifice, it was a source of sustenance for the priests in the Temple.

Later prophets, like Amos and Isaiah, condemn the excessive offering of sacrifices, which often replace the practice of justice and mercy. And as early as the time of the Second Temple the sages began to advocate the replacement of sacrifices with prayers, which in effect became the norm once the Temple was destroyed by the Romans.

The golden calf: why did Aaron let the people betray Moses?

When Moses goes up to Mount Sinai to receive the Ten Commandments, the Israelites, camped at the foot of the mountain, feel abandoned and decide to build a golden calf reminiscent of an Egyptian deity which many of them might have worshiped while enslaves in Egypt (or perhaps because they yearned for the

Moses brings down the Ten Commandments

flesh pots of Egypt which they had left behind). They turn to Moses' brother, Aaron, who is the highest authority among them during Moses' absence, and state their wish. Aaron agrees, and fashions the golden calf they requested.

While the liberation from Egypt and the crossing of the Red Sea were the high point in the early history of the new nation, the building of the Golden Calf which signaled a return to paganism was the low point during that time, and a portent of much backsliding through the Bible and beyond. The philosopher Ahad Haam talks about the essential difference between the priest, represented by Aaron and his descendants, and the prophet, represented by Moses and his spiritual heirs. While the priest is a man of compromise, seeking to accommodate people's wishes, the prophet, who always has a clear idea of what God's will is, never compromises what he or she believes to be right.

The episode of the Golden Calf has serious repercussions. At first God wishes to annihilate the Israelites and start a new nation, with Moses as the founding father. Moses is barely able to talk God out of it, and not before three thousand of the evil-doers are killed does God's anger subside. In the meantime, the two tablets Moses had brought down from Mount Sinai are smashed by an irate Moses, and now the lawgiver must go back to the mountain and fashion a second pair of tablets.

Did Moses have horns?

When Moses comes down from Mount Sinai a second time, we are told that his face radiates and sends forth beams. Now the Hebrew verb form *karan*, or "radiated," is the same as the one meaning "to grow horns." Poor knowledge of Hebrew among Christian scholars writing in Latin resulted in the incorrect use of the second option, and thus artists like Michelangelo painted and sculpted Moses as having horns grow out of his head. Once again, the pitfalls of translating the Bible into another language, altering its meaning.

Why does the Book of Exodus conclude with the blueprint of the Tabernacle?

While the Israelites were trekking through the desert, they began to create a prototype of their future society and religious life. The portable tabernacle which they built in the desert became the model for the future Holy Temple in Jerusalem. This was a matter of grave importance, seeing how easily the people slipped back into pagan practices. Every last detail of the Tabernacle had to be spelled out, so as to centralize and clearly define the rituals and the forms of worship to be practiced by the entire people.

LEVITICUS:
LAWS AND STATUTES

What is the essence of the Book of Leviticus?

The drama of the first two books of the Bible, Genesis and Exodus—beginning with the stories of creation and focusing in particular on miracles like the splitting of the Red Sea—has had a tremendous impact on people's imagination. Leviticus, on the other hand, is about as eventful as a book of laws and statutes can get. It goes into great detail dealing with such areas of religious law as sacrifices, priestly laws, laws of purity, dietary laws, leprosy, forbidden sexual relations, idol worshiping, holidays and festivals, and it admonishes the believers against failure to follow those laws. It is quite possible that Moses let his brother Aaron compose this book, or that later generations of Aaron's priestly descendants put it together. There is something about its style and spirit that clearly sets it apart from the other four books of the Torah, also known as the Five Books of Moses, or the Pentateuch.

Why are the sacrificial laws so prominent in the Book of Leviticus?

Ministering at the altar where the sacrifices were offered was one of the main functions of the priests in biblical times. This, in fact, was the main form of worship. The synagogue and public prayer do not appear until the end of the biblical period, and become the official form of worship after the final destruction of the Jerusalem Temple. The Book of Leviticus focuses on this main priestly activity, as well as other matters pertaining to the priests, such as laws of purity, the prohibition of idolatry, the proper observance of the holidays, and so on. Sacrifices, furthermore, were the priests' source of livelihood, since, for the most part, they did not have their own farms, livestock, or property.

What is the meaning of the biblical dietary laws?

Chapter 11 in Leviticus is dedicated to the enumeration of animals one may or may not eat, depending on whether or not the animal is "clean." Thus, animals with a cloven hoof who chew their cud, such as a cow, are clean, hence can be eaten. A camel, on the other hand, which chews its cud but does not have a cloven hoof, is unclean. A pig, which has a cloven hoof but does not chew its cud, is unclean. Fish must have fins and scales to be clean. A catfish does not have scales, hence it is unclean. Birds of prey are not clean, since they eat carrion.

The full intent of biblical dietary laws is not always clear. The common wisdom in Judaism has been that the underlying reason for allowing or forbidding a certain type of food primarily concerns health, although this is not always apparent, nor does the Bible suggest it. The stated reason in the Bible is that the dietary laws help their adherent to be holy, even as God is holy. In other words, the reason for those laws is spiritual, not physical.

One important aspect of the biblical dietary laws is the prohibition of eating meat without thoroughly draining the blood. The stated reason given for this is that the soul resides in the blood, and one is only allowed to eat the flesh, not the soul. Here again, the reason is spiritual, not physical.

One thing is clear from common experience and from historical records: The dietary laws have a great deal to do with cultural identity. The very act of allowing and prohibiting certain foods creates a group identity, which binds the people together. The exclusion of certain animals, most notably the pig, had to do with their inclusion in pagan rituals. The biblical prohibition against seething a kid in its mother milk has to do with this practice as a pagan ritual among the Ugaritic people who resided to the north of Israel, in today's Lebanon.

What are the implications of "seething a kid in its mother's milk?"

This phrase, which appears three times in the Bible, is responsible for the fact that observant Jews to this day have practiced a complete and total separation of meat and milk products in their diet. This separation is such a major aspect of post-biblical dietary observance, that one feels compelled to take a good look at it and understand it better.

There is, however, no clear reason for this major prohibition. Why does it follow from not "seething a kid in its mother's milk" that no milk and meat products can be consumed in the same meal? Does the Bible mean to say that seething a kid in another she-goat's milk is permitted? What about the above-cited explanation of the pagan ritual? Or the common explanation that it is an act of cruelty to boil the offspring of an animal in its own mother's milk?

No easy answer here.

How do the biblical dietary laws differ from the laws of kashrut today?

Over the ages, the Jewish dietary laws have grown more and more strict and complex. This has followed the Talmudic injunction of "building a fence around the Torah." In other words, safeguarding the biblical laws by adding new restrictions to ensure compliance. Thus, an elaborate system of separating milk from meat products at a meal was added, including separate sets of dishes, with yet another separate set for the festival of Passover, when dietary observance becomes even stricter.

In the Bible, the dietary laws are linked with the laws of the sacrificial offerings. Those offerings are discussed at great length in the Bible. They form the basis of the biblical religion. Food in the Bible is looked upon as something sacred. It can either be clean and holy, or unclean and unholy. An integral part of the process of being a holy people is growing, offering, and consuming food according to strict laws. One is not allowed to harvest the corners of one's fields. Those must be left for the poor. One must bring the first-born of one's flocks and herds to the priest as an offering. And one must eat clean food, consumed in moderation, and give of one's excess to the needy.

After the destruction of the Second Temple, animal sacrifices in Judaism came to an end. Much of the religious energy that had been expended on the sacrifices was now turned to the dietary laws. This is why such matters as separation of milk and meat became more prominent.

It has been proven that the observance of the dietary laws has served as a very strong means of preserving Jewish identity. However, there are many levels in the observance of such laws. Some Hasidic sects have added their own restrictions, going beyond the general practice. Some kosher-keeping Jews, on the other hand, such as Conservative Jews, have eased some of the restrictions, as in the case of fish which have scales when young but lose them later on, hence are considered kosher when young. Jews in the Arab world (Sephardi) have been generally more liberal in their dietary observances (as in the case of foods allowed on Passover) than European (Ashkenazi) Jews. Reform Judaism has left it to the individual Jew to decide on his or her level of dietary observance.

Regardless of any group or individual observance of dietary laws, food continues to play a central part in Jewish faith and culture, as it does in other cultures. The Sabbath and each of the holidays have their own foods. On the other hand, the holiest day of the Jewish year, namely, Yom Kippur, is distinguished by total fasting, or the absence of food, which is the highest level of spirituality.

Why is pork a forbidden food in the Bible, and even more so today?

While the Bible makes no distinction between the prohibition of pork and other types of meat such as rabbit or horse, the pig has become the main symbol of forbidden food.

This is not because of anything intrinsic about pork, bacon, or ham, but rather because of historical and cultural reasons. For over two thousand years, the pig has come to symbolize paganism and pagan antagonism against the Jews. In the Book of Maccabees we are told that the Greco-Syrian King Antiochus, an archenemy of the Jews, placed a pig in the Holy Temple in Jerusalem to humiliate the Jews and to establish his Greek state religion. In refusing to eat pork, Jews are making a cultural statement that transcends the religious one. While in the eating of different kinds of fish and fowl there may be some gray areas, the eating of pork is clear and unequivocal, since it is a reminder of the martyrdom Jews have undergone throughout the ages in affirming their faith.

Yom Kippur and the "scapegoat"—what is the meaning of this ritual?

In Leviticus Chapter 16 we find a description of the atonement ritual associated with the holiest day of the Jewish calendar, Yom Kippur, or the Day of Atonement. Here the high priest performs a ritual of animal sacrifices unlike any of the other sacrifices performed during the rest of the year. In addition to the animals that are sacrificed, namely, an ox, a ram, and a goat, a second goat is not sacrificed but rather kept alive. At the end of the sacrificial ritual, the high priest lays his hands over the live goat and confesses all the sins of Israel, whereupon the goat is taken outside the walls of Jerusalem and pushed over a cliff, so that its death atones for all the sins of the people of Israel. This custom gave rise to the familiar expression "scapegoat."

What is important about this particular ritual is not so much the goat as the fact that the Jews who came to seek atonement at the Temple in Jerusalem on Yom Kippur were not passive spectators at this ceremony. Rather, the text goes on to say that on that day "You shall afflict yourselves," which is taken to mean "You shall fast," making it a day of spiritual dedication, a "Sabbath of the Soul."

Which laws are especially emphasized in the Book of Leviticus?

While at first look the Book of Leviticus appears to be primarily a book of ritual laws, in reality it is a different kind of laws which, while not dwelled upon at length, are given special emphasis and reveal the deeper meaning of the Jewish faith. Those laws, in a word, are ethical, pertaining to the realm of moral conduct and social justice.

Examples:

You shall be holy for I, Adonai your God am holy.

Fear you mother and father, and keep my Sabbaths, I am Adonai your God.

Leave the corner of your field to the poor and to the stranger.

Do not swear falsely in My name.

Do not oppress your neighbor, do not rob him, and do not delay the day-laborer's pay overnight.

Do not curse the deaf and do not make the blind to stumble.

Do not distort justice. Do not favor the poor or the rich, but rather deal justly.

Do not gossip, and do not stand idly by your brother's blood.

Do not hate your brother in your heart, but rather rebuke your neighbor.

Love your neighbor as yourself.

NUMBERS:
THE BIRTH OF A NATION

What is the Book of Numbers about?

Beginning with the census of the tribes of Israel in Numbers, Chapter 1, there is a new feeling in the biblical narrative. The first two years of wandering in the desert are over. As the third year begins, the Israelites have begun to organize themselves as a cohesive union of tribes, each taking its place during the many stops in the desert for the remaining 38 years of wandering at a precise location around the portable temple, or Tabernacle, which becomes the tangible symbol of God's presence among the people. The highly elaborate system of sacrifices and ritual practices is now in place, as it will be during the next thirteen centuries.

Special attention is given in the Book of Numbers to the Tribe of Levi, which is the only one that does not have a territorial tribal presence and is not allowed to own land, since its members are assigned ritual and spiritual duties, assisting the priests, who are Aaron's descendants.

Who are the Levites?

When Jacob gives his final blessing to his children, he condemns his sons Simeon and Levi for disobeying him and for committing acts of violence, and predicts that they will be scattered among the other tribes. Later on, when the Israelites rebel against Moses and build the Golden Calf, the Levites redeem themselves by siding

with Moses, a member of their tribe, helping him fight the evil-
doers.

Consequently, the prediction concerning the scattering of the
Levites among the other tribes turns into a blessing. Unlike the
descendants of Simeon, who simply disappear among the other
tribes, the Levites become religious functionaries, supported by
all the tribes (through tithing). They reside in designated cities,
and perform such duties as officiating in the Holy Temple and
teaching the law.

How historical is the census of the Israelites?

What is most striking about the description in the Book of Numbers of the census of the Israelites, is the great detail in which it is
reported, with precise data given as to the number of battle-wor-
thy males of each tribe. This also applies to the minute description
of the Tabernacle and its ritual objects, and all other ritual and or-
ganizational data in this book.

Was all this information preserved for centuries until it was finally written down, or is this a reconstruction of historical data
long after the fact, in which some of the numbers and physical
details were guessed at?

There is no way of knowing. What seems most likely is that
during their long stay in the desert (and many nations in the ancient Middle East and elsewhere started their career as nomads
and only at a later stage became settled), the Israelites formed a
cohesive community bound by priestly laws, which anticipated a
future settled existence, and conducted itself in keeping with this
eventual reality in mind. Many details, however, may have been
added later on.

The bitter water test—Barbaric or humane?

In Chapter 5 we are told that if a man suspects his wife of having
had sexual relations with another man, whether he is right or not,
he is to bring her to the priest, who will perform the test of giving
her to drink "bitter water." If she is innocent, nothing would happen. If she is guilty, her belly would swell and her hips would
drop and "she would be a curse among her people."

The most natural reaction is to look upon this test as a barbaric ritual which discriminates against women. Seen, however, in the context of its time, it is just the opposite. The first thing this ritual accomplishes is to take the law out of the husband's hands and put it in the hands of the priest. In ancient societies, and still today in some parts of the world, a husband who suspects his wife of adultery is allowed to punish her severely, even kill her. Secondly, the so-called "bitter water test" gave the priest a great deal of latitude as to the outcome of the test. It is quite possible that he might investigate the case and draw his own conclusions. In short, what at first may seem to be a barbaric ritual, may very well have been a humane treatment of an age-old problem.

The Nazirite—what was his role in Israelite society?

Numbers Chapter 6 is dedicated almost in its entirety to the rituals pertaining to the Nazirite. Here too, as in the case of the bitter water test, an age-old human phenomenon is being regulated so as to integrate it in the organized community.

The Hebrew word *nazir* is derived from the verb "to practice abstinence." The Nazirite's counterpart in Christianity is the monk. There must have been many types of Nazirites in ancient Israel. Here their status is regulated by biblical law, prohibiting them from cutting their hair and drinking wine. One famous Nazirite in the Bible is Samson, whose fabled strength resided in his long hair. Another famous Nazirite was King David's son Absalom, whose long hair, after he rebelled against his father, became his undoing, when it got caught in the branches of a tree as he was pursued by David's soldiers.

The Priestly Blessing—the beginnings of prayer?

The chapter concerning the Nazirite ends with God telling Moses to tell Aaron how the priests are to bless the people.

The words are familiar to anyone who has attended synagogue services:

> *May God bless you and keep you;*
> *May God's countenance shine*

upon you and be gracious to you;
May God's countenance be lifted
upon you and grant you peace.
                    (Numbers 6:24-26)

This is one of the most ancient blessing in Jewish history. It shows the beginning of public prayer at an age when sacrificial offerings were the main ritual activity. Here, the prayer is offered by the priests, with the people playing a passive role. In time, this and other prayers will be incorporated in the prayer ritual and practiced not only by the priests and the Levites but by all Jews.

Did Moses celebrate Passover?

In Chapter 9 we are told that Moses is commanded to celebrate the holiday commemorating the exodus from Egypt. This in effect becomes the Jewish Feast of Freedom, the most widely observed of all Jewish holidays to this day. As in all other communal celebrations, here too the central ritual is the offering of a sacrifice, in this case the paschal lamb. It is to be consumed with unleavened bread and bitter herbs, as it is done to this very day (with a shankbone symbolically representing the sacrifice).

It is entirely possible that the celebration of Passover started while the Israelites were still wandering through the desert. In fact, the Israelites start celebrating as soon as they cross the Red Sea and witness Pharaoh's chariots sinking in the sea.

Why were the Israelites punished for eating meat?

During the wandering in the desert described in the Book of Numbers, the Israelites spent much time complaining, murmuring, or even rebelling against Moses. Moses, we are told in this book, "was the humblest of all men." This did not help much, nor did the miracles he kept performing. The people seemed to have forgotten their great suffering and oppression at the hands of the Egyptians, and only remembered the fleshpots of Egypt. It became quite clear to Moses they were not ready to conquer the Land of Canaan and survive as a sovereign people.

At one point (Chapter 12) the people become obsessed with their desire to eat meat, which they recall eating in Egypt. God sends large numbers of quail their way, and they proceed to gorge themselves with the flesh of that bird. God is angered by their gluttony, and kills a large number of them.

Why such an excessive reaction? One way of explaining it is that one of the requisites for entering the Promised Land was self control, being able to curb one's appetite. Otherwise, one could not hope to prevail against stronger enemies. Gluttony in the Bible is a sin. In times of national emergency it can be disastrous.

Why was Miriam punished?

In Chapter 12 Moses is set upon by his own brother and sister. Both come to him and complain about his marriage to the "Cushite woman." They then appear to change the subject, and tell Moses that they too are endowed with the spirit of prophecy, and why does Moses behave as though he alone hears the voice of God? God, we are told, hears them, and is angered.

This brief account is quite puzzling. Who is the Cushite woman? The Hebrew word connotes dark skin. Moses is married to Zipporah, a Medianite. A Cushite woman would more likely be an Ethiopian, hence another woman. Moreover, what has this got to do with Aaron and Miriam also being endowed with the spirit of prophecy?

God proceeds to tell Aaron and Miriam that while they may be endowed with the spirit of prophecy, their brother Moses has achieved a higher level of prophecy, since God speaks to him, and only to him, face to face, while to them God only appears in visions and dreams. God then punishes Miriam with leprosy. Moses intercedes on her behalf, and after seven days she is cured.

It is hard to believe that the same Miriam, who had saved Moses' life when he was born, who led the women in celebrating the victory at the Red Sea, had sunk so low. The storyteller here does not regale us with details. As in many of the desert stories, including the punishment of Moses, much is left unsaid, leaving us to wonder why such excessive punishment, and reminding us that we can never hope to fully understand the will of God.

The spies bring back their report

Was the report of the Hebrew spies correct?

God tells Moses (Chapter 13) to select spies from the twelve tribes of Israel and send them to the Land of Canaan, to gather intelligence about the nature of the land and its residents, in preparation for the forthcoming invasion.

After forty days (a very common number in the Bible), the spies return with a dire report. The land, they say, devours its inhabitants alive. It is inhabited by giants who make the proposition of conquest unthinkable. The people who listen to this report are greatly frightened, and decide to appoint a leader for themselves to take them back to Egypt. The only dissenting view is expressed by Caleb the son of Jephunneh, of the tribe of Judah, and Joshua the son of Nun, of the tribe of Ephraim.

Once again, it becomes clear that the people are not ready to enter Canaan, except for the above-mentioned two. It is interesting, though, to note that two opposite views are expressed by the spies. The history of the Land of Israel shows that both views are correct. It has indeed been a land which exacts many sacrifices from its inhabitants, claiming a heavy toll in human life. It has also been a land of great bounty, both materially and spiritually. In short, a land of great extremes, good and bad.

What is the Red Heifer?

In Chapter 19 we are told of a ritual which has given many a biblical interpreter more than a few sleepless nights. In Hebrew it is known as *parah adumah*, literally red cow, better known as the Red Heifer.

According to Rashi, the Bible calls this ritual a *Hukkah*, namely, a statue whose reason is not disclosed, reminding us that God's will is unfathomable. Briefly, a red heifer is selected and taken outside the camp, where it is entirely consumed by fire. The priest takes its ashes and uses them for purifying an unclean person, as in the case of one who touches a dead body. A clean person, however, who comes in contact with the ashes, is defiled. Thus, the ashes of the red heifer defile the clean and purify the unclean.

This paradox cannot be readily explained. All we know is that

The brass serpent

the red heifer ritual was hardly ever carried out, if only for the reason that it was always difficult to find one that was "without blemish," and the rare ones cost a great deal of money. The red heifer remains one of the Bible's most puzzling rituals.

The brass serpent—magic or authentic Judaism?

The Israelites resume their circuitous journey through the desert, continue to complain, and ask to go back to Egypt. This time God punishes them by sending poisonous snakes that bite them and cause many to die. The people cry out to Moses to save them from the snakes. God tells Moses to mount a snake on a pole, so that the snake-bitten can look at it and be cured. Moses proceeds to fashion a brass snake mounted on a pole, which helps cure the snake bites.

One, of course, is reminded of Adam and Eve's snake in Genesis, and of Moses turning his staff into a snake before the Pharaoh. In all three stories, one fails to see a connection to the letter and spirit of the Jewish faith. Rather, they all smack of magic and paganism. Endowing a snake with magic powers is not Jewish. In all three instances, it seems as though evil is being fought with evil. Six hundred years later, in the time of King Hezekiah (see page 163), we are told that the brass serpent was destroyed, since it became the object of pagan worship. In medieval thought, as evidenced in the commentary of the great medieval Jewish biblical commentator Ibn Ezra, the snake represents the devil. The devil, or Satan, rarely appears in the Bible. In the snake we see vestiges of ancient pagan beliefs, not an expression of authentic Judaism.

Did Balaam's donkey speak?

There are not too many conversations in the Bible between human beings and animals. The first, of course, Is Adam and Eve's conversation with the snake. In Chapter 22 we hear about Balaam, a soothsayer for Balak, king of Moab, who, on a mission to curse the feared Israelites—who have now won several victories over their enemies on their way to the Promised Land—finds himself talking with his she-ass.

God warns Balaam not to curse the Israelites, since they are

Balaam is stopped by the angel

divinely protected. Rather, he should go to see them and God would let him know what to do. Balaam mounts his she-ass and on the way the angel of God appears to the beast and blocks her way. She stops, without her master knowing why. Balaam strikes her, and then God makes her talk in a human voice. She lets her master know that she meant no ill, and they proceed toward the encampment of Israel.

World folklore is full of talking animals. But it is not clear why the biblical writer chose to insert this fable here. Perhaps in order to emphasize that paganism was now confronting monotheism, as it did back in Egypt, where Moses had to fight magic with magic. As happened in Egypt, here again God intervenes in this struggle of faith, and causes Balaam, whose mission was to curse Israel, to reconsider, and to turn his curse into a blessing, as he utters the famous words:

> *How goodly are your tents, O Jacob,*
> *Your dwelling places, O Israel.*
>   (Numbers 24:5)

What is the deeper message of the story of the talking donkey?

Throughout the Bible, the battle rages between monotheism and paganism, between good and evil. This, basically, is what the Bible is all about. And this is what makes the message of the Bible so powerful and timeless. Paganism, as Erich Fromm, the psychoanalyst and social philosopher, has pointed out, is not only the idol worshiping of antiquity. It is also present-day worship of money, power, and self-interest. Godliness, on the other hand, is not primarily about prayer and ritual. It is about living the godly life of justice and mercy and helping build a better world, or, to use the traditional Jewish phrase, "to perfect the world in the image of the divine."

The Daughters of Zelophehad—early example of women's rights?

In Chapter 27 we are told about the five daughters of Zelophehad,

of the tribe of Manasseh, whose father died in the desert and left
no sons. They ask Moses to allow them to inherit their father's
estate, so that their father's name and estate may be preserved.

In antiquity, as in some societies even today, women had no
inheritance rights. God grants the Zelophehad sisters' wish, in
what is one of history's first instances of women's rights. As in
other similar stories, the Bible is thousands of years ahead of its
time in its sensitivity to the rights of the weak and the vulnerable—women, strangers, widows and orphans, the old and the
sick.

Cities of Refuge—what is the broader meaning of this protective measure?

One of the oldest and most common customs in the ancient world,
which continues to this day in the Middle East and in the Mediterranean world, is vendetta, which sometimes lasts for several generations, and causes the death of innocent people. The last chapter
in the Book of Numbers describes a measure to be taken against a
vendetta aimed at a person who has accidentally killed someone,
and therefore is innocent. To protect the innocent, God decrees that
once the Israelites settle in the land of Canaan, they will designate
cities for the Levites to live in, some of which will become cities of
refuge, where anyone who accidently kills someone may stay and
be protected.

The cities of refuge are an early example of the Bible's emphasis
on justice as the supreme means of preserving society and protect-
ing the vulnerable, rather than mercy or charity. In Deuteronomy
19:10 we are told: "Innocent blood will not be shed in the land
Adonai your God gives you for an inheritance." This deep sense of
justice is manifest throughout the Bible, and will become the cornerstone of all prophetic teachings throughout the biblical period.

DEUTERONOMY: MOSES' LEGACY

What does the word "Deutornomy" mean?

The word Deuteronomy comes from the Greek word *Deuter-onomion*, which means second law. Moses, who is now approaching his 120th and final year, is reviewing the history of the exodus and explains the laws which were given to the Israelites during the forty years of wandering in the desert.

The tribes of Israel are now encamped east of the Jordan. They have won several major military victories against the local nations who stood in their way, and are poised to enter the Promised Land. Moses reminds them that God is forbidding him from joining them on this final stage of the long journey, because his faith had failed him during the many trials and tribulations imposed on him by the seemingly endless resistance they had shown him. He mus ac-cept the divine will.

Why are the laws repeated a second time?

When Moses first spoke the law to his people and entrusted it to the priests and Levites, did they not preserve it and transmit it to the next generation? Why was it necessary to repeat everything a second time?

For several reasons. First, the time of the wandering in the desert was a time of great turmoil and conflict, as well as rebelliousness, and now that a new generation is preparing to conquer the Promised Land, it is necessary to repeat the divine message. Second, while in the desert, the people's thoughts focused on physical survival. Now they are thinking of their new life in the new land, and the laws must be explained and expounded with this new life in mind. Third, this second repetition of the law shows that the law is not static, but must be revisited and reinterpreted for every successive generation. The core of the law, as embodied primarily in the Ten Commndments, is immutable and irreplaceable. But the many commandments that surround the core of the law, as we saw in the case of Rabbi Hillel's interpretation of the biblical commandment "An eye for an eye," are to be interpreted and sometimes adjusted for the new realities of future generations.

In repeating the law, what does Moses focus on first, and why?

The people who stood at Mount Sinai and were given the two Tablets of the Law (in Hebrew *luhot ha'berit*, the Tablets of the Convenant), are gone. Now Moses is talking to their children, who did not experience the greatest event in all of Jewish history. At Mount Sinai, six hundred thousand people heard the voice of God, and carried with them the memory of the liberation from Egypt, from where they were liberated with "signs and great wonders." Now we have a new generation that "did not know Sinai." Where should Moses begin?

He begins by reminding his people of God's covenant and promise, and alludes to the sin of the Golden Calf which occurred while he first went up to receive the Law on Mount Sinai, by making the strongest case yet against idol worshiping:

> *Be extremely careful, for you saw no image*
> *on the day God spoke to you in Horeb from*
> *the fire. For you may become corrupted, and*
> *may make any figure, male or female, the*
> *likeness of any beast on the land or any*
> *fowl in the sky, the likeness of anything*
> *that creeps on the earth or the fish in the water*
> *   under the land.*
>
> (Deuteronomy 4:15-18)

In short, idol worshiping is man's worst enemy. Israel exists because it does not worship idols. Having said that, Moses repeats the Ten Commandments for the second time (Chapter 5).

Are the Ten Commandments in Deuteronomy and in Exodus the same?

At the beginning of the exodus, Moses brought down the Ten Commandments from Mount Sinai. Now, some forty years later, he recites to the people the text of those commandments. The text was engraved on stone tablets, which have been kept in the holy ark in the tabernacle. We are not told that Moses took out the tablets and read them, but rather that he spoke from memory. In comparing the two versions (Exodus 20 and Deuteronomy 5), there are variations in the text, both stylistic and substantive. How is this possible?

The most glaring variation is that in the first version the text reads: "*Remember* the Sabbath day," while in the second it reads: "*Observe* the Sabbath day." Now, what did God actually say— "remember" or "observe?"

According to Rashi, God said both words at the same time. But when we examine the entire text, we realize that the second version is actually an interpretation and an expansion of the first. Thus, when the Israelites first leave Egypt, they are told simply to remember. There is no time yet to observe (keep in mind the haste of coming out of Egypt). Now that they are about to become a settled people in their own land, they are told to observe all the laws related to the Sabbath. In the same vein, the second version expands on the reasons for observing the Sabbath. In the first the reason given is that God made the world in six days and rested on the seventh. In the second we are also told that the Sabbath is the day of God, but a second reason is added, namely, "Remember that you were slaves in the land of Egypt, and that Adonai your God took you out of there with a strong hand and an outstretched arm, therefore Adonai your God commanded you to observe the Sabbath day."

Notwithstanding these variations, the essence of the Ten Commandments remains the same.

What is the meaning of "Hear O Israel?"

In Chapter 6 Moses pronounces what has become known as the watchword of the Jewish faith: "Hear O Israel, Adonai our God, Adonai is one."

While these words are the essence of biblical faith, it is not clear when exactly they became the commonly recited watchword. Was it during biblical times or soon thereafter? What is important to note is that they do not contain the words "I believe in God," hence they are not a personal confession of faith. Rather, they are a public proclamation by the community of Israel of its first article of faith, namely, that Adonai is Israel's God, and that Israel recognizes no other deity.

Why does Moses command the people to retell the story of the liberation from Egypt?

Following the proclamation of the oneness of God, Moses instructs the people to teach God's commandments to their children:

> *Teach them repeatedly to your children,*
> *and speak of them when you*
> *sit in your house,*
> *and when walk by the way,*
> *when you lie down,*
> *and when your rise up.*
>
> (Deuteronomy 6:7)

With these words, Moses empowers every Jew to be a teacher and to impart the tradition. Two seemingly different yet interrelated things are to be taught: The laws and precepts of Judaism, and the history of the Jewish people. The reason for this is that the laws and precepts of Judaism grow out of its history and continue to exist within this historical framework. Observing the Seder rituals and retelling the story of the liberation from Egypt on Passover is the best example of this interrelation. In time, key events in the history of the people become, to use Mordecai Kaplan's term, sancta, or consecrated events. The past remembered continues to inform and invigorate the future.

How can you fear and love God at the same time?

In Chapter 10 verse 12 we read:

> *And now Israel what does Adonai your*
> *God ask of you but to* fear *Adonai your*
> *God and walk in all of God's ways and*
> *love God with all your heart and soul.*

How can you fear and love God at the same time?

Maimonides uses the example of raising a child. In the early years of life, a child is taught to fear certain things that are harmful. Later on, fear is no longer necessary, as one begins to make positive decisions.

The rabbis of the Talmud learn from this verse that while God can predict and decide anything, God leaves the fear of heaven to human beings. In other words, God does not *command* Israel to fear and love God. Rather, God is *asking*.

It should also be pointed out that the "fear of heaven" is understood in Hebrew to mean not physical fear but rather piety, which in effect means respectful love and devotion, rather than a state of intimidation.

What is a prophet?

Back during the tumultuous days in the desert, while the people were challenging his authority, Moses made the following statement: "Would that all the people of God were prophets!" This reminds us of a statement attributed to the first president of the State of Israel, Chaim Weizmann, upon visiting President Harry Truman at the White House: "You, Mr. President, are the president of 165 million Americans. I, on the other hand, am the president of a million presidents." Which, by the way, is proof positive that the Jews of today are descendants of the Jews who gave Moses a hard time in the desert.

Here in Chapter 13 Moses discusses the issue of a future prophet who may arise in Israel and try to lead the people astray, and what is to be done in such a case.

What is a prophet? According to the Talmud, prophecy ended at the close of the biblical period. In other words, beginning with Abraham and concluding with the prophet Malachi, during some 15 centuries, the spirit of prophecy was active in Israel. It then came to an end. That prophets arose outside the Jewish tradition and formed other monotheistic religions is another matter. Within the Jewish faith, the time of prophecy ended before the beginning of the common era.

The prophet in the Bible is not primarily someone who predicts the future. Rather, the prophet is God's mouthpiece, and is mainly concerned with promoting faith among his people, and keeping them on the right path. Generally, God chooses someone at a young age to become a prophet, and no one can turn God down, not even Jonah who ran away and was swallowed by the great fish.

But Moses is referring here to another kind of "prophet," which the Bible calls a false prophet. This became a severe problem in Israel, especially during the time of the monarchy. Israel throughout that period is plagued with false prophets, who either promulgate false teachings in the name of the God of Israel, or try to promote pagan religions. Moses shows no mercy for the false prophets. They are to be eradicated, no questions asked.

What is the problem of being ruled by a king?

In Chapter 17 Moses anticipates a time when of the Israelites will be asking to have a king rule over them like all the nations around them (under Moses they are a theocracy). He makes three points: First, the king must be an Israelite. Second, the king must not own many horses or amass great wealth, have many women, or take the people back to Egypt. And third, the king will follow God's teachings, whereby he would recognize God as the supreme authority.

Indeed, a few generations later, once the tribes of Israel are settled in the Land of Canaan, they ask the prophet Samuel to crown a king over them and unify them. Samuel, foreseeing the resulting problems, resists, and only complies very reluctantly. As for the king being an Israelite, that commandment was followed for the most part. As for obedience to God, that, alas, was often disregarded, with dire consequences for Israel. It is interesting to note that King Solomon did have many wives, horses, and great wealth. For this he was punished, as his kingdom was divided after his death.

It appears that the Israelites were not meant to be a monarchy, but rather "a kingdom of priests and a holy people." Crowning a king was a concession. Another concession was the eating of meat, which was only approved in the Bible reluctantly. Thus, "a kingdom of priests and a holy people" remained the ideal, rather than what actually becomes of the Jewish people.

Why the command to destroy Amalek?

In Chapter 25 we read:

> Remember what Amalek did to you when
> you went out of Egypt; what happened to
> you on the way, as they attacked your strag-
> glers while you were tired and weary, and
> they did not fear God. And when Adonai
> your God gives you respite of all surrounding
> enemies in the land that Adonai your God gives
> you as an inheritance to possess, you shall
> wipe any remnant of Amalek from under the
> heavens—forget not!
> (Deuteronomy 25:17-19)

Why such vengefulness? In Jewish history the designation "Amalekite" has always been reserved for Israel's most implacable enemies, such as Haman, Antiochus, the Roman emperors Titus and Hadrian, and, more recently, Hitler. Rabbi Leo Baeck, the leader of German Jewry before Hitler's rise to power and during the Holocaust, secretly wrote a book titled *This People Israel* while interned in the Theresienstadt concentration camp. Clearly alluding to the Nazis, Baeck wrote: "For only if the punishing judgment of God would fall on all of these masters and servants of blasphemy, only then would those lands once again become pure and free and wide, so that humanity would be able to live there" (page 11).

One can only conclude that the evil of the Amalekites was comparable to that of the Nazis (attacking weary stragglers reminds us of the 1945 Nazi Death Marches in which thousands of stragglers were killed), and therefore there was no room for them on this earth, and they could be shown no mercy.

Why all the cursing in Deutoronomy, Chapter 27?

As Moses exhorts the Israelites to keep all the commandments, he introduces a ritual which may give some of us pause. Gathered in the future near the ancestral town of Shehem (today's Nablus), the priests and Levites will present the people with a digest of the commandments, and pronounce a curse on those who fail to fulfill a particular com-mandment, as the people respond to each by saying "amen:"

> Cursed be he who makes a graven image. . .
> Cursed by he who dishonors his father and mother. . .
> Cursed be he who removes his neighbor's landmark. . .
> Cursed be he who makes the blind lose his way. . .
> Cursed be he who denies justice to the stranger, the
>   orphan, and the widows. . .

And finally:

> Cursed be he who does not conform to the
>   words of this law.
>   (Deuteronomy 27:15-26)

The people have been warned over and over again about the dire consequences of breaking God's law. Now this warning is being reinforced by publicly proclaimed curses. The impression one gets is that Moses and the priests were deeply worried people would break the commandments, as history proves people often do. While the covenant in the Bible is usually entered upon with a positive statement, here we have a commitment made in the negative.

Standing before God (Nitzavim)—what do we learn here about the covenant?

> You are standing this day, all of you, before Adonai
> your God. . . that you may enter the covenant of
> Adonai your God and accept the oath. . . And not
> with you alone do I make this covenant and this
> oath. . . but also with those. . . who are not here today. . .
> For the commandment I command you this
> day is not too hard for you or too far. . . Behold,
> I give you today life and good and death and
> evil. . . therefore choose life.
>   (Deuteronomy 29:9, 11, 13-14; 30:11, 15, 19)

These are the most impassioned words in the Bible regarding the covenant. We have here a mention of the divine promise as well as the curse resulting from breaking the covenant. It is made clear that the covenant has no statute of limitation, but rather is made for all time. We are told that it is not beyond human power to keep, and we are urged to choose life by keeping it. This last statement reminds us of the words of Job: "Even if God slays me, still will I hope for God." In short, the covenant is the central concept of the Bible.

What ever happened to the Ark of the Covenant?

In Chapter 31 there is mention of the Ark of the Covenant, in which the tablets of the law were kept, and which was carried in the desert and eventually brought by King David to Jerusalem, where his son, Solomon, deposited it in the Holy Temple.

According to the Second Book of Maccabees, when Solomon's Temple was destroyed, the prophet Jeremiah took the ark on his way to Egypt, and hid it at Mount Nebo, where Moses had died and was buried, to be kept there until the coming of the messiah. All we know is that the ark is not mentioned again during the time of the Second Temple.

The Holy Ark with the Torah scroll in the synagogue has taken the place for Jews of the Ark of the Covenant.

What is the purpose of the Song of Haazinu?

As Moses' life comes to a close, the great liberator and law-giver makes his final exhortation to his people. Here again, as he did forty years earlier after crossing the Red Sea, Moses resorts to a song, rather than a speech. He calls upon the people to listen (Haazinu), and proceeds to tell them about the greatness of God, about their own history of backsliding and disobedience, and about the promise that notwithstanding all their failings, in the end God will redeem them and restore their land to its former glory.

In this song Moses recaps his lifelong mission. He gives his people a constant reminder that God is the ultimate and indisputable ruler of the universe, and that human will is weak, hence prone to error and failure. He gives his people hope, reminding them that the covenant is eternal, and can always be counted on. But he reminds them that breaking the covenant will always elicit a punishment, at times quite severe. "Therefore, choose life."

How does Moses' blessing to the tribes of Israel compare to Jacob's blessing?

Now Moses is ready to bless the tribes, much in the tradition of the patriarchs who bestow their blessing on their successors before they die. It is particularly interesting to compare Moses' blessing to that of the patriarch Jacob, who addressed the same twelve tribes as did Moses.

They both begin with Reuven, the oldest of Jacob's sons. Jacob predicts that Reuven will no longer excel, for he had betrayed his father. Moses predicts that Reuven will survive, but only as a small tribe. The message seems to be the same, although phrased differently.

Jacob groups Simeon and Levi together, and predicts that they will fail for they had also betrayed their father, and as a result they will be scattered among the other tribes. Moses does not even mention Simeon, who disappears as a tribe. On the other hand, Moses, himself a Levite, blesses the tribe of Levi who stood by him in the desert, especially during the Golden Calf rebellion, and turns Levi's curse of being scattered among the tribes into a blessing, in that Levi becomes the preserver and transmitter of God's word among the tribes.

Both Jacob and Moses bless Judah as the one who shall be the leader of his brothers, the nation-builder who shall overcome his enemies.

Moses calls Benjamin "God's beloved," while his father, Jacob, dismisses him as a "Ravenous wolf who hunts in the morning and divides his spoil in the evening."

In blessing Joseph, who actually gave rise to two tribes, named after his sons Ephraim and Manasseh, Jacob only refers to Joseph himself, while Moses mentions the two tribes named after Joseph's sons. What is interesting in the case of Joseph is that this is the only instance where Moses quotes some of Jacob's blessing to one of his sons.

The rest of the brothers receive similar blessings from Both Jacob and Moses.

What is meant by Moses being the only one who knew God "face to face?"

The last chapter of Deuteronomy depicts the death of Moses as the old nation-builder goes up to Mount Nebo and for the last time looks at the Promised Land where he may not enter. Here we are reminded that Moses was the only prophet whom God knew "face to face."

What exactly does this mean? First, as Moses himself made it clear, God does not have a face. Second, in what way was Moses' relationship with God different from that of any other prophet?

According to Maimonides, Moses had reached the highest degree of prophecy. He was not superhuman, or in any way divine. He was an ordinary person, in fact, "the humblest of all people." But God had chosen him when God appeared to him in the burning bush to perform the greatest mission God has ever or will ever entrust to a human being. Through Moses, God gave Israel and the world the divine law. Thus, "knowing someone face to face" can be interpreted as giving someone full authority to transmit the full revelation of God's law, not all of which can be understood by mortals, but all of which is delivered through Moses and becomes humanly operaional, "for this commandment is not too hard for you to do, or too far off."

The Five Books of Moses—random collection or one cohesive unit?

During the nineteenth and twentieth centuries, an enormous effort has been expended by biblical scholars, both Christian and Jewish, in their search for the origins and authorship of the Five Books of Moses. Elaborate theories have been developed regarding the dates of authorship, the types of authors, and the entire process of putting the various texts together before they reached their present order and composition. A clear distinction was drawn between the first four books and Deutoronomy, the latter being seen as an entirely separate version of the Torah. Certain writings have been attributed to the priests, particularly the Book of Leviticus. In Genesis, where we have such repetitions as two stories of creation, some scholars saw two different versions written at two different periods. Eventually, when the Bible was given its final redaction by the rabbis of the second century C.E., the text as we know it today came into being.

Without accepting or rejecting any of the many theories we have today, two things can be determined: First, there is an ideological and logical unity within the five books, which ties them together not as a random collection of writings, but rather as a cohesive unit. Secondly, this unity can be found in the Torah's unequivocal message, namely, that there is an absolute God in the universe, who created the world for a purpose, and made this purpose known through the laws revealed to Moses.

All the stories and laws in the Five Books of Moses fit together and are interrelated, although at first look they may seem disjointed, at times even contradictory. In Genesis we have the beginning of the world and of civilization, leading up to the stories of the ancestors of the Jewish people. In Exodus we have the birth of the Hebrew nation out of slavery in Egypt, and the receiving of the Ten Commandments by this new nation. In Leviticus we have the priestly laws, both ritual and ethical. In Numbers we have the emergence of the twelve tribes as a nation unified by divine laws, and the beginning of the conquest of the Land of Canaan. Finally, in Deuteronomy, we have Moses' recap of God's commandments, his final testimony to his people, and his death on the other side of the Jordan, as he is prevented from entering the Promised Land.

As we saw in the two versions of the Ten Commandments, there is a progression from the first version to the second, which is perfectly logical, once we realize that a process of explication and interpretation takes place within the Bible which, after all, covers a period of centuries.

In short, one should make a distinction between the essence of the Five Books of Moses and the various layers of writing which quite possibly date to different periods during biblical history. The essence, namely, the concepts, beliefs, and commandments are the same throughout. The text may repeat itself in places and vary, but the essence remains unchanged.

PART TWO: PROPHETS

JOSHUA:
THE CONQUEST OF CANAAN

How does the Book of Joshua relate to the Five Books of Moses?

The Book of Joshua is the first book of the second main division of the Bible, known as "Prophets." This division actually consists of two groups of books: The first, starting with Joshua, are history books; the second, starting with Isaiah, are prophetic books.

As a history book, the Book of Joshua marks a departure from the previous Five Books of Moses. The emphasis here is on the conquest of Canaan and the division of the land among the twelve tribes of Israel, rather than on laws and commandments. There are, however, some strong links between this book and the Books of Moses. The first link appears in Chapter 1, when God tells Joshua to be strong and of good courage, and adds:

> *Let not this Torah depart from your mouth;*
> *meditate upon it day and night.*
> (Joshua 1:8)

Moreover, from here to the end of the book, Joshua is busy transmitting Moses' teachings, by reminding the people of the imperative to follow their God, not the idols of their neighbors; by renewing the covenant through circumcision and through a solemn oath; and by implementing Mosaic laws, such as the establishment of cities of refuge.

Did the Holy Ark perform the miracle of the crossing of the Jordan?

As the Israelites begin to cross the Jordan River on their way into the Promised Land, the priests carry the Holy Ark which appears to perform a miracle similar to the crossing of the Red Sea. The waters of the Jordan part, and the people are able to cross without any difficulty.

While this story does not have the epic proportions of the Red Sea crossing, it is clearly reminiscent of it, if only on a much smaller scale. Do we need a rational explanation for it? Should we point out that the Jordan, for the most part, is not a particularly deep river, and crossing it is usually not such a big problem? In any case, Joshua, according to this story, uses the Holy Ark as a magic tool to persuade the people to cross the Jordan, by showing them that God is on their side. No doubt, they are very apprehensive about entering a settled land full of fortified towns and launching a campaign against the various Canaanite nations, who have better weapons and are technologically more advanced than the nomadic Hebrews. They need a sign from heaven, and Joshua provides it.

What does the story of Rahab try to convey?

Joshua knows that he lacks the weapons and resources to launch a frontal attack on his first objective, namely, the town of Jericho, which stands in his way as he crosses the Jordan and enters the Land of Canaan. His approach from the moment he starts his invasion is one of stratagems rather than conventional military strategy. Thus, he starts by sending two spies into Jericho, to find out what can be done to bring down this heavily fortified town.

The spies find their way into the house of Rahab the harlot, located in the wall surrounding the town. They gather their information and leave, promising Rahab to spare her and her family when they conquer Jericho.

This story, told at some length, raises some questions. Why a harlot? Why play up this particular story, while most of the following conquest stories are brief and lacking in human interest?

To fully appreciate this story, we must consider its next part,

The fall of the walls of Jericho

namely, the fall of the walls of Jericho. A good knowledge of the walls was critical for conquering Jericho, and since Rahab lived in the wall, she was the right person to turn to. Moreover, her profession was conducive to betrayal.

Clearly, the story was preserved. It shows that in order for a small nation to overcome numerous enemies, many unconventional methods must be utilized. The Book of Joshua and the Book of Judges which follows it provide several examples of innovative military strategies.

Did the walls of Jericho come tumbling down?

What kind of intelligence did the spies gather regarding the walls of Jericho? For one thing, they were high and thick, and could not be easily stormed. Joshua, like other biblical figures before him, is in a quandary, and as he turns inwardly to search for a solution, the angel of God (or his own inner self?) appears to him and tells him to bring down the walls of Jericho not by attacking them but by having the priests circle the city and blow their horns, which would result in the walls tumbling down.

What are we to make of this story? For one thing, we know that in antiquity the Jordan valley was visited by earthquakes. We also known that Jericho, one of the oldest cities in the world, was destroyed many times and rebuilt, layer upon layer. We can also speculate that the spies who visited Rahab's house in the wall found out that the walls were already full of cracks, possibly from previous earthquakes, and with the vibrations produced by some good blasts of the horns one could precipitate the impending crumbling of the walls. As we have seen in the story of the burning bush and the water coming out of the rock, there are natural phenomena in the Holy Land that, to a stranger, may appear to be miracles.

Did the sun stand still during Joshua's coastal battle?

Having conquered Jericho, Joshua continues his campaign up the foothills near Jerusalem and finally reaches the Valley of Ayalon to the west, having virtually severed the south, or the Negev,

The sun stood still as Joshua fought his battle

from the center of the land and the Galilee. As he prepares for the next battle, he is assisted by a storm with large hailstones coming down on his enemies, and when the sun finally comes out, Joshua commands the sun to stand still in the sky until he finishes the battle. The sun obeys by standing still a whole day in the middle of the sky, "until a nation is done avenging its enemies."

Obviously, here we cannot resort to a natural explanation. We have long known that the sun does not rise and set, but rather the earth rotates, making the sun appear to rise and set. Could it be that this single statement renders the whole Bible unreliable?

In the biblical Book of Ecclesiastes, which is attributed to King Solomon, the wisest of men, we read: "The sun also rises, and the sun goes down, and hastens to the place from where it rises." We know that, scientifically speaking, none of this is accurate. And yet, to this day we keep talking about the sun rising and setting. What we actually refer to is the *appearance*, rather than the actual event, of rising and setting. As for Joshua, having just experienced the phenomenon of hailstones helping him win a battle, he must have shouted at the sun in the heat of the next battle to stand still so he may finish off his enemy. In other words, he ordered time to stand still. Did time obey? Not likely. However, Joshua might have inspired his troops to fight more decisively, so that time *appeared* to have stopped.

Once again we see a natural phenomenon dressed in an ancient people's imagination as a miracle.

Did Joshua set fire to the city of Hazor?

In one of his last battles, Joshua reaches the fortified town of Hazor, north of the Sea of Galilee. Here we are told he scores a great victory, killing its king, Yavin, and burning the town of Hazor to the ground.

This particular story has given biblical scholars many headaches, since we later learn in the Book of Judges, in the story of Deborah and Barak (4:24), that Yavin was defeated in their day, some decades later, and was killed then. How do we settle this chronological contradiction?

Enters biblical archeology. In his book on Hazor, Israeli archeologist Yigael Yadin reports on his excavations in this Galilee site (which inspired James Michener's historical novel, *The Source*), where the digging unearthed many town layers going back to Abraham's time. In the layer corresponding to Joshua's conquest in the 13th century B.C.E., Yadin and his colleagues found a town layer devastated by fire. This provided proof that the story in Joshua is historically correct, while the version in the Book of Judges may be an unedited inclusion of the original story in a somewhat later event.

It is interesting to note in this regard that the first historical record of the actual existence of a people of Israel appears around this time in an Egyptian inscription of the period, in which the Pharaoh refers to a battle in the south of the Land of Canaan where he defeated or actually "routed for good" the "People of Israel." Thus, in effect, with Joshua we are for the first time on firm historical ground, whereas the stories of the patriarchs and Moses still remain shrouded in the mists of history.

Samson destroys the Philistine temple

JUDGES:
THE PRE-MONARCHIC PERIOD

What is the background of the Book of Judges?

The period of the judges, which lasted roughly for one century, preceded the time of the Hebrew monarchy, which lasted for about five centuries. It could therefore be referred to as the premonarchic period. The first thing this book makes clear is that Joshua's conquest of Canaan was far from complete. Local Canaanite towns and town alliances continued to exist and kept attacking the new settlers. To make things worse, new invaders called Philistines arrived from across the sea and settled on the coast, from where they would challenge the Hebrew tribes for over a century. Old invaders, such as the Midianites and the Amalekites, arrived from the desert. And nations from the other side of the Jordan, such as the Ammonites, joined in the fray.

In short, while Joshua won some spectacular victories that enabled the Israelites to settle in parts of the Promised Land, he left the tribes with many unresolved territorial as well as internal problems, not the least of which was the lack of unity, which would continue to plague them for generations.

Did the "judges" really judge?

The term "judges" is misleading, since, with the exception of Deborah, who was both a judge and a prophet, the rest of so-called judges in this book did not judge, but were rather an odd assortment of warlords, appearing in different Hebrew tribes at different times, especially in time of trouble, and acquiring the local status of a tribal leader by virtue of maintaining a state of non-belligerence for a certain number of years.

Why were judges necessary?

The pre-monarchic period is characterized in the Bible as a time of lawlessness, with "everyone doing what seemed right to him." There is disunity among the tribes, and none seems to be able to fend for itself. Moreover, the time of the "judges" is portrayed as a time of constant attempts by the tribes of Israel to assimilate in the local pagan cultures, dominated by deities such as Baal, Ashtaroth, Moloch, Dagon, and others. These attempts never seem to work, causing the tribes conflicts with and subjugation by their pagan neighbors. God, however, mindful of the covenant, "made judges to arise and save them from their persecutors."

Who sepcifically were the judges?

Here is a list of the judges who are included in the book. Some are very familiar, as they had entered world culture. The rest are obscure:

Othniel, son of Kenaz—first of the judges, fought Aram in the north.

Ehud, son of Gera—fought Moab in the east.

Shamgar, son of Anath, fought the Philistine in the west.

Deborah—guided Barak in defeating the Cannanites in the Valley of Jezreel.

Gideon, son of Yoash—fought the Medianites in the northeast.

Abimelech, son of Gideon—the only judge to gain leadership by treachery.

Tola, son of Puah—of the tribe of Ephraim. No battle mentioned.

Yair, the Gileadite—no battle mentioned.

Jephthah, son of Gilead—fought the Ammonites in the northeast.

Ibzan of Bethlehem—no battle mentioned.

Elon, the Zebulunite—no battle mentioned.

Abdon, son of Hillel—no battle mentioned.

Samson, son of Manoah—fought the Philistines single-handedly.

Of the above names, the best known are Deborah, Gideon, Jephthah, and Samson. In the next book, First Samuel, we have two more judges—Eli, the priest, and Samuel, the prophet, before the monarchy is finally established.

Viewed collectively, what do the stories of the judges teach us about the period?

Once the twelve tribes of Israel begin to settle in what will become the kingdom of Israel, much of the unity and cohesion that emerged at the end of the desert years and during the time of Joshua seem to have disappeared. Each tribe finds its own place and becomes isolated from the rest, and although all continue to share a common religion with such unifying elements as priests, Levites, as well as a common history, they are all plagued by local as well as common enemies, they are not able to join together effectively to defeat those enemies, they sometimes even turn on one another, and they remain small tribes who are unable to build a strong political or religious culture.

Unlike the brilliant military campaigns of Joshua's time, now most of the action is more on the order of guerrilla warfare, as in the case of Gideon, or even the exploits of a single larger-than-life individual, such as a Samson. It appears that what saves the day during this time is the fact that the Hebrew tribes do not face a strong alliance of enemies or a major power, such as Egypt or Babylonia, and are able to get by. Later on, during invasions by major powers such as Assyria, Babylonia, and eventually Rome, the balance of power will shift against the now unified tribes.

Deborah the Prophet

What makes Deborah stand out in the Book of Judges and in the Bible in general?

Deborah is the first woman in the Bible, as well as one of the first in recorded history, who assumes a leadership role over her people and wins a spectacular military victory. She is also a prophet, a judge, and a poet. Her victory song is one of the most stirring poems in world literature:

> Awake, awake, Deborah,
> Awake, awake, speak words of song.
> Arise Barak, seize and capture,
> Son of Avinoam.
>
> (Judges 5:12)

Moreover, she has everything working against her, but she finds a way to prevail. First, she is facing a numerically and militarily superior enemy, armed with iron chariots, while her people only have bows and arrows. To win, she must form a coalition of tribes, at a time when the tribes are not only divided, but several of them even refuse to deal with the dire reality facing them and join her campaign. Finally, she selects Barak as her general, but he is hesitant about taking charge, and asks her to assume the command. Reluctantly, she does.

The army of Israel gathers on Mount Tabor, overlooking the Valley of Jezreel. Deborah knows that the ground down in the valley is soft, and that on a rainy winter day the chariots will become bogged down in the mud. She waits for exactly this kind of a day. She gives Barak the order to attack, as the Canaanite iron chariots sink in the mud and the archenemy is routed.

Why did Gideon only select those men who did not crouch while drinking from the brook?

The story of Gideon's campaign against the Medianites is one of the first stories of brilliant guerrilla warfare in recorded history. Gideon could not win this battle by sheer numbers, since he was facing the combined forces of Midian, Amalek, and the "children of the east." Instead, he chose to form a small yet superior unit, consisting of only 300 exceptional warriors. One of the tests he used to select such a force was to bring all the volunteers to a brook where they were told to take a drink. Those who went down on their knees to drink were disqualified, and only those who scooped the water with their hands while standing were selected.

Rashi interprets the act of kneeling down as typical of idol worshiping. It is also, we might add, a sign of servitude. Gideon was looking for truly free and independent individuals, who were always vigilant. He would need them to outsmart the unholy alliance he was taking on, and win the battle of the few against the many.

Why doesn't God spare the daughter of Jephthah?

One of the better known judges is Jephthah, mainly because of the most unusual story of his vow and the sacrifice of his daughter. Briefly, as Jephthah begins his campaign against the Ammonites, he vows that if he return victorious, the first to come out of his house would be sacrificed to God.

The first question here is, was he referring to a farm animal, which was commonly sacrificed in those days, or did he also mean a person? If a person, then it would mean human sacrifice, which was forbidden to Jews. Lo and behold, as he returns home victorious from the battlefield, the first to come out of his house to greet him is his daughter, who is his only child. Jephthah is devastated, but he cannot go back on his word. His own daughter would not let him break his vow, and lets herself be sacrificed.

God, the main character in the Book of Judges as in most of the Bible, remains silent. We are left with a painful question, reminiscent of the question of the sacrifice of Isaac, yet more tragic in its consequences. Why such a sacrifice? Why punish a father who just won a great victory for his people? The question remains open.

Samson—a Nazirite or a playboy?

One of the judges in the book, namely, Samson, is one of the most colorful and contradictory characters in the entire Bible.

Samson and Delilah

At birth, he is dedicated to a life of abstinence, by becoming a Nazirite (see p. 89), commanded not to ever drink wine, and never to cut his hair. As he grows up, "the spirit of God began to move him."

What follows completely contradicts this early report about his life. Samson, rather than lead a life of abstinence, associates himself with the Philistines, who at that time oppress his tribe, the tribe of Dan, leads a dissolute life with Philistine friends, and falls in love with a Philistine woman whom he marries. His parents oppose the marriage, but the biblical narrator tells us that his father and mother did not know it was God's will—he was seeking a pretext against the Philistines.

We soon find out what was meant by "it was God's will." Samson, who is never really accepted by the Philistines, begins to retaliate, and becomes a one-man guerrilla force. He ties burning torches to foxes' tails and lets them loose in the Philistine wheat fields. He smites one thousand Philistine soldiers with the jawbone of a donkey, and so on.

Enters Delilah, the Philistine seductress. She pries the secret of Samson's strength out of him. The rest is history. He falls asleep in her lap. His hair is shorn. He is arrested and blinded. He is put on display in the Philistine god's temple. He prays to God for a last outburst of strength. His wish is granted. He pushes the two main pillars of the temple apart, the temple collapses as Samson cries, "Let me die along with the Philistines," and so "those he killed in his death exceeded the ones he slew in his life" (Judges 16:30).

Samson is included in this book as one of the judges who were doing God's will. The reason may be to show how chaotic that period was. God's ways, of course, are mysterious, and the most unlikely person may become a messenger of God. Naturally, to Jews Samson became a great folk hero, as any person of unusual strength and courage would to a small nation always facing great odds. In the final analysis, Samson was a playboy. Making him a Nazirite was probably meant to show that he was indeed singled out for a divinely appointed mission, in spite of himself, as it were.

The Concubine and the tribe of Benjamin—what do we learn from this harrowing story?

The Book of Judges ends with several unusual stories which help dramatize the state of lawlessness and chaos that prevailed among the tribes of Israel prior to the time of the monarchy, when "everyone did what seemed right to him." These stories reach their climax with the story known in Jewish tradition as the "Concubine in Gibeah. "

According to this story, a Levite residing in the land of Ephraim went to Bethlehem to acquire a concubine. On their way back they stopped in Gibeah, north of Jerusalem, in the land of Benjamin. There some hot headed Benjaminites took the concubine and raped her all night long, leaving her dead in the morning. Apparently, this crime broke some code of hospitality or immunity that must have existed among the tribes. The bereaved Levite cut the dead woman's body into twelve pieces and sent the pieces to the twelve tribes of Israel, asking them what to do. The tribes gathered and asked the Benjaminites to turn over the offenders, but they refused. What followed was a long series of battles in which nearly all the Benjaminites were killed. The tribes now realized that one tribe was about to disappear, and arranged for the surviving Benjaminites to kidnap young women in the town of Shiloh, so that they could start over again.

This closing story of the Book of Judges reveals several things. First, there were indeed some common ties among the various tribes of Israel. Second, this did not prevent them in an extreme situation from turning on one of their own. Third, the tribes were in urgent need of unifying themselves under one authority. It took an act of violence for them to make a common cause, and take joint action to protect their common interest. The groundwork was now laid for further unification and for forging a nation out of the disparate tribes.

The book concludes with the words: "In those days there was no king in Israel, as each person did what seemed right to him."

I Samuel:
The Beginning of
the Monarchy

Why is the Book of Samuel divided into First Samuel and Second Samuel?

The division of the Bible into chapters and verses, as well as the subdivision into two books of Samuel following by two books of Kings, was not done by the sages of the Talmud who produced the final version of Scripture, but by their contemporary Greek scholars who produced the Septuagint, or Greek translation of the Hebrew Bible. The division, however, seems logical, since the central character in I Samuel is Samuel himself, while in II Samuel it is King David, whose many accomplishments required a separate book.

Who is Samuel, and what makes him a major figure in the Bible?

Samuel, the last of the judges, is a pivotal figure in the Bible. He crowns Israel's first king, albeit reluctantly, thus establishing the kingdom of Israel. This elevates him to a rank similar to Moses himself. Indeed, the prophet Jeremiah mentions the two in the same breath (15:1). The story of the birth of Samuel is as compelling as the story of the rescue of baby Moses. Both come along at a time of great crisis, and both are destined to effect a profound change in the lives of their people. Like Moses, Samuel suddenly hears the voice of God and becomes a prophet who proceeds to guide his people's destiny.

The story of Samuel's mother—what do we learn here about everyday life at the end of the period of the Judges?

The narrative concerning the plight of Samuel's mother, Hannah, is one of the finest in all of literature. The genius of the biblical author of weaving an epic story with a few words comes into play in this tale with such intensity, that not only do we have here the plight of one woman who lived over three thousand years ago, but a whole social, religious, and political history of the period.

As for the social history, we learn about the life of an average Hebrew family at the end of the period of the Judges. Typically, it is a polygamous family, with two main wives, and possibly concubines as well. Typically, as in the story of Jacob and his wives Leah and Rachel, one wife is the favorite, but as luck would often have it, the favorite is often barren.

As for the religious history, the head of the family goes each year to the town of Shiloh, which happens to be the religious center for the tribes at that time, to make offerings to God. There, at the temple of Shiloh, the Holy Ark—the holiest religious object at that time—is kept, and the old priest, Eli, presides, with his two sons, Hophni and Phinehas, assisting him. Hannah, who prays for a son, gives us an early example of prayer as a means of communicating with God, rather than the sacrificial offerings her husband brings to the temple. When she is finally blessed with a son, we are given the full text of her prayer, one of the first and most beautiful in the Bible:

> . . .the barren woman keeps giving birth,
> While the fertile one is desolate. . .
> Adonai makes you poor and makes you rich,
> Brings you low, and raises you up.
> Brings up the weak from the dust,
> and lifts the destitute from the dunghill.
> (I Samuel 2:5, 7)

Finally, the political history of the time. Here we learn that the priest, Eli, is the central authority in the land. His authority, however, is limited, since the tribes are politically autonomous, each running its own affairs. Still, he is the only central national authority, since the bond that unites the tribes is not political but rather religious, symbolized by the temple at Shiloh. Eli appears to be a benevolent spiritual leader of his people, but his two sons are corrupt, and they abuse their power. Hannah, who dedicates her son to the temple as a Nazirite (reminding us of the story of Samson), is in effect providing the future leader for the tribes, who will replace the house of Eli.

How does Samuel become the leader of Israel?

When the young Samuel begins to serve Eli the Priest at the temple in Shiloh, we are told that "in those days there was no frequent vision." In other words, God does not appear to his people, because of the weakened state of faith and the idol worshiping among them. It is then that the boy Samuel hears the voice of God, telling him that the House of Eli is doomed. Now Samuel has become a prophet. He keeps hearing the voice of God. As people from all the tribes of Israel flock to the temple in Shiloh to offer their sacrifices, they hear Samuel speak, and they sense the presence of God in his words. "And all Israel from Dan to Beersheba knew that Samuel was trustworthy as a prophet of the Lord." When Eli's corrupt sons are killed by the Philistines, and their old father dies from the shock, Samuel becomes the leader of Israel.

What do we learn here about the leadership roles at that time of the priest, the prophet, and the judge?

Leadership roles here and throughout the Bible are never well defined. The Bible seems to offer a subtle message: the only true leader of the Jews is God. Human authority is always questionable and limited at best. Samuel is the perfect example of this ambiguity. He wears all three hats—priest, prophet, and judge— but none of them endows him with a definitive leadership role. Later, during the time of the monarchy, the tension between the

The return of the holy ark

king, the prophet, and the priest will continue as an internal struggle over the question who is the one speaking for God. Over and over again, the Bible shows us that human authority is short-lived and relative, and only faith in God is long abiding and reliable.

As a leader, does Samuel take on Israel's enemies?

In Samuel's time the main enemy of Israel are the Philistines. The Ammonites, Amalekites etc. are still around, and they too do their share of troublemaking. But the Philistines are the main enemy at the gate. Samuel, however, does not become a military leader. He remains in the background while the tribes go to do battle against the Philistines. At first, things do not go well for Israel, and they decide to carry the Ark of the Covenant with them to the battlefield in the hope of winning a victory similar to those of Moses and Joshua.

What is the message of the failure of the Ark of the Covenant to save Israel?

Despite the initial exuberance of Israel's warriors upon seeing the Ark arrive on the battlefield, the Ark fails to save them. They are badly beaten by their enemy, and to make matters worse, the Philistines capture the Ark and carry it to their land. Soon enough, the Philistines find out that having God's Ark in their midst is not working to their advantage. It only brings them bad luck. They try to move it from town to town, but each time the same thing happens. Finally, in their despair, they return it to the tribes. It finds a home in a place called Kiriat Ye'arim.

The message here appears to be the following: You cannot turn the Ark into a magic object, and expect it to win wars. It is people who win, not so-called sacred objects. To win, the people must truly turn to God, which they didn't do. On the other hand, God's power continues to reside in the Ark, as if sending a message to Israel to let them know that God is still there, waiting.

Samuel blesses Saul

Why is Samuel so opposed to crowning a king?

Back in the desert, Moses provides brief directives as to the nature the emphasis on the adherence of the future king to God's law. The king, in other words, must rule through the divine commandments, as a first among equals, not through personal power and authority.

This is exactly how Samuel himself led the people, not imposing his personal will, but rather persuading them to adhere to the one true God of Israel, which they finally did, whereupon they were able to overcome their main enemy, the Philistines, and live in peace. However, as Samuel grew old, the elders of the tribes realized that his sons did not follow in his footsteps and, worried about the future, they went to see Samuel and demanded that he crown a king over Israel, "like all other nations."

Samuel consults God. The message he receives is that the people are not turning their backs on Samuel, but on God. Rather than become a "kingdom of priests and a holy nation," they want to be a monarchy "like all other nations," that is, like all the other pagan nations with all their abominations.

Samuel tries to dissuade the elders. He does not give the main reason, knowing that the elders would disagree, since they lack his prophetic vision. Instead, he paints a picture of a king who oppresses his people and turns them into his slaves.

The people refuse to listen. It is time for a compromise. God tells Samuel to listen to the people and find them a king.

Was Saul, the first king of Israel, a great king?

Samuel finds a young man from the small tribe of Benjamin and anoints him king. It all happens quite randomly, and the young Saul seems confused by this sudden election. As he begins to assert his authority, the same tribes who for a long time clamored for a king fail to fully unite behind him, and he runs into opposition at every step of the way. He becomes overly dependent on the aging Samuel, who does not always come through for him. He is faced with a formidable foe, namely, the Philistines, who again begin to assert themselves and have now the advantage of iron weapons (this being the dawn of the Iron Age) at a time when the tribes of Israel are yet to have any. Adding to his woes is the rise of a brave and charismatic young man named David, who becomes the boy hero of Israel. Saul becomes depressed and melancholy, and he finds his death in his decisive battle with the Philistines.

This brief portrait of Israel's first king shows a tragic figure, often dismissed as a failure. But in reality Saul was a much greater king than he is usually given credit for. First, we must keep in mind that everything and nearly everyone, including his own mentor, Samuel, worked against him. When he showed compassion to the captured king of the Amalekites, Israel's mortal enemy (see p. 105), he is condemned by Samuel for not obeying God's command to kill the evil king, and told he will lose the kingdom. In short, Saul always seems to operate with his hands tied behind his back.

And yet, Saul is the one who makes the monarchy a reality, paving the way for great kings like David and Solomon. He wins significant victories against Israel's archenemies—the Ammonites, the Amalekites, and, most im-portant, the Philistines, which enable his successor, David, to consolidate the monarchy. As we assess the stories involving Saul and Samuel, and later the young David as well, what we see here are three good men, all of whom are God fearing and devoted to their people. Yet, because of circumstances beyond his control, Saul is not able to get along with either his mentor or his successor. What the Bible clearly shows us here is the great complexity of human relations, when three outstanding individuals, dedicated to the same cause, are unable to pull together.

The witch of En-Dor—did King Saul speak to the spirit of the dead prophet?

Conjuring the spirit of the dead from netherworld must be one of humankind's earliest practices, which has survived to this day in a practice known as seance. After the death of the prophet Samuel, King Saul faces a critical battle with the Philistines, and senses his end is near. In his despair, he goes to see the witch of En-Dor, who specializes in talking to the spirits of the dead. He prevails upon her to bring back Samuel's spirit. He talks to his dead men-

The Witch of En-Dor

tor, who rebukes him for doing so, and reminds him of his disobedience to God in not killing the Amalekite king, which would now precipitate his doom.

In this story we depart from the common biblical view which rejects all witchcraft, and enter the realm of folk beliefs and practices. The reason for including such a divergent story at this point may be to dramatize the extent of Saul's fear and despair. He knows the end is near. He is willing to try anything. Whether he actually hears the voice of Samuel or imagines it is anyone's guess.

The young David—a self-made hero or God's chosen?

While nothing seems to go Saul's way, everything seems to go David's way. Even his name means favorite, or beloved. Few people in the Bible make a more dramatic appearance than David. Before one of those fateful battles with the Philistines, Saul learns that his enemies are introducing an unbeatable warrior named Goliath into the battlefield. The king has no one who can match this giant. Enters a young shepherd boy named David. He volunteers to take on the giant. His weapon? A slingshot and five smooth stones. It all seems ludicrous. But as the giant stands in the middle of the field, the shepherd boy comes close enough to take aim at his forehead, which is not covered by armor. A well-aimed stone strikes Goliath in the forehead, and he falls down, unconscious. David removed the giant's sword and uses it to sever his head. The unknown boy from Bethlehem becomes the boy hero of Israel.

In this and the many subsequent stories about David, one cannot help but feel that David is God's chosen. Jewish tradition has come to regard David as God's anointed, the one who will give rise to the future messiah.

But a careful reading of David's career shows a highly complex human being with a multitude of talents as well as shortcomings. His relationship with God has its ups and downs. His relationship with his family members, friends, and associates ranges from extreme love and devotion to serious conflict. His weakness for women brings him great trouble. David, in the final analysis, is a self-made hero, who because of his unmatched gifts and accomplishments becomes God's favorite.

II Samuel:
The Kingdom of David

David's lament for Saul and Jonathan—sincere grief or a political statement?

Not only was David one of the greatest kings of all time, he was also one of the greatest poets. At the end of I Samuel, Israel's first king and his crown prince lie dead on the battlefield, having fought their last battle with the Philistines. Now the kingdom of Israel, still in its infancy, is without a king or an heir, hanging by a thread, and young David, one of Israel's military commanders, is facing the loss of the king he always obeyed and respected, and his son, Jonathan, whom he loved like a brother.

In II Samuel, Chapter One, David eulogizes the two as he tries to shake heaven and earth with his grief. In Hebrew, there is nothing that surpassed the beauty and majesty of his words. In English, we can only approximate them:

> . . . *Your glory, O Israel,*
> *on your high places, slain?*
> *How did the mighty fall! . . .*
>
> . . . *Saul and Jonathan,*
> *loving and pleasant in their life,*
> *in death did not part. . .*
> (II Samuel 1:19, 23)

As David spoke those words, the legitimate royal house in Israel was the House of Saul. David needed the legitimacy Saul had. He could have composed this moving eulogy to gain the sympathy of the people, and to assert his authority. Indeed, after the death of Saul and Jonathan, Saul's followers crowned another son of his, named Ishboshet,* as king, while David's own tribe, the tribe of Judah, wanted him for a king. Israel was hardly united behind David. His position, and that of Israel in general, was quite precarious.

One, however, will have to be a hopeless cynic to believe that David did not speak those words with all his heart. No one in all of Israel at that time, as we learn from reading the story of David's career, loved his people and their God more than David. He devoted his entire life to continuing the work Saul started, of unifying the tribes and consolidating the monarchy. He knew that Jonathan, whom he loved, in his own words, "more than women," was the one to follow his father as king. In time, he will get used to the idea that he is indeed the founder of the new dynasty, namely, the House of David. But now he is only a bereaved subject and friend, whose pain is reflected perfectly in the words of his lament.

Was King David gay?

The words in David's lament over the death of Saul and Jonathan, where he says that his love for Jonathan was greater than his love of women, has led some to argue that David was gay. Unlike ancient Greece, where homosexuality was fully accepted (some of Greece's great philosophers were known to be homosexuals), in the biblical culture it was not an accepted lifestyle (see Leviticus 18:22), hence being gay was not openly admitted. Consequently, it remains anyone's guess whether or not David was gay.

---

* Literally Man-of-Shame. This was not his real name. It was a pejorative nickname given to him perhaps because his original name was Ishbaal, which referred to the pagan god Baal.

Why did David ask Saul's followers to return his former wife, Michal, as a condition for making peace with them?

In I Samuel we are told that David marries Saul's daughter, Michal, as a reward for killing 100 Philistines. Later, as David falls into disfavor with Saul and runs away from him, Michal is given to someone else as wife.

Now, after a prolonged conflict between David's followers and those of the late king, the latter seek to make peace with David. At that point David asks for his former wife to be returned to him.

The marriage of David and Michal was far from happy, and she never bore him any children. So it appears that this was a political move of gaining legitimacy among those tribes who were still loyal to the old monarchy. It was also David's way of re-claiming what was his in the first place. And, possibly, he was still in love with the woman of his early youth.

Why did David pick Jerusalem as his royal city?

David was originally from Bethlehem, a town near Jerusalem. Later, he moved to Hebron, a little further to the south. Jerusalem at that time was not inhabited by Jews, but rather by a people called Jebusites. The city was fortified and considered impregnable, and neither Joshua nor the Judges nor Saul were able to capture it. Its link to Jewish history goes back to the time of Abraham, who took his son Isaac to be sacrificed on Mount Moriah, where later the Holy Temple was built.

To David, conquering Jerusalem was a military challenge. Additionally, by remaining in the land of Judah, his own tribe, he could be challenged by some of the tribes as a usurper of the monarchy. Jerusalem belonged to none of the tribes, and was a good neutral place to establish the seat of his monarchy, as well as the link to God's covenant with Abraham.

With the establishment of Jerusalem as his capital, David took the greatest step in the process of consolidating the kingdom and shaping the character of the Jewish people. Whether living in their land as a sovereign people, or during centuries of exile, Jerusalem always was and will always be the heart of the Jewish people.

Did God talk to David?

Saul, David's predecessor, tried desperately to communicate with God, but had to content himself with communicating through the prophet Samuel. The same is basically true of David. As the author of the Book of Psalms, the world's most revered collection of prayers, David did a great deal of talking to or about God, but not so much the other way around. Here in II Samuel, David at first has to make his way through life by his own wits, and later becomes the recipient of God's word through the prophet Nathan. In fact, as of David's time, we no longer hear so much about angels coming along as messengers from God, nor do we have God talk to the leaders of Israel. From now on it is a specific class of people known as prophets who get the divine message. Great as David is, he is not a prophet, but rather a political ruler.

Was Michal right in scorning David?

Once David has put an end to the Philistine threat against his people, and has consolidated his power as the central ruler, he decides to bring the Holy Ark to Jerusalem, thus establishing the city as the spiritual center of all Israel. As the Ark is brought in a solemn procession to its future home, King David goes out to greet it dressed in a simple cloth garment, and dances in front of the Ark in public view. When he returns to his palace, his wife, Michal, Saul's daughter, scorns him for behaving like a commoner. David is annoyed by her reception, and reminds her that God has chosen him to take her father's place.

This episode of domestic conflict shows David in a very human light. He is a man of the people. He is not the kind of king Michal remembers from her youth, standing apart from the people. Is she right about decorum? Yes. Is he right about being one of the people? Yes. We recall the words of Moses about the future king, who should not put himself above the people. What we have here is a conflict between two rights, as often happens in human affairs.

Absalom's hair caught in the tree

Why does God turn down David's wish to build the Temple?

Moses' greatest wish was to enter the Promised Land, but God turned him down. David's greatest wish was to build the Holy Temple, and here again God, speaking through the prophet Nathan, turns him down. Why so? Was David not worthy of this task?

David was a man of war. He spent most of life fighting wars, killing people on the battlefield (see I Chronicles 28:3). The Holy Temple was a spiritual center of peace and harmony. The same hands that shed blood could not build God's sanctuary. It was left to David's son, Solomon, to build the Temple. Furthermore, we are about to be told about David's greatest sin, which may also have stood in his way of building the Temple.

David and Bathsheba—how great of a sin?

One evening David strolls on the roof of his palace when he sees on a nearby roof a beautiful woman bathing. He arranges to see her and impregnates her. He then sends her husband to the battlefield on a mission from which he will not return alive.

Clearly, David's behavior in this instance is out of character, and it brings upon him the wrath of Nathan the Prophet. David is told that he stole the poor man's ewe, and God will punish him by seeing to it that the child born to him and Bathsheba will be stillborn.

David's sin is indeed great, and in different ways he will continue to pay for it till the day he dies. The first child born from this union will die. David's sons will give him a great deal of grief, and he will not find peace in his old age.

David and Absalom—is David being punished for his sins?

Apparently, yes. As great a king as David was, as great a believer in God as he was, he broke the rule established by Moses regarding the future king not to have many wives. His wives, particularly in the case of Bathsheba, and his many sons, were the source of his many troubles during his old age. All of this comes to a head with the conflict between him and his son Absalom, who wanted to oust his father. What follows is a civil

war between the followers of the father and those of the son,
which nearly puts an end to David's reign, but turns in David's
favor when Absalom, who has long beautiful hair, finds himself during a hot pursuit in the forest hanging from a tree by his
hair that has become entangled in the branches, and is killed by
his fa-ther's general, Joab. Despite his deliverance, David is devastated by the death of his beloved Absalom, and refuses to be
consoled:

> *David was greatly agitated. He went up*
> *to the chamber over the gate and cried,*
> *saying, as he walked up:*
> *My son, Absalom, my son, my son,*
> *Absalom, would that I died in your place,*
> *Absalom, my son, my son.*
> (II Samuel 19:1)

Here again we see David as very human, a great man with a
highly complex personality, who goes through life experiencing
a great deal of turmoil and conflict.

What do we learn from the life of David about human leadership and God's will?

David was Israel's greatest king, and one of the greatest leaders
in history. Moreover, David, whose name means beloved, remains
to this day one of the most beloved figures of history, not only to
Jews but also to Christians and Muslims. To this day, Jews compose and sing songs of praise, love and yearning for David who,
according to Jewish legend, never really died, but is sleeping in
his secret cave and will rise some day to redeem his people.

But the Bible makes it very clear that David was only human.
Notwithstanding his great accomplishments, he had great character flaws which in the end brought him a great deal of trouble.
David himself says in one of his psalms: "Do not put your trust in
princes, or in man." Only trust God. No doubt, he was thinking
of himself. He was humble enough and aware of his own failings. Great king that he was, he knew that there was only one
true king, the Holy and Blessed One.

What do we learn in the Book of II Samuel about the evolving relationship between God and Israel?

In this book, which covers the career of King David, God is still the main character, but in a different way. Unlike the first great leader of Israel, namely, Moses, who is guided by God nearly every step of the way, David is basically on his own, with God in the background, making the divine will known only in extreme situations, and then only indirectly, or through a designated prophet.

Indeed, there is a clear progression throughout the Bible and in post-biblical times regarding the relationship between God and humanity, and between God and Israel. It begins with Adam and Eve having little say over their own career, living in a controlled environment called Garden of Eden. With Moses, God's law is given to Israel, who are expected to follow it from that time on. At the time of David there is a clear withdrawal of God from human affairs. Gradually, God lets humanity grow up and be on its own, while God's law continues to govern human affairs from a distance. It is no wonder that David composed so many prayers, known as psalms. In his day the people of Israel must have felt that they were on their own, and rather than wait for a divine message, it was up to them now to seek God through prayer (and sacrificial offerings) to find divine favor.

The judgment of Solomon

I KINGS:
THE KINGDOM OF SOLOMON
AND THE DIVIDED KINGDOM

What do we learn from history and archeology about the reign of David and Solomon?

With David and Solomon, the Kingdom of Israel becomes an empire, which rules over a territory stretching from Egypt in the south to Babylonia in the North, with many local nations paying it tribute. One may wonder how twelve relatively small tribes managed in a short time to transform themselves into an empire, and whether this actually happened.

The answer to the second question is yes. There is enough documentary and archeological evidence dating back to the tenth and eleventh centuries B.C.E. to show that during the time of these two kings, the two main powers of the ancient Near East, namely, Egypt and the Babylonia, had lost their primacy and had left a power vacuum in the region. This was actually David and Solomon's lucky break. Coupled with David's decisive victories against Israel's long standing enemies, mainly the Philistines, this window of opportunity was fully exploited by David, and even more so by Solomon. During their long reign (David's 40 years and Solomon's 40), the tribes of Israel were transformed into a highly organized and powerful nation.

As for archeological discoveries related to direct personal data about the two kings, those are yet to take place, but there is a high likelihood that it will happen. Much has been unearthed regarding the times and confirming the activities of both, and their personal chronicles are mentioned in the Book of Kings, copies of which, like the Dead Sea Scrolls which were found in 1947, are lying somewhere in the ground and are waiting to be discovered.

What made Solomon the wisest of men?

Of David's several sons who vied for their father's throne, Solomon was by far the best choice. While David was the best man to unify the tribes, defeat Israel's enemies, and establish the supremacy of God's law among the tribes, Solomon was the right man to rule over a strong nation that was able to build the Holy Temple, replace the tribal loyalties with a national identity, and conduct its affairs like an empire.

The Bible tells us that Solomon was the wisest of all men. "Wise as Solomon" is an old English expression. When the young king first assumes power, God appears to him in a dream and tells him to make a wish. Solomon asks for a "wise heart." This is undoubtedly the wisest thing anyone could wish for. His wish is granted. We are given an early example of this "wise heart" when two women come before the king for a judgment regarding a baby each of them claims to be hers. Solomon knows that if he puts the two women to the test, the biological mother's identity will be revealed. He tells the two he would cut the baby in half and give each one of them one half. The child's mother asks the king to spare her son, while the other woman agrees to the harsh decree, which makes it clear she is the impostor.

The Bible identifies Solomon as the author of two bib-lical books which are part of the wisdom literature of Scriptures—Proverbs and Ecclesiastes. In those books we see Solomon's wisdom transcending the confines of Hebrew culture and reaching into universal culture, notably the works of the Greek poets and philosophers. To what extent Solomon is the actual author of those books we shall see when we reach that part of the Bible.

Why did Solomon prosper even though he did not fit Moses' directives for the future king?

Recalling Moses' directives in Deuteronomy for the future king, two of them are violated by Solomon, namely, not to have too many horses or too many wives. Solomon in effect becomes a leading horse merchant of his time, and is reported to have a thousand wives and consorts (11:3).

How are we to reconcile God's will regarding these matters and Solomon's actions? In Solomon's defense one may point out that both the horse trade and the vast harem were part of his empire-building. The marriages to foreign princesses were part of the process of concluding alliances with his neighbors. The horse trade was a vital part of building his own military power, keeping control over his large domain, and a major source of revenue. But all of this had a downside for a nation that was destined to be "a nation of priests and a holy people." With power comes corruption. With foreign wives comes idol worshiping. Ultimately, the Solomonic lifestyle and empire-building did not fit the Hebrew character and Israel's geopolitical reality, and was doomed to fail after his death.

Who are the Phoenicians, and why do they help Solomon build the Temple?

While the Canaanite nations the tribes encountered in the Promised Land became their enemies and were gradually defeated, one Canaanite people, known to us mainly as Phoenicians and residing on the coast of Lebanon, became an ally of both David and Solomon, and had a major influence on Israel's culture and on the cultures of the world. Two good examples of this influence are the development of the alphabet by the ancient Phoenicians, which is the basis for all Western alphabets and for Hebrew as well, and the cedar wood supplied by the Phoenicians for the building of the Kingdom of Israel, used for both house construction and shipbuilding, and particularly for Solomon's Holy Temple in Jerusalem.

Why didn't David conquer the Phoenicians but preferred to be their ally?

Bringing cedar wood for the construction of the Temple

In effect, the Phoenicians paid tribute to David and later to Solomon, which was far more valuable than an occupation of their land. They were master merchants and builders, and the emerging kingdom of Israel had much to learn and benefit from them. It was a wise decision to become their ally rather than their enemy, and it greatly benefited both David and Solomon.

Why does the Bible dwell at such length on the building of the Holy Temple?

The Bible describes the building and the physical features of the Jerusalem Temple in great detail. This wealth of information begins in the Book of Exodus with the description of the tabernacle, which is the early prototype of the Temple. It is repeated here, and later in the Book of Ezekiel, which predicts the building of the Second Temple, following the destruction of the first. It is also given a prominent place in Chronicles.

Why so much architectonic and artistic detail?

One should bear in mind that the Temple was the fulfilment of a dream of generations, beginning with Moses and even before. It was the only place in its day where a Jew could find atonement, the only dwelling place of Israel's God. Each little detail of this structure was imbued with holiness. Any deviation from the plan, no matter how minute, meant tampering with divine instructions. For the next ten centuries, it will be the wish of every Jew to go on a pilgrimage to this House of God, particularly during the pilgrim festivals (Passover, Shavuot, and Sukkot). When the First Temple is destroyed in the sixth century B.C.E., the Jews, exiled to Babylonia, sit on the banks of the rivers of Babylon and weep as they remember the Temple. Those who return to Jerusalem rebuild it. After the Second Temple is destroyed by the Romans in 70 C.E., the Jews continue to dream of it and mention it in their prayers and songs to this day, associating its future, third rebuilding with the coming of the messiah.

Why did the kingdom split?

This question is answered on two different levels—political and spiritual.

The political answer is that the window of opportunity given to David and Solomon in the form of a power vacuum in the Near East in their time which enabled them to create and maintain their own empire, did not last long. By the time Solomon's son Rehoboam inherited the throne, Egypt had rallied and started to challenge Israel in the south. Meanwhile in the north, the ten northern tribes, or provinces, were complaining to the new king about the yoke of taxes and labor which his father had imposed on them. In other words, the glory and splendor of the great Solomon did not come without a price. The people were heavily taxed, and were pressed into service for small or no pay as they built the palaces and fortifications of the kingdom. The moment Solomon died, rebellion was in the air.

The spiritual answer is that the tribes of Israel became unfaithful to God, and the ten tribes of the north were doomed to break off from the House of David and eventually disappear. Only the tribe of Judah in the south would remain as the enduring remnant of the two kingdoms.

Rehoboam did not have his father's wisdom. Instead of making life easier for the northern tribes, he made it harder, and so they rebelled and started their separate kingdom under Jeroboam, calling themselves Israel, while the old kingdom became known as Judah.

What do we know about the divided kingdom's kings?

With Rehoboam in Judah and Jeroboam in Northern Israel we are on firm historical ground. The many archeological explorations of the past hundred years in the Near East have unearthed a wealth of inscriptions, artefacts, monuments, and remnants of ancient towns and other structures which reveal names of Hebrew kings and their servants, accounts of battles between the kings of Israel and their surrounding enemies, structures mentioned in the Bible such as tunnels, fortifications, and palaces, and fragments of biblical text. We have now fully entered history.

Regrettably, from a political standpoint, this is not exactly a glorious time for the two new small nations, Judah and Israel.

Both are constantly besieged by invading enemies from far and near, and are constantly struggling to survive as political entities. Quite simply, the geographic location of the narrow strip of land they inhabit is a land-bridge for the great powers of the ancient Near East, namely, Egypt in the south and the empires of Mesopotamia—and also lesser powers like Aram (Syria)—in the north. Egypt, which during the time of Solomon posed no threat because of internal weakness, recovers during the time of Solomon's son, Rehoboam, and Pharaoh Shishak invades both Judah and Israel. This kind of invasion results at best in becoming a vassal state, forced to pay tribute, and at worst in conquest, destruction, and exile.

The real greatness of the divided kingdom period belongs to the great prophets who appeared during that time. There were apparently quite a few of them, but the ones who tower above the rest are Elijah, Elisha, Amos, Isaiah, Micah, Hosea, and Jeremiah. They were able to articulate the message of the God of Israel in a way that inspired their people and the world throughout the ages, and ensured the survival of a small people that would have otherwise long disappeared.

How was Judah different from Israel, and why did it last longer?

The northern kingdom of Israel only lasted two centuries, while Judah lasted almost twice as long. There were several reasons for this. First, Judah was the main spiritual center of the Jews, with the Temple as the place where God dwelled. Its population consisted mainly of the tribe of Judah, which had its own cohesive culture and history. It was ruled by a continuous dynasty of the House of David, which had well-established traditions. Additionally, Judah was not directly in the path of the invading powers, which ran along the coast and through the valley of Jezreel. It lay up in the mountains of Judea, and did not offer the same bait to invaders as did the northern plains and coast of Israel.

Israel, on the other hand, was not truly united. Kings were frequently overthrown and replaced by strongmen from outside the royal family. The capital of Israel, originally in Shehem, was shifted several times and ended up in Samaria, and instead of the

Jerusalem Temple, old shrines such as Beth El were used for worship, alongside with pagan shrines which were common, especially when the king was married to a non-Jewish wife, as in the case of Ahab and Jezebel.

Elijah—what is unique about this particular prophet?

Elijah, a native of Gilead, on the far northeastern periphery of the kingdom of Israel, seems to come out of nowhere. Like David before him, he is one of the main legendary figures in Jewish history. He is the one who visits all Jewish homes on Passover. He is the one who will herald the coming of the messiah.

What made Elijah such a figure of legend?

His story makes one think of a near-mythological figure, better yet, a force of nature. He bursts upon the scene of the Northern Kingdom at a time when the people of Israel are being forced by Jezebel, King Ahab's Phoenician wife, to convert to the cult of her gods, Baal and Asherah. The people waver between monotheism and paganism. Many of the prophets of Adonai are killed or go into hiding, as does Elijah. While dodging the law, Elijah becomes a roving country miracle worker. He feeds the hungry and revives a dead child. But he cannot stay away for long. He must confront the evil monarchs and fight back for the God of Israel.

When he meets Ahab, the king asks him if he is Elijah, the "corrupter of Israel." "No," replies Elijah, "you are the corrupter. You have taken your people away from their true God."

Elijah arranges for a contest between himself and hundreds of Baal and Asherah prophets. The people of Israel gather at Mount Carmel to find out once and for all who is the true God. Altars are erected, and Elijah challenges the pagan prophets to bring down fire from heaven to consume the animal offerings on their altar, while he would do the same on his. For hours, his adversaries try to do it but to no avail. Elijah, on the other hand, has no trouble doing it. The multitude falls on the ground and cries out with awe, "Adonai is God, Adonai is God."

Jezebel decides to kill Elijah. He flees to the southern kingdom of Judah, and wanders in the desert. At Mount Sinai, God appears to him:

Elijah goes up to heaven

> *. . . and lo, Adonai passed by. There was a great*
> *and mighty wind, splitting mountains and*
> *shattering rocks by the power of Adonai;*
> *but Adonai was not in the wind. After the*
> *wind—an earthquake; but Adonai was not*
> *in the earthquake. After the earthquake –*
> *fire; but Adonai was not in the fire. And*
> *after the fire—a soft murmuring sound.*
> *When Elijah heard it, he wrapped his mantle*
> *about his face and went out and stood at*
> *the entrance of the cave. Then a voice spoke*
> *to him: "Why are you here, Elijah?" He*
> *Answered: "I am moved by zeal for*
> *Adonai, the God of Hosts; for the Children*
> *of Israel have forsaken Your covenant, torn*
> *down Your altars, and have put Your*
> *prophets to the sword. I alone am left, and*
> *they are out to take my life.*
>
> (I Kings: 19:11-14)

Now Elijah is given his mission, which will altar the politics of the region. He is to anoint new kings for Aram (Israel's northern enemy) and for Israel, and pick a successor for himself, a new prophet named Elisha.

Elijah does as he is told. Now the House of Ahab is doomed to fall, and Israel's prophets will reassert themselves again.

Elijah's life ends as dramatically as it began. His disciple, Elisha, sees him go up to heaven in a chariot of fire. Elisha picks up Elijah's mantle which lies on the ground, and becomes his successor.

As a militant prophet, Elijah is a unique figure in the Bible. So he remains in the collective memory and imagination of the people. He does not accept any human authority. His loyalty is only to the God of Israel. He shows the way to the great prophets who follow him. And in time he becomes part of the messianic hopes and dreams of his people.

II KINGS:
THE TEN LOST TRIBES AND THE
AGE OF THE GREAT PROPHETS

What do we learn from the stories of Elijah and Elisha about the "early" and the "later" prophets?

If Elisha is not as colorful as his master, he certainly comes close. He too becomes a countryside miracle worker, a semi-mythological figure. He too becomes involved in politics. He too lives in the Northern Kingdom at a time of decline, when his master's and his own heroic efforts to restore the faith of Israel's God to the people fail, as the days of the court of Samaria are numbered.

The great prophets who follow Elijah and Elisha are no longer the kind of folk heroes those two are. Instead, they are poets and writers whose words are preserved in books which bear their names: Amos, Hosea, Isaiah, Micah, and Jeremiah. They too will be followed by another group of great prophets, beginning with Ezekiel, whose pronouncements will also be preserved in books named after them. Thus, Elijah and Elisha open the door to the era of Israel's great prophets, whose message is unique in human history.

The fall of the Northern Kingdom—how and why did it come about?

According to the Bible, the Northern Kingdom fell because its rulers and their followers went after pagan gods and did not follow God's law. This may be true, but there was also a more immediate and inescapable reason, namely, the Empire of Assyria in the north, which began its push westward and overran all the small nations in its path. In the year 721 B.C.E., after six years of siege, Israel's capital, Samaria, fell, and the ten tribes of the north were exiled. It was the policy of the occupiers at that time to shift populations from one place to another, thus greatly reducing the chance of an uprising.

Assyrian annals which were discovered in the Near East refer to the Assyrian king, Tiglath-pileser, boasting about the occupation of Samaria and the tribute imposed on it, and mention the names of three of the last four kings of Israel, namely, Menahem, Pekah, and Hoshea:

> As for Menahem, I overwhelmed him [like a
> snowstorm] and he. . . fled like a bird. . . I
> returned him to his place [and imposed
> tribute upon him]. . . Israel [literally "Omri-
> Land"] . . . all its inhabitants [and] their
> possessions I led to Assyria. They overthrew
> their king Pekah and I placed Hoshea as
> king over them.
>   (As quoted in Understanding the Bible
>   by Harry M. Orlinsky).

In this 27-century-old document we have clear confirmation of the end of the Northern Kingdom and the exile of its inhabitants. To this day, scholars speculate as to what ever happened to the so-called Ten Lost Tribes of Israel.

What happened to the Ten Lost Tribes?

The Jews of today are primarily the descendants of the tribe of Judah. However, Jews started to migrate across the ancient world back in biblical times, and by the time the Romans destroyed Jerusalem in the first century C.E., large numbers of Jews lived throughout the Roman Empire, and from there migrated all over the world. In recent centuries, Jewish communities have been discovered in places as remote as China, India, and South Africa. Such discoveries usually led to speculation regarding the "Ten Lost Tribes." Furthermore, theories about those tribes abounded over the years, and have gone so far as to claim that such disparate people as some of the people in the British Isles as well as the Mayan Indians in Central America are descendants of Israel's lost tribes.

The historical truth is somewhat different. There were no ten distinctive tribes at the time of the fall of Samaria, but rather an amalgamation of several of the tribes. The exiled population was not lost, but rather absorbed by local populations in the Assyrian Empire. Some false rumors raised in the course of history never seem to die out.

What was happening in Judah around the time of the fall of the Northern Kingdom?

Prior to the fall of Samaria and thereafter, Judah's history was not particularly spectacular, certainly not stellar. No more Davids or Solomons. The later descendants of the House of David who ascended to the throne alternated between idol worshiping and loyalty to the God of their ancestors. The small kingdom of Judah now found itself squeezed between the Egyptian empire in the south and the northern empires of Assyria and Babylonia. To survive, the Judean king had to make alliances with one against the other, which meant putting oneself in a no-win situation.

Following the fall of Israel, Judah was ruled by King Hezekiah who, we are told, did follow God's law:

> *In the third year of King Hoshea son of Elah*
> *of Israel, Hezekiah son of King Ahaz of Judah*
> *became king. . . He did what was pleasing to*
> *Adonai, just as his ancestor David had done. He*
> *abolished the shrines and smashed the pillars*
> *and cut down the sacred post. He also broke*
> *into pieces the bronze serpent which Moses*
> *had made, for until that time the Israelites*
> *had been offering sacrifices to it. . .*
>
> (II Kings 18:1-5)

Josiah's reformation—too little too late?

About a hundred years after the fall of Israel, Judah was ruled by King Josiah. By now the teachings of Moses had greatly declined among the Judeans, and all manner of pagan cults and beliefs permeated the kingdom. Josiah decided to launch a major reform to eliminate any trace of paganism, and renew the faith of Israel's ancestors and lawgiver. He found, or claimed to have found, a scroll of the covenant, presumably parts of the Book of Deuteronomy, which was now beginning to take its final written shape.

Josiah went about his reform relentlessly. He assembled the people in Jerusalem and renewed the covenant of old. He celebrated the Feast of Passover before a multitude, in a way that it "was not celebrated since the days of the Judges." This comment indicates how far gone the Jews were in having drifted away from their laws and traditions.

But it was to no avail. The kingdom's decline was no longer stoppable. As the Bible puts it, God gave up on Judah, as God had given up on Israel. The days of the southern kingdom were numbered.

Was the fall of Judah the end of the Jewish monarchy?

The fall of Judah in the year 586 B.C.E., in the time of King Zedekiah who was defeated by the Babylonian king Nebuchadnezzar, was not the end of the Jewish monarchy. It was the end of the classical period of the kings in biblical times. During the post-biblical period, the descendants of the Maccabees will establish a new monarchy, taking the place of the House of David, which will last into the beginning of the common era. After that, Jews will no longer have a king.

Who is the central figure in Judah during the time of the fall of Jerusalem and the beginning of the Babylonian Exile?

The leading figure during that time is the prophet Jeremiah. It is interesting that the period of the kings ends with a prophet as the best remembered personality. Here again we are reminded that the kings, or the temporal political leaders, were accidental to the mission of Israel, while the prophets were the dominant figures, the ones who spoke for God, and who charted for their people a direction that has carried them to this day.

Isaiah

ISAIAH:
GOD'S DOMINANCE AND
MAN'S ARROGANCE

What is Isaiah's historical background?

Isaiah lived in Jerusalem before, during, and after the fall of the Northern kingdom, in the second half of the eighth century B.C.E. This event must have had a profound effect on him, echoes of which may be found in the first chapter of his book:

> Your land is desolate,
> Your towns are consumed by fire.
> You see your land eaten by strangers. . .
> The Daughter of Zion is left
> Like a booth in a vineyard,
> Like a doghouse in a melon patch,
> like a besieged city.
> If not for the small remnant
> Adonai of Hosts has left us,
> We would be like Sodom and Gomorrah.
>   (Isaiah 1:7-9)

Judah was now alone, with a vast pagan world surrounding it. Isaiah feels deeply the precarious condition of his people, and is anxious to find a way to preserve the teachings of the one true God.

What is the role of the prophet in the time of Isaiah?

Isaiah continues the task started by Moses and carried on by prophets like Samuel and Elijah, namely, imparting to his people the knowledge of the one God, and their subservience to that God. There is a clear progression from Moses, the lawgiver, to Samuel and Elijah, the activist prophets, to the age of Isaiah, when the words of the prophets are recorded and kept as a lasting legacy for future generations.

What is clear by now is that the task of inculcating the true faith has been most difficult. The prophets are hardly ever satisfied with the state of their people's faith. During the three hundred years that have elapsed since the time of David, hardly any king of Israel or Judah received high marks from the prophets, and the people were scolded nearly all the time. By now it has become a given that the role of the prophet is to scold and to chastise.

And Isaiah does it masterfully. His words are like bolts of thunder. They leave no room for doubt as to who the supreme ruler and judge is, and how miserably people fail to live up to the expectations of the supreme authority:

> *An ox knows its master,*
> *And a donkey its owner's trough;*
> *Israel knows not,*
> *My people have paid no heed.*
>   (Isaiah 1:3)

Does God have unrealistic expectations for the people of the covenant?

Were the people of Israel and Judah really that bad? After all, they did bring offerings to God's Temple in Jerusalem. They did accept the prophets as God's messengers. The people of Judah did remain loyal to the House of David. What, then, was so wrong?

By general standards, not much. They were certainly not worse than the surrounding nations, none of whom the prophets held in high esteem. But the covenant meant that they were not like all other nations, and had to live by a higher standard. Was this realistic?

Isaiah makes it very clear what that standard is:

Put your evil doings away from My sight.
Cease to do evil. Learn to do good.
Devote yourselves to justice, aid the wronged,
uphold the rights of the orphan,
defend the cause of the widow.
                              (Isaiah 1:16-17)

In other words, social justice. A nation founded on social justice can last. Where social justice does not exist, people court their doom. This is the main message of the biblical prophets. It remains relevant to this day. And, while it is difficult, it is not impossible.

What is Isaiah's stand on the ritual of animal sacrifices?

In the first chapter, Isaiah launches an attack on the practice of animal sacrifices in words which are echoed by other prophets as well. What is not clear is whether the prophet would like to see animal sacrifices abolished altogether, or whether he means that sacrifices without true faith are useless.

Whether animal sacrifices were a compromise with pagan practices or an integral part of the early faith of Israel is not clear (see also p. 76). What is clear is that the prophets sensed that material offerings for most people took the place of ethical practices and sincere faith, and thus became idolatrous rather than cleansing.

What is the meaning of paganism and idol worshiping?

The idol worshiping of the pagan nations is seen by the prophet as an abomination. What is it specifically about idol worshiping that the prophet finds to be abominable?

The prophet, living in a world where most people believe a tree, or a rock, or a man-made image to have divine powers and therefore deserving of being an object of worship, is keenly aware of the futility of such belief, and of its offensive nature. Another aspect of idol worshiping is the belief in a human being, such as the Pharaoh, as a divine being. To the prophet, no human being is divine, but rather the handiwork of the one true God. As God's creation, a person is no better than a worm (to use Isaiah's expression). Worst of all, the prophet witnesses how pagan religions lead to immoral practices, such as ritual prostitution, human sacrifices, exploitation of human beings, and the absence of a moral law. Over against the many pagan religions practiced all around him, the prophet posits the one universal and absolute God who transcends all human power and understanding, the creator of all, the one who makes empires rise and fall, and the only one who endures when all other pagan gods are gone.

Why is Isaiah having visions of "Day of Adonai" and the "End of Days?"

Isaiah can tell that the days of the Kingdom of Judah are numbered. Sooner or later, it will go the way of the Kingdom of Israel which has just lost its sovereignty. But he also knows that the covenant God had entered into with Abraham is eternal. It is to last for all time.

Consequently, Isaiah is having two visions, which are shared by other prophets as well. The first is the vision of the Day of Adonai. This is also known as Judgment Day, a time when God comes to judge the world, punish evil, do away with idolatry, and usher a new age. This first phase leads to a second one, called the End of Days:

> *And it shall come to pass at the end of days,*
> *that the mountain of the House of Adonai*
> *shall be at the top of the mountains and*
> *above the hills, and all nations shall come to it.*
> *And many nations shall go and say, Come,*
> *let us go up to the mountain of Adonai. . .*
> *for out of Zion will come forth the Torah,*
> *and the word of Adonai from Jerusalem.*
>   (Isaiah 2:2-3)

In other words, not only will Judah endure, it will, in the words of the prophet Joel, "dwell forever" (4:20). The reason? To impart the Torah, or the knowledge of God, to all the nations of the world.

What is the most common and grievous sin according to Isaiah?

Isaiah accuses not only his own people but all people of one lethal sin—pride. Not pride in the positive sense, but mindless arrogance, over-reliance on human power, flaunting of riches, failure to realize where it all comes from, and how limited human power is:

> *The haughty eyes of man are brought low,*
> *and the arrogance of people is bent down,*
> *and God alone will rise above all.*
>   (Isaiah 2:11)

The prophet Micah, Isaiah's contemporary, makes it clear in one of the most famous verses in the entire Bible, that God expects man to "walk humbly with Adonai, your God" (6:8).

Does Isaiah actually see God in his vision?

The prophets, from Moses on, become aware of their mission at an unusual moment of revelation. For Isaiah, this moment comes one day while he is inside the Temple, presumably during an earthquake. (We know from related records that Judah was visited by some severe earthquakes in Isaiah's time.) The walls shake, and the smoke from the altar or the incense fills the sanctuary. Isaiah sees God sitting on the throne, with six-winged angels hovering about.

Did Isaiah actually see God? Isaiah does not say that he saw God (that is, YHWH), but rather "my Master." There is no physical description of God. There is only a presence. Now, Jews believed that the *shehinah*, or the divine presence, dwelled in the Temple in Jerusalem (*shehinah* means "dwelling"). There was nothing unusual about feeling the presence of God in the Temple. In this case, the prophet reports hearing the voice of God, who sends him on his mission. In short, the prophet experiences the presence of God, but does not actually see God.

What is the prophecy about the "shoot of the stump of Jesse?"

In Chapter 11, Isaiah prophesies:

> *A shoot will grow of the stump of Jesse,*
> *a twig shall sprout from his stock.*
> *The spirit of Adonai shall rest upon him. . .*
> *. . . and the wolf shall live with the lamb,*
> *and the leopard shall lie down with the kid.*
>   (Isaiah 11:1-2; 6)

This is part of the earlier vision of the End of Days. Isaiah believes that the House of Jesse, David's father, will produce a future David, who will bring Israel back its former glory. It will be a time of universal peace, not only between nations, but throughout nature as well.

Why does Isaiah prophesy about Israel's neighboring nations?

Set upon his mission of bringing God's word to his people, Isaiah becomes involved in the politics not only of the royal house in Jerusalem, but also beyond Judah's borders, namely, Babylonia, Assyria, Moab, Damascus, Egypt, Tyre, and so on. All of them will experience the retribution of God.

Isaiah's view of God's plan is universalistic, rather than nationalistic. While the prevailing pagan view in antiquity was that each god is a territorial god, concerned with the local affairs of his or her own subjects, the Jewish view of God gradually developed in the Bible from the covenant between God and Israel to the common destiny of the human race under God's dominance. Thus, Isaiah believed that God used empires like Assyria or Egypt to punish other nations, including Israel, but in turn would punish them as well. No one escapes God's judgment, and all people are bound by a common fate.

Who is the Second Isaiah?

In Chapter 40, the Book of Isaiah no longer deals with the time of the fall of Israel, but moves 200 years ahead to the time of the

Babylonian Exile. Clearly, we have here another, later prophet, who has become known as the Second Isaiah.

We have no data about the person of the Second Isaiah. Nor do we know this prophet's real name. His prophecies, however, like those of the first Isaiah, are written in beautiful poetic language, and his message is consistent with that of his predecessor: God is all-powerful and just. In practicing justice, Israel will be redeemed. In due time, Jerusalem and the Temple will be rebuilt.

Who is the "Suffering Servant?"

In Chapter 53 of Second Isaiah we read about a mysterious person who takes on other people's suffering:

> *Yet it was our sickness that he was bearing,*
> *Our suffering that he endured.*
>
> (Isaiah 53:4)

This obscure passage has given rise to much speculation among both Jews and Christians. For Christians, it became one of the proof texts of the Old Testament regarding the career of Jesus, who was sent to earth to take on the sins of the world and provide vicarious atonement. Jews have tried several possibilities. It is Second Isaiah himself, who is suffering to redeem his people. Or it is the Jewish people as a group, suffering because of the sins of the world. There is no clear understanding of this passage, and there is little to go on to make an informed judgment.

How is the message of the Second Isaiah different from the first?

The two Isaiahs live during a totally different time. The first lives during a time of decline, when the days of the kingdom of Judah are numbered. He spends most of his energy on chastising his people and the rest of the world. He dreams of a better future, and prophesies about the End of Days.

The Second Isaiah lived 200 years later, during the 70-year-long exile in Babylonia, following the destruction of the Temple and Jerusalem. He foresees the return to Zion and the rebuilding of the

Temple. This is not a time for chastising. Israel paid for her sins, and is now ready to be redeemed. It does not need now a prophet of doom, but rather one of consolation. Second Isaiah is a great consoler:

> *Comfort, oh comfort My people, says Adonai,*
> *Speak tenderly to Jerusalem and tell her:*
> *She has served her time, her sin is atoned,*
> *She paid double for all of her sins.*
> (Isaiah 40:1-2)

God will never forget the old covenant:

> *Zion said: God forgot me and left me.*
> *Can a mother forget the child of her womb?*
> *Even if she does, I will not forget you.*
> *I have engraved you on the palms of my hands,*
> *I always behold Zion's walls.*
> (Isaiah 49:14-16)

One is reminded of the words of the psalmist, dating to the same time:

> *If I forget you, Jerusalem,*
> *may my right hand wither,*
> *may my tongue cling to*
> *the roof of my mouth*
> *if I remember you not. . .*
> (Psalms 137:5-6)

Second Isaiah makes it clear that God will not let Israel leave the stage of history. The time has come to go home and rebuild Jerusalem.

Jeremiah dictating his prophecies

JEREMIAH:
DESTRUCTION AND THE
PROMISE OF REDEMPTION

What is Jeremiah's historical background?

Jeremiah lives in Jerusalem at the end of the seventh century B.C.E., during the fall of Jerusalem and the destruction of the First Temple. He is the son of a priestly family of the village of Anathoth, near Jerusalem. His prophetic career begins during the reign of Josiah, and ends at the time of Judah's last king, Zedekiah. This entire period of some 54 years does not mark a high point in the history of the small kingdom of Judah. Two old empires rise in the ancient Near East, vying for control of the region. First, it is old Egypt which invades Judah from the south and makes it pay tribute. Later it is Babylonia, under the powerful King Nebuchadnezzar, who puts an end to Jewish sovereignty.

During this fateful juncture in Jewish history, Jeremiah plays a pivotal role ensuring the survival of Judaism.

What sets Jeremiah apart from all the other prophets?

Jeremiah plays a unique role in Jewish history. Perhaps because of the time in which he lives, he becomes the most well-rounded and multifaceted of all the prophets. He sees his people at their best—during the time of King Josiah's reform and the renewal of the old covenant; and at their worst, during the decline of Jerusa-

lem and the destruction of the city and the Temple. He is destined to start his career as a prophet of doom, which causes him
enormous pain, and in his old age, forced to leave his land, he
becomes a prophet of hope and consolation.

In a way, Jeremiah is the culmination of all the prophets that
preceded him, from Moses to Micah. His prophecies faithfully
mirror theirs. His words sum up their teachings. He spares no
effort in applying those teachings to his day in any way he can,
knowing full well he cannot stop the inevitable.

He has a keen sense of history. He talks about the birth of the
people of Israel during the exodus and the wanderings in the
desert, seven centuries earlier, in the most poetic terms:

> *I remember the kindness of your youth,*
> *The love of your betrothal;*
> *Your going after Me in the desert,*
> *In a land not sown.*
> (Jeremiah 2:2)

Those were the early days of the covenant, full of hope and promise. Now the end of the Jewish people seems to have arrived—at
least outwardly. Jeremiah understands that God has entrusted him
with a very critical mission. He will have to see to it that Israel lives
on.

What kind of a person is Jeremiah?

At a very young age, though born a priest, Jeremiah realizes he is
going to become a prophet. He is overwhelmed by this realization. Like many of his predecessors, including Moses, Jeremiah
tries to beg out. But he knows he has no choice. No one turns
down God. Jeremiah will spend his long life being God's mouthpiece, with hardly anyone willing to listen. he will suffer insults
and physical abuse, coming within a hair of his life.

Through it all, his faith and his love for his God and his wayward people will not falter. He will admonish and implore, cry
and wail, but he will never give up. Though a man of keen intelligence and incredible foresight, Jeremiah is all heart. Few leaders and sages in all of Jewish history show greater love for their

people, or leave us a more powerful message than Jeremiah. His message is as relevant today as it was 26 centuries ago.

Why does God choose such a harsh career for Jeremiah?

There is little happiness in Jeremiah's long life. He comes from a well-to-do family. He has a high social position, and he often has the ear of the king. But he is always at odds with his beloved people, always chastising them, never able to get them to listen, and the terrible fate of his people, which becomes a reality in his lifetime, haunts him and puts him in constant mourning.

Jeremiah realizes that the high hopes God had for the people of Israel have not been fulfilled. After seven centuries of great events, great prophets, and great achievements, the Northern Kingdom of Israel is gone, and Judah's days are numbered. The people have failed over and over again to follow God's teachings. Idolatry is rampant. The Temple is not the holy center it was intended to be. The People of the Covenant have not measured up to the high standards they had set for themselves. Jeremiah sees it all and suffers, knowing the end is near.

Jeremiah in effect takes on the suffering of his place and time, while most of the people in Jerusalem delude themselves that God will save them, no matter what. His prophetic mission forces him to see the terrible scenes of the destruction of Judah and Jerusalem and the Holy Temple long before they take place, day after day. But there is a reason for all of this. Rather than lose his mind or give up, Jeremiah becomes the one who, when the time comes, will leave his people a message of hope that will enable them to do what no other people has ever done, namely, return to their ancestral land years later and once again become a nation with its own distinctive mission.

What does Jeremiah mean when he speaks about "returning?"

Jeremiah calls upon his people to return to God. The concept of "return," *teshuvah* in Hebrew, becomes a key prophetic concept in his time. God does not wish to punish his people, but rather waits for them to return by giving up evil and doing good. This is comparable to the Christian concept of repenting, although repentance is only the first stage of *teshuvah*, which must lead to complete reconciliation with God.

Where there is life there is hope. The prophet refuses to give up. There is still time. Perhaps people will wake up and realize they must do *teshuvah* before it is too late.

Why does Jeremiah single out the observance of the Sabbath?

Like Moses before him, Jeremiah singles out the commandment regarding the observance of the Sabbath as a key to true return to God. Obviously, the Sabbath in his time was desecrated. The nations of antiquity, including the Romans, did not have a weekly day of rest dedicated to spiritual matters. A seven-day work week, particularly for slaves, was the rule. Not until the birth of Christianity does this concept take hold in the pagan world. Along with pagan practices, many in Israel did not observe the Sabbath. This was a blatant rejection of God, which people like Jeremiah could not tolerate.

Was Jeremiah considered a traitor?

Jeremiah spares no words in letting the people of Jerusalem know that the end is near. This does not endear him to the ruling class in the city. He is jailed, tortured, narrowly escaping death. He is denounced as an alarmist, indeed, a traitor. It is only years later, long after the destruction, that people begin to acknowledge Jeremiah was right while they were wrong. To this day, on the Ninth day of the month of Av, Jews sit in mourning and recite Jeremiah's words about Jerusalem's destruction, the most tragic event in biblical history.

Why does Jeremiah decide to record his prophecies in a book?

While no one listens to him, Jeremiah decides to record his words in a book, or rather a scroll, for the future. The book, of course, is the Book of Jeremiah.

What was the reason for recording something that would not stop the inevitable?

Jeremiah knew that the destruction of the Temple was not the end. He knew that wayward as his people were, they were strong enough, and the faith in the one God was compelling enough, to help them endure destruction and exile. He knew that before long the seemingly unbeatable Babylonian empire will fall, and the Jews will be able to return to their land. He even knew that this may happen more than once in the distant future. He understood the cycle of sin and return, of exile and redemption, and he knew that his words will continue to sustain his people long after he was gone.

In our time, his words have sustained those who came back to reestablish the modern state of Israel, particularly after the terrible fate of European Jewry in the twentieth century.

What did the fall of Judah and the destruction of God's Temple do to the faith of the Judeans?

The fall of Judah was taken by many to mean that the gods of Nebuchadnezzar were more powerful than the God of Israel. The exiles who were taken to Babylonia were overwhelmed by the magnificent buildings, the ziggurat towers, and the hanging gardens of Nebuchadnezzar, one of the seven wonders of the ancient world. Many lost faith in God and the Torah and joined their captors. But enough people, known as the "saving remnant," realized that all the glory of Babylonia was transitory, doomed to vanish, while God's teachings were eternal. They were able to endure some 70 years of exile, and when Babylonia was defeated by King Cyrus of Persia, they still had their faith and their memory of Jerusalem, and had the will to return and rebuild the city and the Temple.

What does Jeremiah do after Judah is defeated and the people are exiled to Babylonia?

Judah lies waste. Many communities are completely destroyed. Jerusalem and the Temple are burned down. The surviving remnant is overcome with despair. Many are exiled to Babylonia. Others flee to Egypt. Jeremiah, old and tired, refuses to join those who go down to Egypt, but is forced to go. To dramatize his faith in the eventual return to Zion, he buys a field near Jerusalem (32:6-15). He sets a personal example of faith. He also transforms himself into a new kind of prophet. Doom is now a reality. It is time to lift up the spirits of the survivors. Jeremiah now becomes a prophet of consolation:

> *A voice is heard in Ramah,*
> *Wailing, bitter crying,*
> *Rachel is crying for her children,*
> *Refusing to be consoled,*
> *For her children are gone.*
> *Thus said Adonai:*
> *Let there be no crying in your voice,*
> *No tears in your eyes. . .*
> *For your children shall return to their land.*
> (Jeremiah 31:15-17)

Not only will they return, but a new covenant will be established between them and God:

> *A day is coming, says Adonai,*
> *And I will make a new covenant*
> *With the House of Israel*
> *And the House of Judah.*
> *Not like the covenant which I made*
> *With their forebears when I took*
> *Them by the hand and brought them*
> *Out of the Land of Egypt,*
> *When they broke my covenant*
> *So that I rejected them, declares Adonai;*
> *I will put My teaching into their*
> *Innermost being and write it on their hearts,*
> *And I will be their God*
> *And they will be my people.*
> (Jeremiah 31:31-33).

Why does Jeremiah mention Rachel in his prophecy of consolation?

Jeremiah, as was mentioned before, has a strong sense of history. The patriarchs and the matriarchs, Moses and the exodus, the kings and prophets of the past, all are real to him, ever-present among their people. To him, Rachel is the mother of the Jewish people. When her children suffer, she suffers, when they succeed, she rejoices. Jeremiah has a global view of his people's past, present, and future. He knows the future, down through the generations. One reads his words today and one feels as though he is living now, in the present, and talks to us as if he is living among us.

EZEKIEL:
THE DRY BONES AND THE
GRAND VISION

What is the historical background of Ezekiel?

Along with Isaiah and Jeremiah, Ezekiel forms the trio of the Bible's so-called "major literary prophets." This is not necessarily because they are greater in stature than the following twelve, who are also "literary" (having a book named after them), but because the books of the twelve are rather short, consisting of a few chapters each (Obadiah only has one chapter), while the books of the three "major" prophets have at least 40 chapters each.

While Ezekiel has left us a long book, we know very little about his life. We are told that he was a priest who was exiled to Babylonia a few years before the final exile. But little is known beyond that. Unlike Jeremiah, whose life story is laid out in detail in his book, or Isaiah, who also provides a number of episodes about his career, Ezekiel has little to say about his personal history.

We do, however, obtain from his prophetic activities a clear background picture about his place and time. It is quite clear we are in the same period described in the Book of Jeremiah, namely, before, during, and immediately after the destruction of Jerusalem and the Temple. It is one of the most critical periods in all of

Ezekiel

Jewish history. By all logic, the Jewish people are about to disappear. Yet, visionaries like Jeremiah and Ezekiel see beyond the present, and they are certain God will not abandon his covenant with Israel. The exiles shall return in due time, as indeed they do.

How is Ezekiel different from Jeremiah?

Even though Jeremiah and Ezekiel are contemporaries, and even though both of them are sons of priestly, upperclass families, there are many differences between them. Jeremiah is a very politically involved prophet. He talks to the ruling class in Jerusalem, and lobbies for his beliefs and convictions in any way he can. Ezekiel, on the other hand, seems to live in his own world, even though he calls himself the "watchman" of his people (3:17). It is never clear whether he is addressing his people, either those in exile in Babylonia or those in Jerusalem, or whether he is seeing a vision. Although his language and ideas are rather precise, there always seems to be a distance between him and those he reprimands (or later consoles). Jeremiah, on the other hand, is always in the front of the picture, so to speak, reachable, palpable.

With Ezekiel we enter a new phase of prophecy, which goes beyond the here and now, and presents a global, futuristic view of the world. In Ezekiel we witness the birth of two future philosophies or cultural phenomena, known as eschatology and mysticism. Eschatology is that part of religious thought that deals with the end of time, judgment day, and so on. Mysticism deals with a reality beyond the physical world. Ezekiel is a pioneer in both areas, which makes his prophecy profoundly different from predecessors like Isaiah and contemporaries like Jeremiah.

What is different about Ezekiel's style and language?

Even though a century separates Isaiah from Jeremiah, and even though Jeremiah and Ezekiel are contemporaries, there are greater linguistic and stylistic differences between Ezekiel and the other two than between themselves. It is hard to explain how two prophets like Jeremiah and Ezekiel, who live at the same time and have the same social background, use such different terms and basic expressions.

One explanation might be that some of the words we now accept as Hebrew, were borrowed by Ezekiel from languages in his land of exile. One example is the word *hashmal*. It appears nowhere else in the Bible. In today's Hebrew it means electricity, while its original usage by Ezekiel is obscure, and could mean either a bright metal, polished bronze, or some kind of a precious stone.

As for expressions, Ezekiel keeps using the term *ben-adam*, or "son of man," which none of the other prophets in the Bible uses. In today's Hebrew this simply means a person. In the Bible it could mean "mere mortal," or, conversely, an important person.

Much about Ezekiel, in addition to his language, is enigmatic. Nevertheless, his prophecies are well within the mainstream of biblical prophecy, and they form a major link in the cycle of prophecies which help move Jewish history from the time of the First Temple to the Second.

What is the "Chariot Vision?"

In Chapter 1, and also in later chapters, Ezekiel describes his encounter with God. His is one of the most detailed and complex visions of God in the entire Bible. It became, along with the story of the creation of the world in the beginning of Genesis, the basis of Jewish mysticism, which seeks to reach a closer and deeper understanding of God. We are told in the opening chapter:

> . . . the heavens were opened and I saw visions
> of God. . . I looked and behold, a stormy wind came
> out of the north, a great cloud, with fire flashing up,
> so that a brightness was round about it, and inside
> it as though the color of hashmal [electrum?], inside
> the fire. And inside it the likeness of four living
> creatures, who had the appearance of a person. Each
> had four faces, and each four wings. . .
> . . .and when the living creatures went up above
> the ground, the wheels went up with them. . .
> . . . and above the firmament over their heads
> the appearance of sapphire, and upon the like-

ness of the throne was the likeness of a man upon
it above. And I saw as the color of electrum,
as the appearance of fire round about enclosing
it, from the appearance of his loins and upward;
and from the appearance of his loins downward
I saw as it were the appearance of fire, and
there was brightness round about him. As the
appearance of the rainbow that is in the cloud
on a rainy day, so was the appearance of the
brightness around it as the likeness of the glory
of Adonai. . .

(Ezekiel, Chapter 1)

This vision has been understood to refer to a heavenly chariot upon which the glory of God appeared to Ezekiel.

One is reminded of Isaiah's vision of God in the Temple in Jerusalem. One basic difference is that Isaiah's vision was simpler and only took place inside the Temple, while Ezekiel's vision reaches from heaven to earth, with a great deal of mobility and apparitions which have given rise to many theories and interpretations.

A careful examination of the vision of the so-called chariot (the word chariot is never mentioned, and the entire structure only barely makes one think of a chariot), has been taken by some to mean a scale model of the world. Thus, the top of the chariot is the sky, and the bottom is the earth. The creatures have four faces, namely, the human face, the lion, the ox, and the eagle. Those represent the four rulers of nature—man, the ruler of all creatures; the lion, the king of the animals; the ox, the king of the domesticated beasts; and the eagle, the king of the birds. All the four known elements of which nature was believed to be composed are here as well—earth, water, fire, and air. Above it all is God, the divine providence controlling the world. Here the God of Israel does not reside only in the land of Israel, but rules over the entire world (contrary to the common belief in Ezekiel's time, according to which each nation had its own territorial god whose power was limited to its own geographical area).

Finally, the dominant number here is four. Four and forty are very common numbers throughout the Bible, and seem to have a special power. Later Jewish mysticism will make a great deal out of numbers, developing a whole ancillery science within mysticism called numerology, or *gimatria*, namely, the science of discovering hidden meaning through numbers.

Did Ezekiel actually see God in human form?

The closest we ever get in the Bible to a prophet reporting an encounter with God in near-human terms is when Ezekiel says he saw "the likeness of a man." Earlier we have been told that the only prophet who "saw God face to face" was Moses, and even there it does not mean "face to face" in human terms, but in the sense of direct contact. Did Ezekiel actually see God in human form?

The answer is no. What Ezekiel sees is the *glory of God*. That is as far as a mortal can see. In his vision, Ezekiel sees a fire with a glow around it which he imagines looks like a human figure. In short, he does not see a human figure. Rather, he imagines the fire to look like one.

While the prophet never actually sees God, he or she can hear a voice which is attributed to God, even though God does not have a human voice. Indeed, after the vision, which transcends ordinary human experience, God speaks to Ezekiel and sends him on his mission. The vision is suspended while the prophet hears the divine message. Later it is resumed. Ezekiel goes through a ritual of eating a scroll given to him by a divine emissary which contains his con-demnation of the rebellious people of Judah, thus preparing himself for his mission of denouncing their evil deeds.

How did Ezekiel give rise to Jewish mysticism?

The essence of mysticism is the human striving for a union with God. In Jewish mysticism, the ultimate reality of God is beyond human reach. There are, however, lower levels, so to speak, of the divine presence, which are reachable. The Jewish mystic, or Kabbalist, focuses on reaching those levels.

Ezekiel's visions of God have fueled the mystic yearnings of Jews, which may have started or at least became more urgent during the time of the destruction of the First Temple and the

Babylonian Exile, since Jews felt God had abandoned them, and new ways had to be found to reach a reconciliation with God. After the destruction of the Second Temple by the Romans and the loss of Jewish sovereignty, mysticism intensified even further, with Rabbi Shimon Bar Yohai of the second century being its major exponent. Ezekiel's visions gained more and more currency, and along with the story of creation, his vision of the chariot became one of the two pillars upon which Jewish mysticism rests.

Why does Ezekiel bring up the issue of the righteous and the wicked in the middle of his initial visions?

Ezekiel has barely begun his prophetic mission, when God tells him:

> *Son of man, I have set you as a watchman*
> *for the House of Israel, and you will hear*
> *this message and you will give them a*
> *warning from me, as I say to the wicked,*
> *you will surely die. . . And if you warn the*
> *wicked and he does not turn away from*
> *his wickedness. . . he will die in his iniquity. . .*
> (Ezekiel 3:17, 19)

Ezekiel's main task is to warn the people of Judah against the coming destruction in the hope that they will repent and be saved. Many of them refuse to believe that God will abandon them, and are confident that despite the impending doom, a miracle will happen at the last minute. Ezekiel is out to dispel such notions. Rather than address them collectively, as a community protected by God because of the covenant between God and Israel, he addresses them individually.

Individual responsibility becomes one of Ezekiel's main messages to his people. God is judging them individually by examining the actions of each and every one of them. They cannot hide behind the collective merit of the nation.

This, indeed, is a new and revolutionary concept in the development of biblical belief. It is further refined in Chapters 18 and

33. It marks a departure from the teachings of Moses, according to which God is described as "visiting the iniquity of the fathers upon the children" (Exodus 20:5).

What could have possibly prompted Ezekiel to depart from one of the key concepts of the Torah?

The rabbis of the Talmud were divided in their opinions about this question. Some tried to reconcile the divergent views of Moses and Ezekiel. But this seems too facile an answer. The question must be addressed in light of Ezekiel's time and place.

Ezekiel was exiled from his land, and he knew the end of Judah was near. He was laying the groundwork for the new reality his people had to face. Individual Jews had to find a way to survive in foreign places like Babylonia, or Egypt, or even farther away, without the support system they had in Jerusalem and in Judah. The Northern Kingdom had been gone for over a century. Judah was hanging by a thread. A new approach had to be found for asserting one's own faith and identity.

Ezekiel's answer is individual responsibility. There is no longer anyone to hide behind. Nor should one be able to say that with the fall of Judah there is no hope for individual Jews, since, without the Temple, atonement is no longer possible. Each person must find a way to return and be reconciled to God. Each individual and each generation from now on will be judged on their own merit. This is Ezekiel's way of dealing with the new reality, and it becomes the basis for Jewish belief and survival to this day.

Who does Ezekiel address?

It is never clear whether Ezekiel is addressing his fellow Jews in Babylonia, or whether he is addressing the people of Judah. It is quite possible he is addressing neither. He may be recording his prophecies for future generations. In the closing chapters of his book he deals with the future, culminating with the construction of the future Temple. Clearly, here he is addressing a future generation, not his own contemporaries.

Ezekiel performs some most unusual acts to dramatize his prophecies. He isolates himself and does not talk to anyone for a long time. He lies for a long time on one side. He makes a scale model of Jerusalem and acts out its destruction, and so on. We never hear of anyone reacting to his outlandish acts. Quite possibly, no one ever witnessed any of it. He did it for himself and recorded it to show that all that was happening to the Kingdom of Judah was the will of God which he, the prophet, predicted and dramatized, rather than the will of Nebuchadnezzar, the Babylonian king.

Is Ezekiel miraculously transported to Jerusalem?

We read in Chapter 8:

> *And the likeness of a hand took me by the*
> *hair on my head and a spirit lifted me*
> *between earth and sky and took me to*
> *Jerusalem in the visions of God.*
> (Ezekiel 8:3)

This makes Ezekiel the first airborne prophet, with the exception, perhaps, of Elijah, who instead of dying to went up to heaven in a chariot of fire.

Here again we have a vintage Ezekiel activity which crosses the line between reality and imagination, and which in time will become part of the lore of Jewish mysticism, with famous mystics like the sixteenth century Holy Ari of Safed being able to transport himself through the air from one place to another.

Why doesn't Ezekiel ever mention Jeremiah, and vice versa?

In Chapter 13 Ezekiel excoriates the false prophets of Judah who lull their listeners into a state of false security. This makes one wonder why he never mentions his contemporary, the true prophet Jeremiah.

This is a question for which a good answer is yet to be found. At a minimum, one may argue that Ezekiel operated in Babylonia, and only went to Jerusalem in his imagination. Hence, he was not familiar with Jeremiah's activities, and was referring to either false prophets he knew in Babylonia, or to those in Judah of whom he only heard from other exiles.

Why does Ezekiel go into the history of the Israelites in the desert in such detail?

Ezekiel does not leave any stone unturned in condemning Judah and showing why it deserves to be destroyed. He goes into a detailed description of the Israelites in the desert failing to live up to the covenant, and he also dwells in great detail on Judah's sins in the present. The descriptions of the various forms of idol worshiping in Jerusalem show a complete breakdown of the Mosaic and monotheistic faith, and a moral degradation that leaves no room for doubt that God has no choice but to allow the destruction and the exile. Ezekiel does not spare anyone. Like a prosecutor arguing his case in a court of law, he brings forth any possible argument to condemn the defendant.

What is the purpose of the prophecies against Judah's neighboring nations?

Like the prophets before him, Ezekiel takes on all of Judah's neighbors and prophesies their fate. He addresses the Ammonites, The Moabites, the Edomites, the Phoenicians, and the Egyptians, paying special attention to the last two, and predicts that they all will disappear from the stage of history, as indeed they do.

The message here is clear. All is in the hands of God. The destruction of Judah, in which all those nations had a hand, was an act of God. So is the future destruction of those nations. The difference is that Judah will eventually come back, while those others will not.

How does Ezekiel react to the destruction of Jerusalem and the Holy Temple?

In Chapter 33 we hear about a fugitive who arrives in Babylonia and breaks the news to Ezekiel about the fall of Jerusalem. One would expect at this point to see the prophet go into mourning, give voice to his sorrow, lament the destruction. But none of this happens. One almost gets the impression Ezekiel is devoid of compassion and acts strictly as a conduit of God's words, which he is quick to voice in a new attack on the failed shepherds, i.e. leaders, of Judah, who were not able to lead their people onto the right path and avert the evil decree.

Is Ezekiel strictly a prophet of doom?

Up until now we have seen Ezekiel as the prophet of doom par excellence. He seems to put both Isaiah and Jeremiah to shame when it comes to prophesying doom. But now it is over, and doom is a reality. Ezekiel wastes no time in making it known that this is not the end as far as God is concerned , but rather the beginning. In Chapter 34 he declares on God's behalf:

> *I will rescue them from all the places where*
> *they have been scattered, on a day of clouds*
> *and fog. I will take them out from among*
> *the nations and gather them from the lands*
> *and bring them to their land and shepherd*
> *them on Israel's mountains along the streams*
> *and in all the habitable places of the land.*
> (Ezekiel 34:12-13)

At once, Ezekiel has become a prophet of consolation. All doom is forgotten. He is now a visionary of redemption and of a messianic age to come.

What is the vision of the dry bones?

The vision of the dry bones in Chapter 37 is undoubtedly the most famous episode in the Book of Ezekiel. Briefly, Ezekiel finds himself in a valley full of dry human bones. Obviously, they represent people who are long dead. God asks Ezekiel if those bones can come back to life. The prophet does not know. God orders Ezekiel to prophesy the resurrection of the dead bones, which he does. Soon the bones come together, become covered with flesh and skin, and a large multitude of people rises, alive.

The valley is Babylonia. The dead bones are the exiles, who are spiritually dead, and have lost hope. Their coming back to life means that they will once again rally as a people and return to their homeland.

The vision of the dry bones

This vision has been taken to mean that the Bible believes in the resurrection of the dead. This is incorrect. Rather, it is a vision, or a parable, dramatizing the prophet's conviction that the Judeans will return to their land, as indeed they do. Ezekiel goes further to say that the other tribes of Israel will also return and form part of one united people under one king of the House of David, who will renew their covenant with God and rebuild the Temple.

Who are Gog and Magog?

Having prophesied the redemption of Israel, Ezekiel goes a step further and looks into the more distant future, where he envisions powerful future enemies of Israel, who go under the name of Gog from the land of Magog, who will turn on Israel, but will be defeated by God.

This prophecy is rather obscure. In rabbinic literature, Gog and Magog are seen as two persons of an apocalyptic nature, leading hostile armies against Israel before the coming of the Messiah. The Jerusalem Talmud identifies Magog with Gothia, the land of the Goths. In the Babylonian Talmud it is Kandia, possible the island of Crete. In short, there is no clear idea what Ezekiel is referring to here. Once again, he reaches beyond the prophetic realm covered by his predecessors.

Why does Ezekiel provide a description of the future Temple?

In the last nine chapters of his book, Ezekiel provides a very detailed description of the future temple, with minute details of its courtyards, chambers, and so on. He goes on to delineate the functions of the priests, the observances, the sacrificial offerings, the festivals, and finally the division of the land among the tribes.

In other words, Ezekiel is repeating the legacy laid down by Moses in the Torah, albeit with some variations. By doing so, he makes it clear to the exiles in Babylonia that their exile is not the end, only the prelude to a new beginning. One is reminded of the words of England's prime minister in the nineteenth century, Disraeli, who wrote that the Jews, in celebrating agricultural holidays such as Sukkot and Shavuot, will one day go back to their land and cultivate it again. Here Ezekiel does not engage in mystical visions, but rather performs a very practical task in predicting the future return to the land and describing the future Temple.

What is the difference between Ezekiel and the Jeremiah?

These two major prophets, who are contemporaries living through the same fateful events in their people's history, are as different from each other as day and night. Although both of them are members of the priestly upperclass of Jerusalem, they represent two totally different human types.

Jeremiah is a man of the people. He is all heart. He argues with God and bemoans the suffering of the righteous. He is in constant pain over the fate awaiting his people. He tries in every way he can to bring his people back, to avert the evil decree. His language is poetry, full of solicitation and disappointment. When he predicts doom, he cries. When he consoles, he is at his best, speaking healing words, as in his address to Mother Rachel: "Cry not, your children will come back."

Not so Ezekiel. Here we have the prophetic tradition carried to its extreme—uncompromising, unflinching, relentless. It is as though Ezekiel has no mind of his own. Once God makes him eat the scroll at the beginning of his prophetic mission, he almost seems to have become an automaton. He does exactly as told, never questioning anything, never showing any emotions. He is a perfect soldier in God's service. He does, indeed, play his part well. Perhaps too well.

HOSEA:
GOD'S LOVE FOR
WAYWARD ISRAEL

Why is the book of Hosea and the remaining "Twelve Prophets" so brief?

While each of the first three "literary prophets," namely, Isaiah, Jeremiah, and Ezekiel, have left us a fully developed book, the remaining twelve prophets have only left us a few chapters, in one case only one, and in Hosea's case—the second longest of the twelve—fourteen brief chapters. The impression these books create is one of fragments, rather than a fully developed message. Is what we have here the full text of their prophecies?

In general, the Bible covers vast topics with few words. Many major events are dismissed with one or two verses. Here, however, we have the writings of a given person, one who spent a lifetime speaking out on the major issues of the day. Is it possible that so little is recorded?

Quite possibly, what we have here are indeed mere fragments of longer books. We must keep in mind that the prophets were scorned in their lifetime by their contemporaries, the object of their own scorn. Jeremiah's book was publicly burned, and had to be rewritten. Some prophets were killed. Certainly, their books were not kept in any official libraries. Rather, their words must have been committed to memory, passed on, and eventually recorded, edited, and canonized.

How much do we know about Hosea?

Not very much, mainly because of the above reason, namely, the brevity of the book. As happens with many other biblical books, the editor must have added an opening line to the book, letting us know the time during which the person was active. Here we have the century prior to the destruction of the Northern Kingdom of Israel.

It is a time of political turmoil, outside danger, and moral decline in that kingdom. Hosea senses the doom of Israel, as do the other great prophets of his time—Amos, Isaiah, and Micah. The inevitable doom is a function of external factors such as the rise of Assyria in the north and its expansionist policy, and attacks by Egypt from the south; and of internal factors, such as the social and moral decline of the kingdom.

How does Hosea become a prophet?

Hosea becomes a prophet in a most unusual way. God tells him to marry a prostitute. She gives him two sons and one daughter. His unusual marriage becomes a symbol of the "whoring" of Israel after foreign military alliances and after foreign gods, instead of putting its trust in the God of Israel, who is Israel's true "husband."

There is nothing unusual about a prophet using his own private life as a metaphor for the greater issues of the day. Isaiah, for example, gives his son a name which predicts a military disaster for Israel. But none of the prophets went to the extreme of marrying a woman ineligible by Jewish law for marriage to prove a point. This has given many headaches to traditional Jewish biblical commentators, such as Rashi and Maimonides, and has elicited a large number of conflicting commentaries and theories.

Why does Hosea use his marriage as a metaphor?

Hosea, like Jeremiah after him, is a man of heart (the prophets seem to fall into one of two categories: those who are guided by their heart, and those who are guided by their mind). He sees the political and spiritual issues of his time through the prism of personal relations and feelings. Unlike an Ezekiel, with his relentless prophecies of doom, Hosea manages in the first chapter of his book to speak both doom and consolation. He predicts Israel's destruction at the hand of her enemies, and immediately turns to redemption and a new covenant, typically in images of marriage:

> *I will betroth you forever,*
> *I will betroth you in righteousness*
> *And justice, and in kindness and mercy,*
> *I will betroth you in faith, and you will*
> *Know Adonai.*
>
> (Hosea 2:21-22)

What does "you will know Adonai" mean?

In Genesis we read that Adam "knew" his wife, Eve. Hence the expression "to know someone in the biblical sense," namely, carnal knowledge. But this is only one aspect of the biblical concept of knowledge. Hosea, who uses the term "knowing God" frequently, is making the point that it is not enough to know through one's reason that there is a God. One must feel it inside oneself. True knowledge of God means leading a godly life, being in harmony with God. This is the goal the prophet wants his people to strive for.

What is God's attitude toward Israel according to Hosea?

One of Hosea's most touching passages conveying the feelings of God toward backsliding and wayward Israel is the following:

> *I fell in love with Israel*
> *When he was still a child;*
> *And I have called him my son*
> *Ever since Egypt. . .*
> *I have pampered Ephraim,*
> *Taking them in my arms,*
> *But they have ignored*
> *My healing care.*

I drew them with loving human feelings. . .
(Hosea 11:1, 3-4)

No prophet speaks about the relationship between God and Israel in more tender and loving terms. The only one who comes close is Jeremiah.

How does Hosea see the eventual return of Israel to God?

The idea of the return, or *teshuvah*, is one of the key concepts among the literary prophets. God does not wish the death of the sinner, Ezekiel affirms, but rather that the sinner may return to God and be forgiven. If not for *teshuvah*, the human race could not endure.

In Chapter 6 we hear the people of Israel say:

> *Come, and let us return to Adonai;*
> *For Adonai has devoured, but will also heal,*
> *Struck, but will dress the wounds.*
> *After two days Adonai will revive us,*
> *And will raise us on the third, and*
> *We shall live before Adonai. . .*
> (Hosea 6:1-2)

The prophet realizes that the people are saying these words, but are not sincere. They are not ready for true return. While they are saying these things they continue to persecute the prophets, they show no kindness or mercy to the weak, their priests are corrupt, and they shed blood. No true return can be effected under such conditions.

In the closing paragraph of his book, however, Hosea urges his people to pursue true return:

> *Return, O Israel, to Adonai your God,*
> *For you have stumbled in your wrongdoing.*
> *Take with you words, and return to Adonai;*
> *Say to Adonai, Forgive all wrongdoing,*
> *And accept that which is good;*
> *And let the offering of our lips be like*
> *The sacrifice of bullocks.*
> (Hosea 14:2-3)

JOEL:
THE LOCUST AND THE
END OF DAYS

Who is Joel?

The short book of the prophet Joel, consisting of four short chapters, provides no clue as to who Joel was, when exactly he prophesied, or any other particulars. He could have lived at any time from the time of the early kings to the end of the monarchy. His book consists of two seemingly unrelated subjects. The first is a major plague of locust, and the second is a vision of the end of time, or judgment day.

What, then, makes Joel a prophet?

Joel speaks in the name of God. While we have no clear idea as to the time and context in which he speaks, his words are well within the biblical prophetic tradition. His vision of the final judgment is as powerful as any in the Bible. Some of it, such as the text "blood, and fire, and pillars of smoke," has found its way into the Passover Haggadah.

Joel concludes with the vision of the end of time:

> *And the mountains shall drip with wine,*
> *The hills shall flow with milk,*
> *And all the brooks of Judah shall*
> *Flow with water. . .*
> *And Judah shall dwell forever,*
> *And Jerusalem throughout all generations.*
> (Joel 4:18-21)

Amos

AMOS:
GOD SPOKE, WHO WILL
NOT PROPHESY?

What distinguishes Amos?

The Book of Amos consists of nine short chapters. But short as it is, it packs more prophetic power than any other book in the Bible. In fact, Amos was the first of the literary prophets, and much of what they had to say was first said by him. Unlike some of his illustrious successors, such as Isaiah, Jeremiah, and Ezekiel, Amos was not a member of the upperclass, but rather a herdsman from the countryside of Judah, or possibly Israel. This is reflected in his language, which is not nearly as elaborate as theirs. Yet his prophetic utterances are clear as a bell and strike out like thunderbolts.

Amos refuses to accept the title of prophet, and utters the famous words: "I am neither a prophet nor the son of a prophet." But he adds: "God spoke, who will not prophesy?" He hears the voice of God like the roar of a mighty lion, and he knows he must speak up:

> *Will two walk together if they did not*
> *Agree to meet?*
> *Will a lion roar in the forest without prey?*
>
> *. . .*

> *A lion roared, who is not afraid?*
> *God spoke, who will not prophesy?*
> (Amos 2:3, 8)

With Amos, biblical prophecy expands its horizons from dealing strictly with the people of Israel, to presenting a global view of the human race. In antiquity, gods were considered territorial. Each god had power over the territory of the people who followed that god. Amos and his successors took a new stance: the God of Israel is the only ruler of the universe, the master of all the nations. While Israel was singled out for a covenant with God, which puts more demands on Israel than on other nations, God is concerned with all the nations, and all of them are responsible for their actions and accountable before the universal Master.

What is the earthquake Amos alludes to?

In the opening verse of his book, Amos refers to the earthquake that took place in his time. This earthquake is mentioned by several other prophets. It could well be the earthquake Isaiah experienced when he was inside the Temple and saw the presence of God (see p. 171). It is also mentioned by the prophet Zechariah (14:5). Clearly, it was an event that left a deep impression on the people of Jerusalem, and was used by the prophets as an example of God's power.

Is Amos' chastising of Israel's neighbors nationalistic or universalistic?

The prophecies of Amos begin with a listing of crimes committed by Israel's neighbors—Damascus, Gaza, Tyre, Edom, Ammon, and Moab:

> *For the three crimes of Damascus,*
> *And for four, I will not reverse it;*
> *For they have threshed Gilead*
> *With iron combs.*
> (Amos 1:3)

At first look, it seems that the prophet's intention is to chastise the nations for their crimes against Israel. But without pausing, Amos goes on to chastise Judah and Israel as well. No one is being spared. God judges all people according to what is expected of them. What is interesting are the particular crimes of each nation. In the case of Israel's neighbors, the crimes are invariably committed against the kingdoms of Judah and Israel. Judah's crime is abandoning God's law, while Israel's crime comes down to some very specific social issues:

> *For the three crimes of Israel,*
> *And for four, I will not reverse it;*
> *For selling the righteous for money,*
> *And the poor for a pair of shoes. . .*
>
> (Amos 2:6)

With Amos, no one escapes God's judgment. Israel's neighbors will be punished for what we would call today war crimes. But the Northern Kingdom of Israel—which is the main target of Amos' prophecies—will be punished for what most people would hardly pay attention to, namely, the lack of sensitivity toward the poor. With this prophecy, Amos takes a giant step in the development of biblical religion, from the traditional ritualistic view, to a world view of social justice, that will leave its mark on civilization to this day. One could safely say that the world's sense of morality and social justice as we know it today stems from biblical passages such as the above passage from the Book of Amos.

Does Amos believe Jews are the chosen people?

In Chapter 3, Amos tells Israel:

> *Listen to what Adonai has said regarding you,*
> *children of Israel, the entire family I brought*
> *out of Egypt: Only you have I known of all the*
> *families of the earth. . .*
>
> (Amos 3:1-2)

This kind of statement easily creates the impression that the prophet believes the Jews to be God's chosen. To dispel this misconception, Amos later says:

> To Me, you are equal to the people of Africa,
> Children of Israel, declares Adonai.
> I did bring Israel from the Land of Egypt,
> But I also brought the Philistines
> Out of Crete, and Aram from Kir.
>   (Amos 9:7)

Amos goes on to say that Israel has become so sinful that God has a good mind to wipe it off the face of the earth. Yet, God will not annihilate the House of Jacob. The Covenant cannot be broken.

Why is Amos so hard on Israel?

Amos is the first prophet to predict the destruction of the Northern Kingdom of Israel. Interestingly, he lives in the time of King Jeroboam II, some fifty years before the fall of Israel, which is a time of prosperity and territorial expansion. This prosperity is alluded to in his condemnation of the rich who oppress the poor in Samaria:

> Listen to this word, the cows of Bashan
> Who are in the mountain of Samaria
> Oppressing the poor, who keep saying,
> Let us drink and feast.
>   (Amos 4:1)

The prophet, who started out in life as a herdsman tending his own flock, realizes one day that the people of both Judah and Israel have failed to live up to the covenant of old. Idol worshiping is the order of the day in Jerusalem, the city of God. It is even worse in the north where, in addition to idolatry, moral corruption has reached its peak. This state of affairs can only mean one thing: the people of Israel are courting their doom. While God is waiting for them to repent and return to the right path, it has become clear to Amos that this is not going to happen. Amos is trying to impress upon his people the dire consequences of their behavior, but to no avail. He only invites the anger of the king of Israel, whose priest tells Amos:

> *Seer, go, run to the Land of Judah,*
> *and eat bread there, and there prophesy.*
> (Amos 7:12)

The people won't listen to Amos or to his successors. But that does not stop any of them, from Amos to Jeremiah, from prophesying. They know that a time will come when the people, banished from their land, will begin to listen. Thus, their words will not have been spoken in vain.

What does Amos have to say about the future of Israel?

Amos foresees a time when Israel, chastised and chastened, will begin to look for God:

> *Behold, a day is coming, says Adonai,*
> *When I will send a famine to the land,*
> *Not a famine for bread,*
> *And not a thirst for water,*
> *But for hearing the words of Adonai.*
> (Amos 8:11)

This will be the beginning of redemption. It will be followed by a restoration and a messianic age:

> *On that day I will raise David's fallen*
> *tabernacle,*
> *And mend its breaches and clear*
> *Its ruins, and build it as in the days of old.*
> . . .
> *Days are coming, says Adonai, when the*
> *Plowman shall overtake the reaper,*
> *And the treader of grapes him that sows,*
> *And the mountains shall drip with wine,*

And all the hills will melt.
And I shall return the captivity of
My people Israel,
And they shall rebuild the waste cities,
And they shall plant vineyards
And drink their wine,
And plant gardens and eat their fruit.
And I will plant them on their land,
And they shall not be taken away again
From their land which I have given them,
says Adonai.

(Amos 9:11-15)

OBADIAH:
JUDGMENT ON EDOM

Who is Obadiah and what is his message?

Both questions are hard to answer. This is the shortest book in the Bible, consisting of a single chapter with only 21 verses. All we know is that Obadiah has a vision about Edom.

The rabbis of the Talmud identified Obadiah with the person of the same name who lived in the time of King Ahab (I Kings 18:3-4). They actually thought he was an Edomite proselyte (Sanhedrin 39b). That would put him in the ninth century B.C.E. Textual analysis, however, shows similarities between Obadiah and parts of Jeremiah, Chapter 49. That would put him in the sixth century B.C.E., some three hundred years later.

That would make more sense, since the Edomites, who lived on the other side of the Jordan and were believed to be descendants of Esau, Jacob's brother, hence cousins of the Jews, helped Nebuchadnezzar in defeating Judah and destroying Jerusalem. Obadiah has a dire prediction for the Edomites, who will be destroyed for their evil deed. Indeed, in Jewish history, Edom becomes synonymous with hatred of Israel, and the Roman Empire is often referred to as Edom, the Evil Kingdom.

The prophet concludes with a prediction of Judah's restoration:

And the House of Jacob shall possess

Its inheritance.
. . .
And rescuers shall come up in Mount Zion,
To judge the Mountain of Esau,
And the kingdom shall be Adonai's.
(Obadiah 1:17, 21)

JONAH:
RUNNING AWAY FROM GOD

Was Jonah swallowed by the whale?

The Book of Jonah is one of the best known stories of the Bible. There are two reasons for this: first, the story itself is intriguing and memorable. Second, it is read in the synagogue every year on the afternoon of the Day of Atonement in its entirety.

Like all popular folk stories, there are misconceptions about the story. The most common is that Jonah was swallowed by a whale. The Bible never mentions a whale, but rather a "great fish."

Who is Jonah?

The prophet Jonah, the son of Amittai, is mentioned in II Kings 14:25, in the time of King Jeroboam the Second, in the ninth century B.C.E. It is difficult, however, to know with certainty when Jonah actually lived. The style of the book and some of the words used could place it centuries later.

Unlike the other literary prophets, whose text consists mainly of prophecies and written in a rich poetic style, the Book of Jonah only contains a few words of prophecy, and consists strictly of a short story told in a prose style.

Briefly, God sends Jonah on a mission to the great city of Nineveh, in Mesopotamia, to exhort its people to repent. He refuses to go on that mission, and instead goes to sea and boards a

Jonah tossed ashore

ship. Out at sea, a storm suddenly threatens to sink the ship. Everyone prays to his or her own god for deliverance, but to no avail, when they discover that Jonah is a fugitive from God. Jonah tells them to cast him overboard to appease God. They do, and the sea quiets down, as Jonah is swallowed by the big fish. God rescues him from the fish, making Jonah realize he cannot run away from God.

What makes the book different from the other books of the prophets?

Besides being a story written in prose while most prophetic texts are written in poetic language, the Book of Jonah is clearly a morality tale, a background story about the mission of the prophet, who cannot escape his calling. The story seems to be a composite of several versions, written at different times. It must have been very popular from the start, and might have been included in the Bible not because of its great prophetic message, but because of popular demand.

Its great popularity is attested by the fact that it was included in the ritual of Yom Kippur. Jonah also became a popular figure in Christianity and in Islam. To Christians the story indicates the capacity of the gentiles for salvation, and in Muslim tradition Jonah is one of the apostles of Allah.

Why is the Book of Jonah read on Yom Kippur?

Yom Kippur is the day on which Jews are expected to fully repent and atone for their sins. The story of Jonah dramatizes the search for repentance. It also dramatizes the struggle of the individual with his faith in God and his mission on this earth. Each Jew on Yom Kippur turns inwardly and examines his or her own relationship with God, and his or her life's mission.

The Prophet Micah

MICAH:
DO JUSTICE, LOVE MERCY,
WALK HUMBLY

Who is Micah, and what sets him apart among the prophets?

Micah is a contemporary of Isaiah. Unlike Isaiah, who is a member of the priestly upperclass in Jerusalem, Micah is a country boy from the southern coast of Israel. He too witnesses the fall of the Northern Kingdom of Israel, and predicts the fall of Judah. In fact, Micah is the first to utter the shocking prediction of the destruction of Jerusalem. His words make such a deep and lasting impression on the people, that they are mentioned again over a century later in the Book of Jeremiah:

> *Micah the Morashtite, who prophesied in*
> *the days of King Hezekiah of Judah, said to*
> *all the people of Judah: Thus said the Lord*
> *of Hosts, Zion shall be plowed as a field,*
> *Jerusalem shall become a heap of ruins,*
> *and the Temple Mount a shrine in the woods.*
> (Jeremiah 26:17-18)

Micah actually says:

> *Hear this, rulers of the House of Jacob*
> *You chiefs of the House of Israel,*

215

Who detest justice,
And make crooked all that is straight;
Who build Zion with crime,
Jerusalem with iniquity.
Her rulers judge for bribery,
Her priests make rulings for a fee
And her prophets divine for pay.
Yet they rely on Adonai, saying:
Adonai is in our midst,
No calamity shall befall us.
Therefore, because of you
Zion shall be plowed as a field,
And Jerusalem shall become heaps of ruins,
And the Temple Mount a shrine in the woods.
                                (Micah 3:9-12)

Micah, like Amos before him, is a man of the people. He feels deeply the moral crisis that brought the fall of Israel and is now threatening the survival of the Kingdom of Judah. His prophetic utterances are not carefully thought out or arranged in any particular order. He speaks directly from the heart, and uses rural imagery. He is deeply offended by the glib use made of God's name by the prophets and the priests and the ruling classes in Samaria and Jerusalem, who live with a false sense of security, ignoring the idolatry and injustice which are prevalent throughout the land. At the same time, he is overwhelmed by his own words of doom, and quickly turns to predicting a future time when the remnant of Israel will be brought back by a loving God:

I will gather all of Jacob,
I will bring together the remnant of Israel,
I will put them all like sheep in a fold,
Like a flock inside its pen.
They will be teeming with people.
                                (Micah 2:12)

Did Micah copy Isaiah's vision of the End of Days?

In Chapter 4, We find Isaiah's vision of the End of Days ("And it shall come to pass in the end of days that the mountain of the House of Adonai," etc.) repeated almost word for word by Micah. It is unlikely that the two of them made such a similar statement. From a literary and conceptual standpoint, the text belongs to Isaiah, and might have either been repeated by Micah, or interpolated in his text by a later editor. This interpolation clearly shows that the texts of the books of the prophets did not reach us intact from their original source, but underwent various stages of editing. One example is the scroll of Isaiah that was found among the Dead Sea Scrolls around 1948. On the one hand, it is quite amazing that this version, at least 2000 years old, is nearly identical to the Book of Isaiah as we know it today. On the other hand, there are a few verses in this scroll which are different from the ones we have.

How does Micah sum up all the teachings of Judaism in one sentence?

Perhaps the most famous verse in Micah is the following:

> *It has been told you,*
> *O man, what is good,*
> *And what Adonai asks of you—*
> *But to do justice,*
> *And to love mercy,*
> *And to walk humbly*
> *With Adonai your God.*
>
> (Micah 6:8)

Perhaps better than anyone else in the Bible, Micah was able in this verse to sum up in three words what God expects of Israel and of humankind: Justice, mercy, and humility. Here we have the entire essence of the prophetic teachings. According to Judaism, God's two main attributes in dealing with humankind are justice and mercy. It is incumbent upon every person to *do* justice, which is an unconditional action one must never deviate from. Thus, for example, giving to the poor is considered an act of justice, rather than mercy or charity. It must be done regularly, rather than occasionally, when one feels moved to do it. In Hebrew, giving to the poor is called *tzedakah*, a word derived from *tzedek*, or justice. This is different from the concept of charity, which is derived from the Latin word *caritas*, meaning love or affection.

Next to doing justice comes *loving* mercy. While justice is an action, mercy is a feeling. When one is imbued with the feeling of what Micah calls *hesed* (translated here as mercy, but also meaning kindness, grace, charity and so on), one is compelled to do justice. Explained in legal terms, justice is the letter of the law, while mercy is the spirit of the law. The two go together to create the harmony necessary for the well being of the individual and society.

Finally, "walking humbly with God" means being aware at all times that there is a higher authority one is always accountable to. One must never play God. Rather, one must always remind oneself that human power and human judgment are limited, and must always be used with discretion.

What is the background of Micah's closing prayer?

The Book of Micah ends with a prayer, in which the prophet asks God to have mercy on his people, and restore them to their former prosperity and glory. As in the rest of the book, which consists of prophetic statements without any particular sequence or order, it is not quite clear what the prophet has in mind, or whether this text is indeed Micah's own words rather than a later addition. But if we attempt to put it into a historical context, it is quite possible that Micah utters these words soon after the fall of the Northern Kingdom of Israel. Judah is now alone (the prophet alludes to "God's flock that dwells alone"), and the provinces of Bashan and Gilead are lost. The prophet reminds Israel's enemies that the ultimate power is in the hands of God, and there is nothing they can do to defy it. He ends with a the following prayer to God:

Who is a God like You who forgives iniquity,
And pardons the sins of the remnant of your
Heritage;
Who does not keep his anger forever,
Delighting, rather, in mercy.
Returning to console us, You will cast
In the depths of the sea all our sins,
Giving truth to Jacob,
Mercy to Abraham,
As you swore to our ancestors
From the days of old.

(Micah 7:18-20)

Nahum:
The Enigmatic Prophet

Who is Nahum and what is unusual about him?

Nahum's three short chapters raise more questions than provide answers. To begin with, we have no idea who he is or where exactly he comes from. His place of birth, Elkosh, could be in the Galilee, or on the southern coastal plain, or even in northern Mesopotamia. He seems to have prophesied either shortly before or shortly after the fall of the Assyrian Empire, which occurred in the year 612 B.C.E.

And this is only the beginning. While he employs beautiful poetic language, he does not concern himself with either the moral or the ritual issues of the people of Judea. Instead, his entire book is devoted to a prophecy about Assyria and its capital, Nineveh. Assyria at the time was Israel's archenemy, the destroyer of the Northern Kingdom. Its fall in the hands of the Babylonians is a major event for Judah and for the rest of the region, and Nahum launches a frontal attack on the evil of Assyria which brings upon it the vengeance of God. One may wonder why this book which does not provide the usual prophetic teachings was included in the Bible.

Did Nahum fail to see the imminent fall of Judah?

After his initial statement about Assyria, Nahum goes on to say:

Behold upon the hills the feet of the
Announcer of good news, who speaks peace.
Celebrate your festivals, O Judah,
Perform your vows,
For the evil one will no longer
Pass through you,
He is utterly destroyed.

(Nahum 2:1)

In other words, the destroyer of Israel will not come back to destroy Judah. However, less than thirty years later, the destroyer of Assyria, namely, Babylonia, will come and destroy Judah. Nahum seems to be unaware of this, as he joyously let Judah know it is safe. This would disqualify him as a true prophet of the God of Israel.

How do we work our way through this problem?

Biblical commentators and scholars have offered a variety of answers, none of which seems to be satisfactory. Nahum remains an enigma among the prophets of the Bible. One can only wonder if his colleagues, prophets like Isaiah or Jeremiah, are comfortable having him in their august company.

HABAKKUK:
MIGHT IS RIGHT AND THE
FAITH OF THE RIGHTEOUS

What does Habakkuk have in common with his two contemporaries, Jeremiah and Nahum?

Habakkuk prophesies at the time of the rise of the Chaldean, or Babylonian Empire, following the fall of Assyria. While Nahum rejoices in the fall of Assyria, Israel's archenemy, Habakkuk is shaken by the rise of Babylonia, another evil empire poised to destroy every nation in its path. In this regard, Habakkuk resembles Nahum in that both are basically "one issue" prophets. Neither one goes into the moral and ritual issues which deeply concern other prophets, but instead concentrate on one particular issue of their time.

Habakkuk confront the issue of the rise of another evil empire in a novel way. He engages God in a dialogue, in which God responds to the prophet's questions. Habakkuk starts out by questioning God's justice. Here we recall Jeremiah's question to God about the same issue, one of the major issues not only in the Bible, but in all cultures and religions throughout the world. God, instead of giving a direct answer, tells Habakkuk about the rise of the Chaldeans, "the bitter and swift nation," who will devastate many nations.

What is Habakkuk's answer to "might is right?"

Now Habakkuk's question changes from a general observation about good unrewarded and evil unpunished, to a specific historical phenomenon, which makes him the only prophet who raises this question: Why does God use evil empires to punish what the prophet perceives to be not only sinful nations, including Israel and Judah, but the innocent as well?

This question has enormous implications regarding theodicy, that is, whether indeed there is divine justice. Were people like Isaiah, Jeremiah, or Ezekiel right? Were Israel and Judah so sinful that they deserved to be destroyed?

What Habakkuk is saying in effect is that generation after generation, since time immemorial, there always seem to be one evil empire after another that causes great suffering and destroys many innocent lives. In the twentieth century we could mention, besides Naziism in Germany, many other evil regimes in Russia, Spain, Italy, Japan, and many other places, who murdered many millions of innocent people. Is this really all part of the divine plan?

Habakkuk does not seem to have a thorough answer for this question. In fact, his answer seems to boil down to three Hebrew words, which translate as follows: "The righteous lives by his faith" (2:4). In the midst of all the evil in the world, one can achieve a state of righteousness, and find the true meaning of life in this state of grace.

Having struggled with his faith and found more questions than answers, Habakkuk concludes by saying:

> *I will rejoice in Adonai,*
> *Celebrate the God of my salvation;*
> *Adonai my God is my strength,*
> *Who sets my feet like deer's feet,*
> *Making me walk upon my high places,*
> *For the leader of my song.*
> (Habakkuk 3:18-19)

ZEPHANIAH:
THE DAY OF THE ALMIGHTY

What is the background of Zephaniah's prophecy?

Zephaniah's book consists of three chapters which deal with a vision of the Day of Adonai. Zephaniah prophesies in the time of King Josiah, before this righteous king performs the great reform (see p. 196). Jerusalem is reeling from the pagan cults introduced by King Manasseh, and suffers from moral decline. This is the time following the fall of the Northern Kingdom of Israel and prior to the fall of Judah. Zephaniah, like his predecessors—Hosea, Isaiah, and Micah, and like his younger contemporary, Jeremiah, realizes that the Kingdom of Judah is facing cataclysmic events. He invokes the common vision of the literary prophets, namely, the Day of Adonai, a day of judgment that will put an end to paganism and will be followed by a rebirth of the remnant of Israel.

What is the meaning of Zephaniah's "Day of Adonai?"

Zephaniah carries the vision of the Day of Adonai to its final extreme. It is, in effect, a reversal of the story of creation in the first chapter of Genesis:

> *I will utterly sweep all things*
> *From the face of the earth,*
> *Says Adonai.*
> *I will sweep man and beast,*

I will sweep the fowl from the heaven,
And the fish from the sea,
And the stumbling blocks of the wicked.
And I will cut off man from
The face of the earth, says Adonai.
And I will stretch out My hand upon Judah,
And upon all the inhabitants of Jerusalem;
And I will cut off the remnants of
Baal from this place,
*And the names of the pagan priests**
*With Israel's priests;*** *
And them that worship the stars
Of the heavens on the rooftops. . .
                    (Zephaniah 1:2-5)

Zephaniah spares no one. The judgment is global, and it encompasses the idolatrous nations as well as Israel and Judah.

Does Zephaniah tell us what will happen after the destruction of God's creation?

Here we are left in the dark. We can only surmise that some restoration of nature would take place, or that the prophet does not have in mind total global destruction.

What will happen to Israel after the Day of Adonai?

Like all the other prophets, Zephaniah predicts a restoration of the remnant of Israel:

Sing, O Daughter of Zion,
Shout, O Israel;
Be glad and rejoice with all your heart,
O daughter of Jerusalem.
Adonai removed your judgment,
Cast out your enemy. . .

---

* *Kemarim* in Hebrew.
** *Kohanim* in Hebrew.

> *At that time I will bring you,*
> *and at that time will I gather you,*
> *For I will make you renowned and glorious*
> *Among all the people of the earth,*
> *When you will behold the return*
> *Of your captivity,Says Adonai.*
>
> (Zephaniah 3:14-15; 20)

Has the "Day of Adonai" predicted by Zephaniah and the other prophets taken place already, or is it still in the future?

The Day of Adonai is clearly a day of judgment. In a limited way, it has taken place more than once. In its ultimate manifestation, it will take place in what Isaiah called "the end of time," that is, the end of life as we have known it for thousands of years, and the beginning of a whole new stage of human existence, completely different from the cumulative experience of the human race.

In the Jewish year cycle, a day of judgment occurs once a year on the Day of Atonement. In Jewish history, the destruction of Jerusalem and the First Temple was a day of judgment, which was followed by the return from Babylonia and the rebuilding of the Temple. One could argue that the destruction of the Second Temple was a repetition of the Day of Adonai announced by the prophets, and that the return of the Jews to their land in our time is, in the words of the new liturgy of Israel, the "Beginning of our redemption."

In both Judaism and Christianity a belief exists in the eventual day of judgment that will usher a new world. The prophets are the ones who gave rise to this belief, which even during biblical times and thereafter has undergone many transformations.

HAGGAI:
THE REBUILDING OF
THE TEMPLE

Are we still in the age of prophecy with Haggai?

The last two giants of the era of the biblical prophets are Jeremiah and Ezekiel. Looking back on biblical prophecy, the first great prophet is Moses, also known as the "Father of the Prophets." Other giants are Elijah, Amos, and Isaiah. When Jerusalem and the Temple are destroyed in the year 586 B.C.E., an era of some 700 years of great prophets comes to an end. The people of Judah are exiled to Babylonia, where they remain for about 70 years. When Cyrus the Great of Persia defeats the Babylonians in 539 B.C.E., he allows the Jews to return to their land and take with them many of the vessels of the Holy Temple plundered by King Nebuchadnezzar of Babylonia. A certain portion of the exiles go back to Jerusalem and the surrounding area.

Back in their land, now a Persian province with a Persian-appointed Jewish governor named Zerubbabel, some new prophets emerge, who no longer are part of the great age of prophecy. Three of them are known to us, namely, Haggai, Zechariah, and Malachi.

In effect, the classical biblical period has now ended. Gone is the kingdom, the great prophets, and Solomon's Temple. As the remnant of Israel attempts to restore a semblance of political and spiritual independence, it is clear that many things have changed. the Israelite society is now in transition as a theocracy, a province ruled by priests, rather than a monarchy. New ideas, new beliefs are being tested. Haggai is one of the new spiritual leaders who seek to prepare the people for the new age.

What is Haggai's specific role?

More than a prophet, Haggai, along with his contemporary, the prophet Zechariah, is a spiritual leader who is dedicated to a specific mission, namely, encouraging the returned exiles in Jerusalem to rebuild the Temple:

> In the second year of King Darius, in the
> sixth month, on the first day of the month,
> the word of God came from Haggai the
> Prophet to Zerubbabel son of Shealtiel,
> governor of Judah, and to Joshua son of
> Jehozadak, the high priest, saying: Thus
> said Adonai of Hosts, saying, These people
> have said, It is not time for the House of
> Adonai to be rebuilt.
> And so the word of Adonai came through
> Haggai the Prophet, saying: Is this the time
> for you to be ensconced in your houses
> while this House lies waste?
> (Haggai 1:1-4)

Haggai and Zechariah are able to prevail upon the people to begin the work, which in four years results in the completion of the basic structure of the Temple.

How does Haggai convince the people to Rebuild the Temple?

Haggai uses several arguments to get the people going on this major project. First, he points out to the poor harvests they have had since their return, and argues that without God dwelling in their midst they cannot prosper. Next, he evokes the grandeur of the original Temple, and assures them that the new Temple will be even greater (which does not exactly happen). He also predicts that God will punish the neighboring nations, and as a result much of their wealth will be used to beautify and enhance the new Temple. Finally, he shows that the sacrifices administered by the priest are not ritually acceptable, and only after the Temple is completed will Israel's sacrifices be acceptable to God.

Are Haggai's prophecies accurate?

Haggai's last prophecy refers to Zerubbabel, the Persian-appointed governor of Judah, who Haggai believes will be chosen by God as the ruler of his people, namely, the new king.

This does not happen. In fact, Haggai's prophecies are somewhat off the mark. But the intent is clear, and the results are positive. In other words, the returned exiles, some of whom have now been back for several years, do not have the courage and the determination to undertake the great task of rebuilding the Temple. Haggai is able to inspire them to overcome their fear and their misgivings and get the work done. Thus, his mission is accomplished.

ZECHARIAH:
NOT BY MIGHT, NOR BY POWER, BUT BY MY SPIRIT

What role does Zechariah play in the rebuilding of the Second Temple?

Along with Haggai, Zechariah advocates the rebuilding of the Temple after the return from the Babylonian Exile. But while Haggai is pragmatic and programmatic, Zechariah is a visionary, or a mystic, who keeps having visions which express his ideas about the rebuilding of the Temple, the redemption of Judah and Jerusalem, the installation of Joshua, the high priest, and the re-dedication of the people to God and to God's law of justice and mercy. While Haggai deals directly with the business of the rebuilding, Zechariah provides inspiration and spiritual guidance.

What are we to make of Zechariah's visions?

Zechariah's visions in Chapters 1 through 8, and his symbolic acts, remind us of similar visions and acts seen and performed by the prophet Ezekiel, who precedes Zechariah (see p. 164). With Ezekiel we have the beginning of mysticism, eschatology, and apocalyptic visions, which seem to result from the time of the fall of Judah and later the return of some of the exiles during the time of Zechariah. It is quite natural for people living in times of great crisis to look for

230

another form of reality beyond the here and now, and both Haggai and Zechariah, who yearn for full redemption for their people after the loss of the monarchy, are having visions of a better future.

What are we to make of Zechariah's first vision?

Zechariah's visions are not easy to explain. In the first vision, an angel of God takes the prophet at night to a deep valley where he shows him a man riding a red horse and stopping near mirtle trees, followed by red, sorrel, and white horses. The angel tells the prophet he will explain to him the meaning of all this. Then the horseman speaks, and explains that the horses are messengers of God, who search the earth. They find out that all is peaceful on earth. Then the angel asks God why, seventy years after the destruction of Jerusalem, God has not yet taken pity on Jerusalem and the towns of Judah. God replies that now the time has come to rebuild the Temple and for God to return to Jerusalem.

It is to be assumed that Zechariah communicates this vision to the returned exiles in Jerusalem, and inspires them to rebuild the Temple. But the details of his vision are far from clear. One could attempt various interpretations, but much remains in the realm of speculation.

Is there a consistency among Zechariah's various visions?

After seeing the horseman, Zechariah sees four horns which symbolize the enemies attacking Jerusalem. Then he sees a man with a rope measuring Jerusalem. Then he sees Satan rebuking Joshua, the high priest, while Joshua wears soiled garments, which represent the sins of Israel. Then he sees a seven-branched golden candlestick, representing the presence of God in the world. Then he sees a flying scroll, representing punishment for stealing. Then he sees scales with a woman, representing evil. Then he sees four chariots com-ing out of mountains of brass, representing the four corners of the earth.

Once Zechariah is done with his visions, he reminds the people of the need to return to God, and prophesies regarding Jerusalem:

> *Thus said Adonai the God of Hosts:*
> *Old men and women will sit*
> *In the streets of Jerusalem,*
> *Each leaning on his and her cane,*
> *Steeped in years.*
> *And the city will be filled*
> *With boys and girls playing*
> *In the streets.*
>
> (Zechariah 8:4-5)

Seen in this context, the visions are the prophet's way of inspiring the people to take heart. The present may be grim. The Temple is still in ruins. The returned exiles are few in number. But this is a temporary situation. There is a reality greater than the dreary sight of Jerusalem still in ruins. It appears in visions from God, which the prophet sees and reports to his people. Those who believe in his visions will be able to carry on and fulfill the divine promise.

Who is Satan?

Satan, known to us as the devil, makes its appearance here for the first time. It is not a well-established biblical character. In earlier biblical stories, such as the story of Balaam and his she-ass in the Book of Numbers (see p. 95), the word Satan appears in the sense of adversary, not the devil. Here, and also in the Book of Job (see p. 263), Satan makes its debut as God's evil messenger. In early Christian lore, and more so in the Middle Ages, Satan becomes a major figure, mostly among Christians but also among Muslims and Jews. The appearance of Satan here may be the result of foreign influences picked up by Zechariah in Babylonia prior to returning to Jerusalem.

Why does Zechariah proclaim: "Not by might, nor by power, but by My spirit, said Adonai of Hosts" (4:7)?

This is one of the most famous verses in the Bible. One should bear in mind that it was preceded by seven centuries of nearly constant wars, which began with the exodus in the desert, and ended with the fall of Jerusalem seventy years before the time of Zechariah.

The prophet is making a revolutionary statement. Judah is too small and weak to wage wars. The time has come to realize that Jewish survival is predicated on the spirit, not on physical force. Indeed, for the next 24 centuries, with the exception of the Maccabean wars and the Bar Kokhba rebellion, Jews will rely on their faith rather than their sword to survive.

What are we to make of Chapters 9 through 14 of the Book of Zechariah?

The prevalent opinion among biblical scholars is that these chapters are not part of the original book. In the first eight chapters we have a historical figure operating in a historical context. The last six chapters, on the other hand, contain various unrelated subjects and terms which are not part of the style, the language, or the themes of the first eight chapters. Most likely, these last six chapters are pre-exilic text which found its way into this book by mistake.

MALACHI:
THE END OF THE
PROPHETIC ERA

Who is Malachi?

The word Malachi in Hebrew means "my messenger." It is quite possible that what we have here is an anonymous writer, not necessarily a prophet. In fact, this last book of the second division of the Bible, or Prophets, consisting of three chapters, reads like a compendium of prophetic ideas, or a summary of the teachings of the prophets, rather than the utterance of one particular prophet.

What we can gather from the text is that these words were written after the time of Haggai and Zechariah, when the Second Temple was already rebuilt, and life in the newly rebuilt city of Jerusalem began to normalize.

What prophetic teachings does Malachi emphasize?

Malachi applies the prophetic teachings to his place and time. The returned exiles are striving to establish a renewed Jewish life in the small province of Judah. Not only the Temple, but also the social, ethical, and religious structures have to be rebuilt. Malachi emphasizes the need for strong Jewish families, based on respect for parents and elders:

A son will respect his father,
and a servant his master.
If I am your Father,
Where is My honor?

(Malachi 1:6)

And The heart of the parents will
Return to the children,
And the heart of the children,
To their parents.

(Malachi 3:24)

The community must band together to survive under the covenant of the ancestors. Husbands must remain loyal to their wives. As for charitable and ritual observances, the tithing and the offerings must be faithfully followed. Social justice, however, must take precedence over everything else.

Once all of this is accomplished, the prophet envisions a time of full reconciliation between Israel and God:

Then shall the offering of
Judah and Jerusalem
Be pleasant to Adonai
As in the days of old
And as in ancient times.

(Malachi 3:4)

In his concluding words, the prophet mentions the Day of Adonai, and introduces what becomes a post-biblical Jewish belief, namely, before the coming of that Day and of the messianic age, the prophet Elijah will come to announce those great events.

Malachi's conclusion, which provides a proper ending to the books of the prophets, is believed to be a later addition.

Why are the biblical prophets different from all the oracles, soothsayers, and other religious functionaries of antiquity?

All ancient cultures had a class of people who invoked the gods and made predictions. Israelite society was no different. As we read through the books of the prophets, we come across many such people who spoke both in the name of the God of Israel and pagan gods. The biblical prophets refer to them mostly as false prophets.

Prophets from Samuel to Malachi grew out of this universal tradition. They too spend much of their time predicting future events. But this is not where their strength lies. They are not always right in their predictions. What they are always right about is their sense of justice and morality. Their passion for justice is unsurpassed in all of human culture. "Justice, justice, you shall pursue," is their watchword. This conviction is never compromised. Micah put in better than anyone else: God expects humankind to do justice, love mercy, and walk humbly with God. These things, which seem all too obvious, always were and continue to be difficult to follow. The prophets, however, believed that a world imbued with justice, mercy, and humility was possible. They dedicated their lives to promoting such a world, and their words will continue to inspire many people and nations to work towards that goal.

PART THREE: WRITINGS

Saul attacks David

The Psalms:
The Language of the Soul

What is the Book of Psalms?

The Book of Psalms is a reflection of the soul of the Jewish people. It is a compendium of liturgical, or ritual songs, which were originally sung or chanted to the accompaniment of string, percussion, or wind instruments, or a combination thereof, mostly at the Temple in Jerusalem, on festivals, national events, or simply on the days of the week. As such, the Book of Psalms represents one of the oldest forms of formal Jewish prayer. In its words we find the beliefs, hopes and concerns of both the individual and the nation, and, by extension, the entire human race.

King David, to whom the Bible refers as the "Sweet Singer of Israel," is considered the original author of The Book of Psalms. David was a poet and a harpist, and during his reign Temple music became a prominent aspect of the religion of Israel. The era also gave rise to many outstanding liturgical poets, and to guilds of singers who arose from among the Levites and others, and played a prominent role in the spiritual and cultural life of the nation.

But the Book of Psalms is not only the product of David's reign. As the national repository of Jewish liturgy, pre- as well as post-Davidic compositions found their way into this canon, dating back to the Exodus and forward to the time of the return from Babylon and possibly even to the time of the Maccabees, a period of close to one thousand years.

This poetic collection is also the most influential book of liturgy in the history of the world. The various Catholic and Protestant religious services are inconceivable without the Psalms. Jesus' last words before dying on the cross were taken from the Book of Psalms ("My God, my God, why have You forsake me" [22:2], and "In Your hands I entrust my soul" [31:6]). Jews routinely recite from the Book of Psalms at all critical moments, as well as on all joyous occasions. When the decision was made at the end of the nineteenth century by the new Zionist movement to bring the Jews of the world back to Zion, the words that galvanized the delegates of the Zionist Congress and unified all the various ideological factions were the famous words of the psalmist:

> *If I forget you, Jerusalem,*
> *May my right arm wither;*
> *May my tongue cleave*
> *To the roof of my mouth*
> *If I remember you not,*
> *If I do not place Jerusalem*
> *At the top of all my joy.*
>   (Psalms 137:5-6)

What does the word Psalms mean?

A psalm is a song of praise to God sung to the accompaniment of a string instrument, such as a lyre or a harp. This large book of 150 chapters contains, however, many different types of songs, not only psalms. Somehow, the word Psalms, or *Tehillim* in Hebrew (a derivation from the word *tehillah*, praise), is the name by which this collection has become known.

Are the Psalms strictly prayers to God? Can one find inspiration in the Psalms even if one does not pray to God?

The Psalms are primarily songs of praise to God. They are an expression of a deep religious faith which reaches a high point with King David and continues through the ages. The Book of Psalms gives us a word which does not appear anywhere else in the Bible, namely, *Hallelujah*, meaning "praise God." This word has found its way directly from Hebrew into many other languages and religions.

But the Psalms go far beyond strictly offering praise to God. They cover a wide gamut of human experience, both individual and national. They offer words of solace to a broken heart, and words of encouragement to a people in the middle of a national crisis. As such, they have given comfort and spiritual sustenance to many individuals and nations around the world. Ironically, when we look back at history we often find two Christian nations going into war against each other, with the clergy on both sides reading to their troops words of inspiration from the Book of Psalms, each believing that those words were written for them and against the other side. One should, however, mention the Bishop of Canterbury who, on the eve of the Falkland War between Britain and Argentina, realized the absurdity of this act and refused to bless the troops in the name of the same faith shared by both countries.

What is the message of the First Psalm?

The First Psalm reads:

> *Happy is the man*
> *Who did not walk in*
> *The counsel of the wicked,*
> *Nor stood in the way of sinners,*
> *Nor sat in the company of the frivolous.*
> *For his delight is in the law of Adonai,*
> *And on this law he meditates day and night.*
> . . .
> *Adonai knows the way of the righteous,*
> *But the way of the wicked shall perish.*
> (Psalms 1:1-2, 6)

The Bible begins with the story of the first man, Adam, who is not a heroic, superhuman figure, but rather man plain and simple. The Psalms begin with a portrait of the righteous man, the *tzaddik*.

The righteous is not a saint, or someone spiritually superhuman. The portrait presented here is within everyone's reach. The purpose of the Psalms is to help every individual reach a state of righteousness.

Two other compelling psalms about the righteous person are Psalm 15 and Psalm 112.

Why does the author of the Psalms repeat each idea twice in different words?

> For his delight is in the law of Adonai,
> And on this law he meditates day and night.

This biblical poetic style, which is used throughout the Bible, beginning with such ancient poems as the Song of Moses upon crossing the Red Sea, or the Song of Deborah, is known as biblical parallelism. It dates back to the time when the Israelites were nomads, roaming through the desert. To this day, Middle East nomads, such as Bedouins, pass the time while riding their camels by having a song-leader begin a chant, with everyone responding with the same idea conveyed in different words. This style of singing follows the rhythm of the marching camels.

During Temple times, psalms were chanted by the Levites and other Temple singers, with people responding, thus preserving the desert tradition.

The Second Psalm: Does David proclaim himself "son of God?"

The Second Psalm is ambiguous. It is not directly attributed to David, but it is believed to describe David's career. Some commentators, however, believe that it deals with a future, messianic time. It describes the deliverance of God's chosen from his enemies, and it contains the following puzzling verse:

> God said to me: You are My son,
> Today I gave birth to you.
>
> (Psalms 2:7)

A careful reading of those parts of the Bible dealing with the life of David show that, for one thing, God did not speak to David, but rather communicated with him through the prophet Nathan (see II Samuel 7:14 ff). If David is indeed the one speaking here, then he is taking poetic license in saying "God said to me." As for "I gave birth to you," the meaning here is metaphoric. David is spiritually reborn when he is anointed king of Israel.

The Third Psalm: What do we learn from this psalm about the structure of the book as a whole?

Here we have the first psalm specifically attributed to King David. What is interesting about this early psalm is that it deals with events late in David's life, namely, the rebellion of Absalom, David's son. What we learn here is that the Book of Psalms is not arranged in any particular chronological order, or in any order of authorship.

The Eighth Psalm: A little lower than the angels?

The Eighth Psalm is a meditation on the puzzling reality of human life, at once sublime and meaningless:

> *What is man that you are mindful of him,*
> *Or the son of man, that you take account of him?*
> *And yet, You made him a little less than God,*
> *Crowning him with glory and honor.*
> (Psalms 8:5-6)

The words "a little less than God" have baffled biblical scholars over the ages. The more common English translation has been "a little lower than the angels," since the word *elohim*, or God, can also mean angels. Here again as elsewhere, this can be taken as a poetic expression, or it can be theologically challenged.

Psalm 18: Why were war songs included in the Book of Psalms?

David was a warrior king. He spent most of his life waging wars against Israel's enemies, from the Philistines in the west to the

Ammonites in the east, and from as far south as Egypt and as far north as Babylonia. Clearly, some of the psalms composed by him or in his day were war songs, intended to assure the troops God was on their side, and to inspire them to overcome great odds.

Psalm 18 is one example of the above:

> *The God who girds me with strength,*
> *And protects my way;*
> *Who makes my feet nimble as does,*
> *And sets me upon the high places;*
> *Who teaches my hands the skills of war,*
> *And my arms how to bend a bow of brass.*
> (Psalms 18:33-35)

One may wonder why those psalms were kept as part of the holiest collection of biblical prayers. Aren't they contradictory to the spirit of peace?

They may very well be, but the Book of Psalms is a true reflection of a people's history, not only of the quest for peace. Both throughout Jewish history, up to our days, and throughout the history of Western Civilization, the Psalms have been recited during time of war as well as time of peace. One is reminded of a paraphrase once offered by an American fighter plane pilot, who rewrote the opening verse of the 23rd Psalm, "The Lord is my shepherd," as "The Lord is my copilot."

Psalm 19: what do we learn here about science and faith?

In this psalm, the sky, the earth, and the sun reveal the glory of God who created them all. As in Greek mythology, where Apollo, the sun god, rides his fiery chariot across the sky, here too we read:

> *. . . set a tent for the sun,*
> *Which, like a groom emerging from his chamber,*
> *He will rejoice like a hero to run his course;*

He departs from the start of the heavens,
and his course is to the end thereof. . .
(Psalms 19:5-7)

Having said that, the poet concludes:

The law of Adonai is perfect,
Restoring the soul;
The testimony of Adonai is sure,
Making wise the simple.
(Psalms 19:8)

Paraphrasing this psalm in simple English, one would have to say that the poet is using the motion of the sun as proof that "God's law in perfect," when, in effect, the motion of the sun is an optical illusion.

This question has already been dealt with in the story of Joshua's battle in the Valley of Ayalon (see p. 118).

Psalm 22: Who is saying, "My God, my God, why have You forsaken me?

The opening question of this psalm, "My God, my God, why have you forsaken me," is among the best know questions in the entire Bible. The reason is self evident. Being forsaken by God is one of the most common human experiences. Jews have certainly felt that way throughout the ages, and even more so during and after the Holocaust. In the New Testament, Jesus speaks these words while suffering on the cross. Interestingly, English-language Christian Bibles have kept those words in the original language, so as not to detract from their impact.

But this psalm, which is attributed to King David, presents difficulties for interpreters. The language and style are not exactly David's. Some attribute it to a much later period, such as the time of Esther, centuries later, when the Jews of Persia faced annihilation in the hands of Haman. But whatever the case may be, the words have been used throughout time by people in distress, and are still used today by many who struggle with their faith and with the question of existence.

Is the 23rd Psalm the most famous and inspirational of all the Psalms?

The answer is yes. When people are in the greatest need of faith, during a time of bereavement or great stress or fear, this psalm is commonly recited. The best known version of the 23rd Psalm in the English-speaking world is the King James, dating back to 1611. People still recite it today, many from memory, using this old version:

> *The Lord is my shepherd, I shall not want.*
> *He maketh me to lie down in green pastures,*
> *He leadeth me beside the still waters.*
> *He restoreth my soul;*
> *He guideth me in straight paths for His name's sake.*
> *Yea, though I walk through the valley of the*
> *shadow of death*
> *I will fear no evil, for Thou art with me;*
> *Thy rod and Thy staff they comfort me.*
> *Thou preparest a table before me in the presence*
> *of mine enemies;*
> *Thou hast anointed my head with oil,*
> *My cup runneth over.*
> *Surely goodness and mercy shall follow me all*
> *the days of my life,*
> *And I shall dwell in the house of the Lord for ever.*

For the past one hundred years, countless attempts have been made to render these immortal words in modern English, while keeping the beauty and power of the original, but all have failed. No one to this day has been able to improve on the old version, which preserves to an amazing degree the meaning and music of the original Hebrew. It is no wonder that the King James translation of the Bible (actually, it was borrowed from an earlier English translator named Tyndale) is considered, along with the work of Shakespeare, the apex of English literature.

A quick look at some new translations of this psalm elucidates the point. A recent Jewish translation begins with the words:

> *The Lord is my shepherd,*
> *I lack nothing.*
> *He makes me lie down in green pastures,*
> *He leads me to water in places of repose.*

A recent Catholic translation starts:

> *Yahweh is my shepherd,*
> *I lack nothing.*
> *In meadows of green grass he lets me lie.*
> *To the waters of repose he leads me.*

Both translations have given up the poetic rhythm, or music, of the original. Much of the inspiration is lost.

This author, somewhat presumptuously, would like to offer his own translation. Gender terms, such as "Lord" or "He," are omitted:

> *God is my shepherd,*
> *What more do I need?*
> *I lie down in green meadows,*
> *I Walk by quiet streams,*
> *My soul is revived.*
> *I am led in the paths of righteousness*
> *For the sake of God's name.*
> *Though I may walk through*
> *The valley of the shadow of death*
> *I will fear no evil for You are with me.*
> *Your rod and your staff they comfort me.*
> *You prepare a table before me*
> *In the face of adversity;*
> *You have anointed my head with oil,*
> *My cup overflows.*
> *Only goodness and mercy shall follow me*
> *All the days of my life,*
> *And I shall dwell in my God's house*
> *Forever.*

Actually, the original Hebrew does not say "forever," which may imply eternal life. It literally says "for a long time." But in English "forever" does not only mean "to all eternity," but also "for a long time" (as in: "It seemed to go on forever").

Psalm 37: Is it possible that the righteous are never forsaken and their offspring never starve?

Psalm 37 deals with the problem of evil. Here the psalmist takes on life's most troublesome question—why do bad things happen to good people? The author's answer is one of the most powerful statements anywhere regarding the ultimate triumph of good over evil:

> *Do not be vexed by evil people,*
> *Do not envy evildoers.*
> *For they will quickly wither like grass,*
> *And fade like green herb.*
> (Psalms 37:1-2)

Good eventually is rewarded, and evil eventually is punished, the author asserts. How does the author know? He tells us:

> *I was a young boy, and now I am old,*
> *But I have not seen the righteous forsaken,*
> *Nor his seed begging for bread.*
> (Psalms 37:25).

We all know that the children of good people often do go hungry, which seems to contradict this assertion. The answer seems to lie in the word "eventually." Things can never be judged by one particular moment or situation. One must look at the greater picture. The psalmist's point is that evil carries the seeds of its own destruction within itself, while good carries the seeds of its own reward. While this is not always apparent, in due time good always prevails.

Psalm 72: Is this the last of David's Psalms?

This psalm ends with the words: "The prayers of David son of
Jesse have ended." Whether this editorial note belongs here is
doubtful. What it does is separate the first 72 psalms from the
next group, which is attributed to a writer named Asaph.

Thematically, however, this psalm does seem to signal the end
of David's career. Here the old king is talking about his son,
Solomon, who is about to succeed him. The psalm is dedicated to
Solomon, and describes the kind of king his father hopes he will
be. It is important to note that the emphasis is placed on justice
for the poor and the weak. This is the supreme test of the good
ruler, which Solomon, to judge from the story of the two women
and the baby, passed beyond anyone's expectations.

Who is Asaph?

With Psalm 73 we have a group of psalms attributed to Asaph,
who was one of the poets or singers of David's time. He gave rise
to an entire family of singers, the Asaphites, who are mentioned
among those who returned from the Babylonian Exile some five
hundred years after the time of David. It is not clear whether the
ancestral Asaph mentioned here actually wrote these particular
psalms, or only sang them. It is possible that he and his successors had their own particular style of psalm singing.

Psalm 90: Was it written by Moses?

It is quite strange to run in the middle of the Book of Psalms into
a solitary psalm written by Moses. But given the style and subject
matter, it is quite possible that the attribution is authentic. It is
also a beautiful poem about the brevity of life and God's eternity:

> A prayer of Moses, the man of God:
> Adonai, you have been our home
> In every generation.
> Before the mountains were born,
> You formed the earth and the universe.
> From everlasting to everlasting you are God.
> You bring man low

And You say: Return, children of man.
For a thousand years in Your eyes
Are like yesterday that is gone,
Like a watch in the night.
They are swept away by sleep,
Gone in the morning like grass.
In the morning it sprouts again,
In the evening it withers and dries up.

(Psalms 90:1-6)

Psalm 92: Why is this a hymn for the Sabbath?

This psalm begins by briefly introducing the Sabbath:

A psalm, a song for the Sabbath day.
It is good to give thanks to Adonai,
To sing to Your name, O Most High!
To declare Your mercy in the morning,
And Your faith at night.
With the instrument of ten strings
And with the psaltery,
With a solemn sound upon the harp.

(Psalms 92:1-4)

Having said this, the psalmist goes on to discuss the wicked and the righteous, rather than talk about the Sabbath day itself.

Good and evil, one of the major themes of the Book of Psalms and of the entire Bible, is indeed also the theme of the Sabbath. The Sabbath is not only the day of rest, but also the day of righteousness. During the week one is caught up in the rough and tumble daily struggle of bread-earning and problem solving. But on the Sabbath one's thoughts and prayers turn to the world of the righteous, the kind of person one may not have been during the past week, but would like to become in the days ahead.

Psalm 103: Is it by or related to King David?

This is a clear example of a psalm attributed to David which was written centuries after the time of David. The clear giveaway here is the language which dates to the time of the return from the Babylonian Exile. Here the returning exiles are thanking God for divine mercy and forgiveness, and make it clear that God's mercy is far greater than what they deserve:

> *God dealt with us not according to our sins,*
> *And repaid us not according to our iniquities.*
> *For as high as the sky is above the earth,*
> *So is God's mercy toward the faithful.*
>   (Psalms 103:10-11)

What one is inclined to conclude from the attribution of this psalm to David is that what is actually meant here is a psalm written in the Davidic style.

Psalm 104: What does this psalm tell us about the Jewish view of nature?

In all the cultures of antiquity, nature itself was viewed as a god, or a series of gods. The ancient Egyptians, Greeks, Babylonians, Romans and others worshiped the sun, the moon, mountains, various animals, and so on. The Hebrew religion was the only one that realized early on nature was not divine, but rather the creation of a power which transcends nature.

All of this is conveyed in this majestic poem, in which, at one point, the psalmist exclaims:

> *How manifold are Your works, Adonai,*
> *In wisdom have you made them all,*
> *The earth is full of Your creation.*
> *Behold the great and boundless sea,*
> *With creatures without number,*
> *The tiniest with the largest ones.*
> *There ships sail; there is*
> *The whale You created to sport with.*
> *They all turn to You for their sustenance,*
> *That You may give them their food in due season.*
>   (Psalms 104:24-27)

Here nature is presented as a marvelous creation, rather than a divine force controlling the destiny of mankind.

What does Psalm 114 tell us about the Jewish view of the exodus from Egypt?

The exodus from Egypt is mentioned over and over again throughout the Bible. It is without a doubt the pivotal event in all of biblical history. Here, however, we have a song of exaltation recalling the exodus, unsurpassed anywhere else in the Bible:

> When Israel came out of Egypt,
> Jacob from a foreign land.
> Judah became God's sanctuary,
> Israel, God's domain.
> The sea saw and fled,
> The Jordan turned back.
> The mountains danced like rams,
> The hills like young sheep.
> What made you flee, O sea?
> Jordan, why did you turn back?
> Mountains, you shall dance like rams,
> Hills, like young sheep.
> Tremble, O earth, before the Almighty,
> Before the God of Jacob.
> The one who turns the rock into a pool of water,
> Flint into a bubbling brook.
> (Psalms 114:1-8)

Psalm 118: What do we learn from this psalm about life in Jerusalem after the return from the Babylonian Exile?

This psalm is a festive hymn sung at the Temple in Jerusalem on one of the pilgrim festivals, most likely Sukkot. It is dated to the early days of the Second Temple, shortly after the return from Babylon. Those were difficult times for the renascent community in Jerusalem, taking its first steps after the national ordeal of the Babylonian conquest and exile. The diminished community was surrounded by old and new enemies in its own land, and had to overcome great odds to survive.

What is remarkable about this psalm and others like it which date to the same period, is that the religious fervor and poetic beauty of King David's earlier psalms is preserved here, nearly five hundred years later. Much of the text of this psalm has found its way into the daily and festival prayers of Israel:

> *Praise Adonai's goodness,*
> *For God's mercy is forever. . .*
> *Let Aaron's House say:*
> *God's Mercy is forever.*
> (Psalms: 118:1, 3)

Another interesting aspect of this and subsequent psalms is the borrowing of text from earlier parts of the Bible. For example, verse 14, "God is my strength and song; indeed, God has become my salvation," is borrowed from Moses' Song of the Sea in Exodus 15:2.

Psalm 119: What sets this psalm apart from the others?

This psalm, which is in effect a love song to the Torah, is remarkable in many ways. First, it is the longest chapter in the entire Bible, consisting of 176 verses. Second, it is an alphabetic acrostic, in which each of the 22 letters of the Hebrew alphabet is given a section of 8 verses, each beginning with that letter. This intricate poetic construction holds together and flows from verse to verse, brimming with emotion and with expressions of faith and love of Torah:

> *Where it not for Your Torah, my delight.*
> *I would surely perish in my affliction.*
> (Psalms 119: 92)

The other remarkable thing about this psalm that sets it apart is the time of its writing and the message it conveys. It dates to the time of the return from the Babylonian Exile, when the written text of the Torah becomes all important to the returning exiles. This psalm signals a point in time when little is being

added to the Bible, which has now become the "holy history" of
the Jews, the completed message of God, and the law by which
future generations will live. The author exalts in this divine message written in human language. Without the Torah, he would
perish in his affliction. Without the Torah, Israel would disappear, and God's law would be forgotten. Elsewhere in the Book
of Psalms we read:

> The dead do not praise God,
> Nor those who ascend into silence.
>   (Psalms 115:17)

Psalm 122: How is this psalm about the love of Jerusalem relevant to us today?

> A song of ascents, of David.
> I rejoiced when they said to me,
> We are going to the House of God.
> Our feet were standing
> Within your gates, O Jerusalem;
> Rebuilt Jerusalem,
> A city interconnected.
> There the tribes ascended,
> God's tribes, a testimony to Israel
> To give thanks to the name of Adonai.
> For there were the seats of judgment,
> The seats of David's House.
> Pray for the peace of Jerusalem,
> May those who love you be at peace.
> May there be peace within your walls,
> Tranquility in your palaces.
> For the sake of my brothers and friends
> I will speak peace to you.
> For the sake of the House of Adonai, our God
> I will seek your good.
>   (Psalms, Chapter 122)

These words, written after the return to Jerusalem from Babylonian Exile, could have been written today. The entire human race today prays for the peace of Jerusalem, the city holy to a vast portion of the human race, the city where King David composed his Psalms, where both Judaism and Christianity were born, and where the founder of Islam ascended to heaven.

Proverbs:
Folk Wisdom

Why is the Book of Proverbs included in the Bible?

Going through the Torah, the Prophets, and the Book of Psalms, one becomes immersed in Jewish history, beliefs, moral teachings, and laws. All this changes once we begin to read the Book of Proverbs. Consider the following passage:

> *Go to the ant, you who are being lazy,*
> *Study its ways, and become wise.*
> *Without leaders, officers, or rulers,*
> *It prepares its food in the summer,*
> *It stores its provisions in the harvest time.*
> *Until when will you be lying down,*
> *When will you rise from your sleep?*
> *A little more sleep, a little more slumber,*
> *And your ruin will come walking,*
> *Your want like a man with a shield.*
> (Proverbs 6:6-11)

This is a piece of universal folk wisdom, having nothing to do with Israel's faith, law, or history. Why did the compilers of the Bible see fit to include this type of literature in the biblical canon?

256

A careful reading of the Book of Proverbs shows that this book which, together with the Books of Job and Ecclesiastes forms the Wisdom Literature of the Bible, complements the teachings of the prophets and the priestly laws.

The wisdom Literature embodies the teachings of the elders, or the folk teachers of biblical times. According to both Jeremiah (18:18) and Ezekiel (7:26), there were three types of teachers in their day: priests, prophets, and wise elders. It was the function of the priest to transmit the law, while the prophet delivered divine messages and visions. The wise, or the elders, taught the practical lessons of life in the spirit of the law and the prophetic teachings.

Proverbs, then, while not directly dealing with matters of faith and law, should be seen as complementary to—rather than separate from—the priestly and prophetic teachings. The elders laid no claim to prophecy or to expertise in Jewish law. Their task was to transmit practical advice to the people, particularly to the young. Their advice, as we shall see, is well within the teachings of biblical Judaism.

Was ancient Israel's understanding of the concept of wisdom different from that of ancient Greece?

There is a fundamental difference between the biblical concept of wisdom and the Greek one. The ancient Greeks cultivated the science of wisdom, which they called philosophy, or the love of wisdom, elevating human wisdom to a high level, apart from the religious beliefs of their culture. Western civilization and religion are deeply influenced by the Greek concept of wisdom.

The approach to human wisdom in the Bible is different. The Psalms proclaim: "The beginning of wisdom is the fear of (or faith in) Adonai" (111:10). Proverbs adds: "The fear of Adonai is the beginning of knowledge" (1:7). In other words, any human wisdom or knowledge which is not based on one's acceptance of the supremacy of God and the subordination of the human intellect is erroneous. Human knowledge by itself is insufficient. It can only have meaning once it begins to operate within the belief system enunciated in the Bible.

To whom are the proverbs mainly directed?

They are directed mainly to the young. Both in form, in which an unnamed elder speaks to "my son" (which could also be his student), as well as in substance, given the type of advice that is given and the observations made, it is clear that an older person is addressing someone with much less life experience.

Is the Book of Proverbs a national or a universal document?

While the teachings of this book are well within the context of the beliefs and concepts of the Bible, they address the universal, rather than the national aspects of life. They cover such questions as prudent living, family values, and industriousness. They should be seen in the context of sayings and aphorisms that are common to all cultures around the world, and particularly to the cultures of the ancient as well as the modern Middle Eastern and Mediterranean worlds. They are also similar in tone, style, and ideas to proverbs of ancient Egypt and other countries in the ancient East during the time of the kings of Israel.

Did King Solomon write the Book of Proverbs?

Officially, the Book of Proverbs is attributed to King Solomon, who the Bible says was the wisest of men. It is entirely possible that parts of this book date back to Solomon's time, and were written, most likely, by some of his elders. But the varying Hebrew style and some of the varying statements show that the book was written and compiled over a long period of time, and, like the Book of Psalms, it is a compendium of proverbs rather than the work of any one person.

Love, sex, and marriage—why do they figure so prominently in the Book of Proverbs?

Perhaps the most famous chapter in the Book of Proverbs is the one about the ideal wife, or the "woman of valor." But the book has a great deal to say about the other kind of woman as well.

The first reference to a woman one should guard against warns a young man as follows:

To save you from the strange woman,
The alien woman who speaks smoothly;
The one who has left the man of her youth,
Who has forgotten her God's covenant.
For she brings her house down to death,
And her paths lead to the shadow world.
Those who go to her do not return,
Nor do they reach the path of life.

(Proverbs 2:16-19)

The woman described here is a seductress who is unfaithful to her own husband, and in addition to being adulterous is also idolatrous. In the context of biblical folk wisdom, this kind of a woman spells trouble, and any man who pursues her can only come to grief.

The ideal woman is described as follows:

A woman of valor who can find,
For her price is far above rubies.
Her husband's heart trusts her,
And he has no lack of gain.
She does him good and not evil
All the days of her life.
She looks for wool and flax,
And works willingly with her hands.
She is like the merchant ships,
Bringing her bread from afar.
She rises when it is yet night,
And gives food to her household
And a portion to her maidens.
She considers a field, and buys it,
And with the fruit of her hands
She plants a vineyard. . .
She opens her mouth with wisdom
And the law of kindness is on her tongue.
She watches the goings on of her home,
And does not eat the bread of idleness.
Her children rise and call her blessed,

Her husband praises her:
Many daughters have done valiantly,
But you have excelled them all.
Grace is deceitful and beauty is vain,
But a woman who fears Adonai
Shall be praised.
Give her of the fruit of her hands,
and let her works praise her in the gates.
(Proverbs Chapter 31)

The focusing on the issues of love, sex, and marriage in this kind of a book is not surprising. Clearly, these have been and remain to this day the most difficult issues for people to handle, particularly for the young. The first passage, which is repeated in different variations throughout the book, is meant to warn the young and not so young against romantic liaisons which can only lead to problems and to unhappiness. The above-quoted final chapter of the book, dealing with the ideal woman, offers a model of a woman one should pursue, whose main virtues are devotion to her family, industriousness, practical skills, wisdom, compassion, serenity, lack of vanity, and faith in God. In short, a woman whose character and substance outweigh any easy charm and good looks.

Together with the description of the righteous man in Psalms Chapter 1, we have here the Bible's portrait of the ideal couple.

To what extent are these proverbs folk wisdom rather than the sayings of a particular individual?

This would be hard to say, since a great deal of folk wisdom starts with one person making an observation which then becomes part of the general folklore. Most likely, the bulk of the Book of Proverbs originated with individual statements and observations which either took hold among the public or were gathered and put into this collection. Consider the following examples:

A wise son makes his father rejoice,
A foolish son is his mother's sorrow.
(Proverbs 10:1)

Like a gold ring in a swine's snout
Is a beautiful woman with no good sense.
(Proverbs 11:22)

A dry loaf eaten peacefully is better
Than a house full of the feasting of strife.
(Proverbs 17:1)

Job and his friends

JOB:
HISTORY'S GREATEST
QUESTION

What is the essence of the story of Job?

Job lived long ago in the land of Uz, presumably in Edom, or today's southern Jordan. He could have been a Jew or an Edomite. He could have lived in the time of Abraham, or Moses, or centuries later during the return from Babylonia. A careful reading of the book shows that it was rewritten and expanded over the centuries, so that while the original story may be quite ancient, some parts were written much later.

Job is a prominent citizen of his place and time. He is exceedingly wealthy, pious, and charitable. People refer to him as "Father to the Poor." God takes notice of him, and considers him the most righteous person alive. God, unfortunately, is not the only one who takes notice of Job. The other one is Satan, a figure of folklore, who rarely appears in the Bible. Here Satan is presented as one of the "Children of God," or angels. He appears before God, having returned from a tour of the earth. God asks Satan if he saw anyone on earth more righteous than Job. Satan replies that God has showered so much good fortune on Job and protected him from misfortune, that it was only natural for him to be God-fearing and righteous. It is agreed that Job's faith will be tested by Satan.

In quick succession, Job's property, consisting of vast numbers of livestock, is gone, and his seven sons and three daughter are killed. When Job gets the terrible news, he says:

Nake came I from my mother's womb,
And naked will I return there.
Adonai gave and Adonai took away,
Blessed be Adonai's name.

(Job 1:21)

Job passes the first test. But Satan is not satisfied. He argues that if Job's own skin and flesh were assailed, he would change his tune. God agrees. Job is afflicted with a terrible skin disease. He is forced to leave the community, and he finds himself in the town's garbage dumb, where he keeps scratching himself with a potsherd to assuage the pain.

Job's three friends come to console him. They sit there for seven days and seven nights without uttering a word. At that point, Job finally breaks down and curses the day of his birth.

Job's friends counter with some long discourses. In essence, they justify God, and insinuate that Job must have sinned to be so sorely afflicted. The reader, of course, knows that this is not the case, and Job adheres tenaciously to his innocence. Job questions God's justice. He realizes that God is all-powerful and beyond questioning, but cannot accept what happened to him after the kind of life he has led, while so many wicked people continue to prosper.

Finally God joins the discussion. Job and God enter into a dialogue, without God letting Job know he is actually being tested by Satan. God never gives Job or, for that matter, the reader, an answer to why innocent people must suffer while evil people prosper. Job, however, realizes that he has no right to question God. Once all arguments seem to have been exhausted, we are told that God rewards Job for his faith and goodness, and gives him even greater wealth and new children.

Who is Job and did he ever exist?

One rabbi in the Talmud states: "Job never existed and was never created. He is only an allegory" (Baba Batra 15a). While this may be true, the fact remains that Job does exist in every generation and in every land. Whenever a person is going through a series of misfortunes without any apparent reason, one speaks of such a person as "going through the suffering of Job." Another common expression in English is "to have the patience of Job," referring to someone who endures a long and unusual ordeal.

Any folk story of this kind has some kernel of historical truth to it. But in terms of biblical history, Job is not necessarily one particular person who lived at a particular place and time. He is someone who embodies faith in God as well as the questioning of God, an age-old human phenomenon which has been with us for thousands of years and will probably be with us for many more years to come.

What is the place of the Book of Job in the Bible?

Along with the Books of Proverbs and Ecclesiastes, Job forms part of the Bible's Wisdom Literature. But there is a sharp difference between Proverbs and Job. While Proverbs is a compendium of folk wisdom which does not question God's ways, but rather seeks to teach how to live a good, productive life, Job is an open and eloquent challenge to God's justice. One marvels at the rabbis for allowing this book into the biblical canon. It takes strong faith to include a book like Job in the Bible. After all, Job did not deserve such suffering. And we, the readers, are left in the dark as to why a just and caring God would allow this to happen.

But there is another way of looking at it. The rabbis must have known that the question of God's justice causes many to lose their faith. They needed a story that would show the most extreme case of a good man suffering the most unspeakable and unjustifiable calamity. This man, in spite of everything that befalls him, manages to say: "Though God may slay me, still I hope for God" (Job 13:15). In the end, he is rewarded. The moral of the story is that great and unshakable faith can overcome anything.

But what about Job's children who died for no reason whatsoever?

This question, for some odd reason, is not raised by either the old or the new commentators. All the scholars seem to concentrate on what happened to Job himself, but the death of his children is conveniently ignored. And yet, here we have what is by far humankind's most difficult question. The death of an innocent child (although one may argue that Job's children were actually adults) is beyond explaining. The death of an innocent adult is not much easier to explain either. This question remains open.

What do we learn from the Book of Job about reward and punishment in the next life?

The question of the afterlife does not come up in this book. Job, in the end, is rewarded in this life, because, according to biblical belief, this is the only life one has. The belief in a life after death is post-biblical. Clearly, the belief in an afterlife has made the question of justice in this life much easier to deal with, since one could look forward to a reward in the next life.

An interesting question would be: Has the belief in an afterlife done more good or more harm to humankind? Did it help perpetuate poverty and oppression, or did it provide hope and comfort to the poor, the afflicted, and the oppressed? This question is outside the scope of this book.

Does Job remind us of Abraham?

In many ways, Job reminds us of Abraham. Both were great believers in God. Both were affluent and charitable. Both were put to a severe test by God—Abraham with the would-be sacrifice of Isaac, and Job by the loss of his possessions, children, and health. Both were communal leaders, and both lived a long life. Some rabbis in the Talmud even argue that Job might have been more righteous than Abraham, which posed a theological problem for the rabbis.

What do we learn from Job's friends' arguments about the place of wisdom in the Bible?

As we saw in the discussion of the Book of Proverbs, human wisdom in the Bible is seen as inferior to prophetic and priestly knowledge and faith. Job's friends are typical biblical elders, who have life experience and human wisdom. But this does not endow them with the insight of the prophet, or the faith of the priest. They fail to grasp that there is more to Job's suffering than simple punishment for sin. They have their conventional wisdom, which is static, rather than dynamic. Much of what they say are platitudes, failing to take account of the unusual nature of Job's calamity. The author here seems to say: Wisdom is very important, but cannot penetrate God's ultimate intent. Man must accept the limitations of wisdom.

When are Job's friends at their best?

Job's friends are at their best in the first seven days of their visit with Job. They say nothing. They just keep him company. Once they begin to speak, they only make matters worse.

There is an important lesson here for anyone who happens to visit someone who is in mourning, as Job is. One is not expected to speak too much, but rather to listen and to offer comfort and, if necessary, material help. Bereavement, material loss, and loss of health are not something to philosophize about, as Job's friends do at great length. Human empathy is what is needed here, not human wisdom.

What are some of the difficulties inherent in this book?

The Book of Job is a dramatic poem, a great work of literature. All the characters in it speak with great eloquence, and as the discourse between Job and his friends unfolds, we are touched more and more deeply by Job's fervor and his steadfastness through all his sorrow and pain. But, as was mentioned before, the book was written and rewritten over a period of centuries. As a result, the language became extremely hard to follow. We have here Hebrew at different stages of development, as well as words taken from Aramaic and Arabic. Many key words have to be guessed at, and it is not always clear what a character is trying to say. Furthermore, the frame of reference of each character keeps changing. Sometimes it seems that they are in Egypt, and sometimes in Arabia, and other times in the land of Israel or even in Babylonia. Of all the books in the Bible, Job is the most linguistically complex and most difficult to decipher.

SONG OF SONGS: SOLOMON'S LOVE SONG

What is the Song of Songs, and how did it find its way into the Bible?

The Song of Songs is a short collection of love poems. In modern Israel, many of its lines are set to music, and become popular love songs. It is quite remarkable that words written nearly 3000 years ago can still be used today by songwriters to elicit romantic feelings:

> I am the rose of Sharon,
> The lily of the valley.
> Like a rose among the thorns,
> So is my beloved among the maidens.
>
> (Song of Songs 2:1-2)
>
> Let me see you,
> Let me hear your voice.
> For your voice is sweet,
> Your looks so fair.
>
> (Song of Songs 2:14)
>
> You are beautiful, my beloved,
> You are beautiful, your eyes are like doves
> Through your braids. . .
>
> (Song of Songs 4:1)
>
> Put me as a seal upon your heart,
> As a seal upon your arm,

For love is as strong as death.
(Song of Songs 8:6)

Biblical poetry concerns itself with faith, national events, prophetic visions and teachings, and personal questing. Only in this small book are we treated to love poetry, pure and simple.

The Song of Songs is attributed to King Solomon, but as in the Book of Job, here we have text, imagery, and words which date a few centuries later, to the time of the Second Temple. It is quite possible that Solomon composed some love poetry, part of which is preserved in this book. But it is hard to believe that this is a Solomonic composition from beginning to end, for the above-cited reasons, and because the story involves not only the king but also a shepherd boy who is the shepherd girl's true lover, and the object of her desire.

Why did the rabbis allow a book of love poetry into the Bible?

An examination of the traditional sources shows that the rabbis had a hard time deciding whether or not to admit this book into the biblical canon. It was probably Rabbi Akiva who prevailed over his colleagues in getting their consent for this inclusion, when he explained that this book was "the holiest of the holy." By that he meant that this book was not simply a love poem, but rather an allegory of the love between God, represented by the king, and Israel, represented by the beautiful young country girl.

Over the centuries, this book has been read as both a love poem and as a spiritual allegory. In fact, of all the books in the Bible, Song of Songs comes closest to meeting all the criteria of how the Bible is to be understood—on literal, allegorical, allusive, and mystical levels (see p. 13). Its literal meaning is self-evident. Its above-cited allegorical meaning took hold of the Jewish and later also the Christian mind (who saw it as a love poem between God and the Church), and became firmly entrenched. Additionally, the mystics found a great deal of hidden meaning in the male-female aspect of the book, which is one of Jewish mysticism's main ways of understanding the relationship between God and man.

Did Rabbi Akiva fail to see the romantic love aspect of this book?

Rabbi Akiva was fully aware of the romantic love aspects of the Song of Songs. When we read the stories about Rabbi Akiva in the rabbinical sources, it becomes clear that he was an extremely romantic personality himself. This is reflected in his love for his wife, Rachel, whom he idolized, and in many stories about his personal approach to human relations. He was fully aware of the secular aspects of this love poem, but at the same time he was taken by its beauty, and he must have sincerely believed that it was written on different levels, as indeed it came to be understood to this day.

RUTH:
A STORY OF DEVOTION

Who is Ruth, and what makes her special?

Ruth, after whom this book is named, is a Moabite woman who marries a man from Judah, whose family had been driven out of Judah by famine and settled in Moab, on the other side of the Jordan. Ruth's claim to fame is being the great-grandmother of King David.

But Ruth is an outstanding woman in her own right. After her Judean father-in-law, husband, and brother-in-law die, her mother-in-law, Naomi, decides to go back to Judah. She tells Ruth to stay in Moab and start a new life, since she, Naomi, is old, and has nothing to offer her. Ruth refuses to abandon her bereaved mother-in-law, who has lost both sons as well as her husband. She responds with a statement that has echoed through the ages:

> *Do not urge me to leave you and go back.*
> *For wherever you go, I will go,*
> *and wherever you stay, I will stay.*
> *Your people are my people,*
> *and your God, my God.*
> *Wherever you die, I will die,*
> *and there will I be buried.*
> *May Adonai do so to me, and more,*
> *if anything but death will part*
> *you from me.*
>
> (Ruth 1:16-17)

Did any mother-in-law ever hear kinder words from her daughter-in-law, Jewish or gentile?

If one were to rank Ruth among the great women of the Bible, she would certainly be placed near the top of the list.

Is the story of Ruth fictitious?

There is reason to believe that Ruth and the other characters in the book are indeed fictitious. For one thing, the names of the characters describe their personality or their fate. Naomi means pleasant. Her sons, Mahlon and Chilion, mean the sickly ones who will die, and so on. The book was clearly written and added to the Bible to provide a genealogy for King David.

Why does the Bible highlight a non-Jewish ancestor of David?

It is entirely possible that David came from a mixed stock, and the story is built around that historical fact. From the time of Jacob's sons on, non-Jewish women become important players in Jewish history. They include Tamar, Judah's daughter-in-law (also an ancestor of David); Zipporah, Moses' wife; and possibly Bathsheba, Solomon's mother, who was probably a member of a Jebusite family that lived in Jerusalem before it was conquered by David.

Does the Book of Ruth reflect life in the time of the Judges?

The story of Ruth, according to the opening verse, takes place in the time of the Judges. While the language and style of this story is similar to the prose of the Book of Judges, the picture painted here about life during that time is totally different from what we read in the book that covers the history of the period. The time of the judges, from beginning to end, was a time of strife and lawlessness, when "each person did what seemed right to him." The tribes of Israel lived under a succession of chieftains who for some odd reason were called "judges." There was danger everywhere. There seemed to be no respite from the repeated attacks by Israel's neighbors.

Here, on the other hand, we have idyllic country life, with generous, caring people, living in a peaceful community, steeped in tradition. How can we explain such a contradiction?

Ruth refuses to leave Naomi

One answer is that it is possible to find a peaceful community of good, caring country folk even during a time of national strife and conflict. The other answer is that this story, which was written during the time of David's or possibly Solomon's reign, reflects only partially the reality of life during the time of the Judges, but more so life during the peaceful years of David's, or, more likely, Solomon's reign.

LAMENTATIONS:
AN ELEGY FOR JERUSALEM

What is the purpose of the Book of Lamentations?

This short book of five chapters has a clear purpose: to lament the destruction of Jerusalem at the hands of the Babylonians in 586 B.C.E.

The fall and destruction of Jerusalem and the ensuing exiling of its inhabitants to Babylonia was the most tragic national event described in the Bible. It was repeated six centuries later, in the year 70 C.E., when the Romans once again stormed the city and destroyed it, putting an end to Jewish sovereignty in the Land of Israel for the next twenty centuries. Ironically, both events happened on the same day, the ninth day of the month of Av. To add to the irony, the expulsion of the Jews from Spain in the year 1492, also one of the most cataclysmic events in all of Jewish history, also occurred on that day. Consequently, it became a day of national mourning for Jews, during which the Book of Lamentations is chanted.

Lamentations was enshrined in the biblical canon as a perpetual reminder of the worst calamity that befell Israel. It served as a catharsis for the people's unbearable sense of loss and humiliation, and as a reminder that horrible as this event was, it was not the end. To quote the conclusion of Lamentations:

> *Bring us back to You, Adonai,*
> *And we shall return,*
> *Renew our days*

The people lamenting the destruction of Jerusalem

As in the days of old.
For indeed You have found us loathsome,
You were exceedingly angry with us.
                    (Lamentations 5:21)

Did Jeremiah write the Book of Lamentations?

The Greek translation of the Bible (Septuagint) attributes this book to Jeremiah, and this view has prevailed to this day. But there is no official attribution in the Bible of Lamentations to this prophet, who was the most prominent figure in Jerusalem during the events described in the book, and who began lamenting the destruction before it even happened. Moreover, Jeremiah's ideas and style are not exactly reflected in this book. It is possible that Jeremiah provided the basis for this book, but the hands of subsequent authors are visible in both the style and the contents.

What is the predominant imagery in the laments?

The author keeps referring to the "Daughter of Jerusalem," or the "Daughter of Zion." The allegorical comparison of a nation to a woman becomes common in later times, emanating not only from biblical language but also from Greek and Roman mythology. Woman is the source of life, the one who gives birth. At the sight of so much life destroyed, one invokes the woman image as a symbol of the nation:

> *What will I use for testimony,*
> *What will I compare you to,*
> *Daughter of Jerusalem?*
> *What will I liken you to and console you,*
> *virgin daughter of Zion?*
> *For your rupture is as wide as the sea,*
> *Who will heal you?*
>   (Lamentations 2:13)

What does the imagery of Jerusalem's destruction remind us of?

The imagery of the devastation in Jerusalem is extremely graphic and stark:

> *See, Adonai, and observe,*
> *To whom You have done this.*
> *For women are eating the fruit*
> *Of their womb,*
> *The children they have raised.*
> *Shall prophet and priest be slain*
> *In the Temple?*
> *Young and old are lying in the streets,*
> *My virgins and my boys died by the sword.*
> *You have killed in the day of Your anger,*
> *You slaughtered mercilessly.*
>
> (Lamentations 2:20-21)

The imagery conjured by this lament is that of the destruction of the Jews in Europe during the Holocaust. One can see scenes of the Warsaw Ghetto, for example, with people taken to slaughter on the death trains, while others are lying in the streets of the ghetto, dying of disease and starvation.

The author of Lamentations could as well have written this book to describe these and similar events of our time. Apparently, we have made little progress since the days of the ancient Babylonians.

How does the author explain such a catastrophe?

The author reflects the feelings of those who survive the destruction:

> *Let us search our ways,*
> *Let us question and return to Adonai.*
> *Let us lift our hearts on our hands*
> *To the God up above.*
> *We have transgressed and rebelled*
> *And You did not forgive us.*
>
> (Lamentations 3:40-42)

In other words, the people were punished for their sins. But once they were punished, they can hope for forgiveness. God would not abandon them. Once they repent, the road back will open up. It may not happen right way, but it will happen in due time.

ECCLESIASTES:
VANITY OF VANITIES

What is the essence of the Book of Ecclesiastes?

The essence of this book is summed up in its opening verses:

> *The words of Koheleth,*
> *Son of David, king in Jerusalem:*
> *Vanity of vanities, said Koheleth,*
> *Vanity of Vanities, all is vanity.*
> *What profit has man in all his work*
> *Which he performs under the sun?*
> *A generation goes and a generation comes,*
> *but the earth abides forever.*
>   (Ecclesiastes 1:1-4)

The book can be summed up in one word—resignation. The author is resigned to the seeming futility of life. Having said this, this book raises as many questions as any book in the Bible.

Who is "Koheleth?"

David's son who ruled in Jerusalem was Solomon. Is Solomon "Koheleth?"

The word is derived from "a group of people." This does not easily lead into the name Solomon. More likely, this name means "collective wisdom." The author was too self-effacing to append his or her own name to this book. Instead, what we have here is collective wisdom, attributed to King Solomon. It is possible that the text is built around some sayings of Solomon in his old age. It is also possible that, since Solomon was considered the wisest of men, this particular life-wisdom is attributed to him.

Is Ecclesiastes influenced by Greek philosophy?

Some biblical scholars have argued that this book was writ-ten under the influence of such Greek philosophers as the Stoics, or perhaps the Cynics. That would date the book to around 300 or 200 B.C.E., centuries after the time of Solomon. They point to the fact that many of the ideas in this book are not typical of the period of the biblical kings, but rather resemble the ideas of classical Greek philosophy. While this may be true, it is not proven conclusively. It is entirely possible that the Hebrew author ante-dated the Greek philosophies with the ideas expressed in this book.

How is wisdom treated in this book?

Not very well:

> I spoke to my heart, saying: Behold, I have
> acquired great wisdom, more than anyone
> who was before me in Jerusalem, and my
> heart perceived much wisdom and knowledge.
> And I directed my heart to know wisdom
> and knowledge, as well as merrymaking
> and foolishness, and this too is striving
> after the wind. For in much wisdom there
> is much frustration, and in increasing
> knowledge there is much sorrow.
>   (Ecclesiastes 1:16-18)

This observation can be understood if we put it in the context of the Book of Job, another biblical book which belongs to the Wisdom Literature, along with Ecclesiastes and Proverbs. As we saw there, human wisdom does not occupy as high a place in the Hebrew Bible as it does in Greek philosophy, for example. The fear of God and the adherence to God's commandments rank much higher in the Bible than human wisdom. To the prophets, human wisdom is limited and insufficient. "There is no wise man in his wis-dom," proclaims Jeremiah. Accepting God's supremacy is the beginning of wisdom. Reliance on human wisdom is a grave error.

The entire Book of Ecclesiastes is a warning against reliance on human wisdom.

Does Koheleth confirm the limitation of human wisdom when he talks about the sun rotating around the earth?

In Chapter 1 the author talks at length about the movement of the sun in the sky:

> *The sun also rise, and the sun goes down,*
> *And hastens to the place where it rises.*
> (Ecclesiastes 1:5)

Obviously, the author did not know that the sun does not move, rather the earth moves. We today have greatly advanced in our knowledge of the universe, but we are still in the dark as to many questions related to the nature and origins of this universe. Scientific knowledge was limited in biblical times. It continues to be limited today despite all the progress we have made. Certain questions may never be answered.

Is it true that "there is nothing new under the sun?"

The above expression is one of the most famous quotes this book has given us, indeed one of the most famous quotes in the entire Bible.

According to Koheleth, everything that happens on this earth has happened before. Nevertheless, we have to ask ourselves: Were there astronauts before the twentieth century? Were there antibiotics in past centuries? And, if every human being is unique, did you and I exist before you and I existed?

Clearly, we are entering the domain of Greek philosophy by raising such questions, rather than the domain of biblical faith and beliefs. Koheleth says that a generation goes and a generation comes, but the earth abides forever. According to one school of thought in ancient Greece, the earth is never the same, but rather changes constantly.

Is prosperity something we should avoid?

In Chapter 2 Koheleth tells us:

> *I amassed more wealth than anyone that*
> *was before me in Jerusalem, and my wisdom*
> *stood me in good stead. I did not deprive*
> *myself of any joy for I rejoiced in my labor*
> *and my portion. And so I looked at all my*
> *works that I made, and behold, it is vanity*
> *and striving after the wind.*
>
> (Ecclesiastes 2:9-11)

This is a direct attack on prosperity, achievement, and the good life. It is all for naught. And yet, when God rewards Job in the end, God gives job great wealth. Indeed, in many places in the Bible we find people praying to God for prosperity, as people do to this day. How can prosperity be bad?

Seeing it through Koheleth's eyes, here we have a man in old age who has done it all and yet feels that when life's end is near, one looks back and sees that it makes no difference if one was a pauper or the greatest king who ever ruled in Jerusalem. Both go to the same place. In the end, prosperity is an illusion. "You can't take it with you," although the ancient Pharaohs may have tried. Certainly, this is one way of looking at life, but is it the best way?

What does "For everything there is a season" mean?

Chapter 3 starts with yet another very famous passage:

> *Everything has its time and season under*
> *the heaven:*
> *A time to give birth, and a time to die,*
> *A time to plant, and a time to uproot,*
> *A time to kill, and a time to heal,*
> *A time to destroy, and a time to build.*
>
> (Ecclesiastes 3:1-3)

This passage has been taken completely out of context to mean that "for everything there is a season." In other words, there is a right time for everything, hence it is wise to do the right thing at the right time. This is not quite what Koheleth has in mind. Seen in context, the author is saying that everything is predetermined, hence there is little point in trying to take an initiative, since what must happen will happen no matter what one does.

Is life worth living?

In Chapter 4 we read:

> *And I went back and I saw all the oppression*
> *under the sun, and behold the tears of the*
> *oppressed and no one to comfort them while*
> *their oppressors have power, but no comforter.*
> *And so I find the dead better off than the living.*
> *And best off is the one who has not yet been,*
> *and has not seen the evil deed committed*
> *under the sun.*
>
> (Ecclesiastes 4:1-3)

One is reminded of a poem by Heinrich Heine, the great Jewish German poet, which argues that "sleep is good, death is better; however, best of all is not to have been born at all." According to an old Mexican folk song, life in this world is worth nothing, since it always begins with crying and likewise ends with crying.

However, having passed judgment on life, the author goes on to give some practical advice about living a good life. Thus, he decries envy, laziness, avarice, and the pursuit of wealth. Instead, he recommends peace of mind, compan-ionship, and friendship: "Two are better than one. . . and the threefold cord is not quickly torn" (4:9, 12).

Is it better to be rich or poor?

In Chapter 5 Koheleth makes it clear where he stands on this issue:

> *He who loves money will never be*
> *satisfied with money. . .*
> *The laborer's sleep is sweet,*
> *whether he eat little or much,*
> *But the satiety of the rich won't let him sleep.*
> *There is a great ill under the sun,*
> *Wealth kept by its owner to his hurt.*
> *This wealth will be lost in a bad venture,*
> *and if he begets a son he has nothing left.*
> (Ecclesiastes 5:9, 11-13)

In other words, wealth does not by itself bring happiness, peace of mind, and security. The author seems to imply that many people either pursue wealth or wish they were wealthy, without stopping to think that money is a means, not an end in itself. Money itself is not evil. The pursuit of money for its own sake is.

What does Koheleth mean by "Do not be too righteous?"

In Chapter 7 we find the following statement:

> *Do not be too righteous,*
> *and do not be too wise,*
> *why should you destroy yourself?*
> *Do not overdo wickedness,*
> *and do not be too foolish,*
> *why should you die before your time?*
> (Ecclesiastes 7:16)

Cardinal Cushing used to say one should beware of a saint. It is hard to believe that either Koheleth or Cushing meant that righteousness should have its limits. Yet what seems to be implied in this text is practical advice. One should not go to any excess of giving too much of himself or being too selfish. Extremes are harmful, and result in untimely death. Life must be lived in moderation.

What is Koheleth's attitude towards women?

There are several contradictory statements in Ecclesiastes, but the most puzzling one seems to appear in the two following passages:

> *I find woman more bitter than death.*
> *For her heart is full of snares and nets,*
> *And her hands are chains.*
> *He who pleases God will run away from her,*
> *While the sinner will be trapped by her.*
>   (Ecclesiastes 7:26)
> *Enjoy life with the woman you love*
> *All the days of your vanity. . .*
>   (Ecclesiastes 9:9)

These two seemingly contradictory statements actually complement each other. The giveaway word in the first quote is "sinner." This implies dealing with a woman who is wayward, which is what a sinner would do, in which case one often invites a great deal of trouble. Some have taken this statement to mean that all women are evil, but this of course is a case of pure male chauvinism. The second statement is part of Koheleth's overall philosophy of moderation and prudent living. Marital bliss is the best way to have peace of mind and stability in one's life.

Later in the chapter the author argues that he has met more virtuous men than women. This is hard to believe, since common experience proves just the opposite. The only explanation one could attempt is that Koheleth experienced a time of moral decline, when many women were engaged in immoral behavior.

What does Koheleth means by "for God has already accepted your works?"

In Chapter 9 Koheleth says:

> *Go eat your bread with joy and drink your wine with*
> *A merry heart, for God has already accepted your*
> *works.*
>   (Ecclesiastes 9:7)

Here, as in the rest of the book, Koheleth lets us know he believes in predestination. There is little one can do about the final outcome of things, hence it is best to enjoy life while you can. This reminds us of the Greek belief in *moira*, or fate, which even the gods themselves cannot escape.

Does Koheleth change his mind about wisdom in Chapter 9?

In this chapter we find the statement that "wisdom is better than strength" (9:16). There are other statements in the book which praise wisdom in comparison to foolishness, which seems to contradicts the author's derisive comments about wisdom in the beginning of the book.

Actually, there is no contradiction in these statements. The author has not changed his mind about the limitations of human wisdom. Everything, however, is relative. In the practical affairs of everyday life, wisdom is better than foolishness. Strength only succeeds temporarily, while wisdom will ensure long-term results.

What does "Send your bread on the face of the water, for in the fullness of time you will find it" mean?

This statement in Chapter 11:1 has given rise to different interpretations. Some thought it had to do with taking risks in pursuing one's affairs. The traditional Jewish view is that it means performing acts of kindness and charity, which later on may pay off. The next verse reads:

> Divide a portion into seven, even into eight,
> For you do not know what evil may be
> Upon the earth.
>
> (Ecclesiastes 11:2)

Here again the two interpretations apply. You could argue that this too is business advice, namely, do not put all your eggs in one basket. On the other hand, it could mean that one should give charity to different causes to make many friends. One is then more likely to receive help later on in time of need.

The ambiguity continues throughout the chapter, as it does in many places in Ecclesiastes.

Does Koheleth soften his views in the last chapter?

In Chapter 12 we have the conclusion of the Book of Ecclesiastes. Here the author begins to sound more like the author or authors of the Book of Proverbs:

> Remember your Maker in the
> days of your youth,
> Before the evil days come,
> And the years come when you will say:
> I have no use for them.
> (Ecclesisastes 12:1)

In other words, after pondering at length the futility of life, Koheleth does uphold the value of life and tries to give sound advice to the young. But true to form, Koheleth concludes with these words:

> Vanity of vanities, said Koheleth,
> Everything is vanity.
> And besides being wise, Koheleth
> taught the people knowledge,
> and he listened to and tested the
> soundness and corrected many maxims. . .
> (Ecclesiastes 12:8-9)
> The end of the matter:
> Revere God and obey God's commandments,
> For this is all man is.
> For God will judge every act
> And every hidden thing,
> Whether good or bad.
> (Ecclesiastes 12:13-14)

Esther accusing Haman

ESTHER:
THE QUEEN WHO
SAVED HER PEOPLE

What is the Book of Esther?

The Book, or Scroll, or, in Hebrew, the Megillah of Esther, is one of the best known and most popular books of the Bible. It is read every year in the synagogue on Purim, the Jewish holiday of merrymaking, from a scroll made of parchment or paper. Its story about the evil Haman, the foolish Persian king Ahasuerus, the pious Mordecai, and his cousin, Esther, the beautiful Jewish Queen who rescues her people from Haman's evil decree, enjoy a popularity similar to the Arabian Nights.

Of all the books in the Bible, this book is the only one told tongue-in-cheek, in a fanciful style, without any religious or moral overtones, simply as a good story. It is also the only book in the Bible in which the name of God is not mentioned even once.

What is the historical background of the Book of Esther?

The story takes place in Persia around 474 B.C.E., about one hundred years after the Babylonian Exile, in the time of one of the Persian kings who succeeded Cyrus the Great, the king who had allowed the Jewish exiles to return to Jerusalem. By that time the Jewish Diaspora had begun, and people like Mordecai and Esther were descendants of Jews who were born in the Diaspora. The

289

great detail the description of Ahasuerus' court is rendered in makes it clear the author was quite familiar with the story's place and time.

Did Persia actually have a Jewish queen at that time?

This is not known. Considering the fact that the Persian Empire was founded by a king who favored the Jews, it is quite possible that Jewish women had access to the court and one might have even become a queen. But as we see in the story, this did not prevent Haman, the king's courtier, from turning against the Jews.

What do we make of names like Mordecai and Esther?

Neither name was originally a Jewish name, although in time both became very popular Jewish names. We are told that Esther's original name was Hadassah, which means myrtle in Hebrew. The name Esther is derived from the name of the Babylonian goddess Ashtoreth, while the name Mordecai is derived from the name of the Babylonian god Marduk. Clearly, the two of them were born in Persia and given local names. Ironically, Mordecai, despite his pagan name, is the only person in the Bible who is referred to specifically as "the Jew."

Why doesn't the name of God appear in this book?

There is no ready answer for this question. One can only speculate. It is possible that since the book was associated with Purim, the time of merrymaking and levity, the author wished to protect God's name from profanation. It may also be because the story is not to be taken as fact, but rather as fiction.

Why did the rabbis include this book in the biblical canon in spite of the absence of God's name?

By the time the Bible was given its final form in the second century C.E., the feast of Purim had already become a popular holiday. Furthermore, divine providence is felt throughout the book. One gets the distinct impression that it was preordained for Esther to be chosen as the new queen of Persia, so that in time she would

Mordecai honored by the king

be in a position to save her people from the harsh decree of
Haman, the king's courtier.

What do we learn from Haman's argument against the Jews about their condition during that time?

Haman, in seeking to destroy the Jews, tells his king the following:

> *There is one people which is scattered and*
> *dispersed among all the other nations in all*
> *the lands of your kingdom, and their religion*
> *is different from all other people and they*
> *do not follow the religion of the king, and*
> *it is not profitable for the king to let them be.*
> (Esther 3:8)

In this short statement we learn a great deal about Jewish history during the early years of the Diaspora. Jews had been scattered not only in Babylonia and Persia, but also in other parts of the ancient Middle East. While all other conquered nations accepted the religion of their conqueror, the Jews remained loyal to theirs. This was taken by people like Haman, and later by such rulers as the Syrian king Antiochus and the Roman emperors as disobedience and rejection of the official state religion, and caused the Jews a great deal of trouble.

Were the Jews justified in massacring their enemies?

After Esther succeeds in persuading the king that Haman's request to destroy the Jews must be turned down and Haman must be punished, the Jews are given permission to defend themselves against their enemies throughout the empire. The Jews take advantage of the opportunity, and massacre thousands of their enemies.

This rather harsh turn of events, coupled with the fact that the Jews never give thanks to God for their deliverance, but rather celebrate it among themselves, has raised questions over the ages among both Jewish and Christian scholars and commentators.

One should, however, keep in mind that this book is more fiction than fact, and was never meant to be taken as objective history, but rather a national expression of deliverance from a mortal enemy. In the context of the carnival-like celebration of Purim, this episode is more of a flight of fancy than a recounting of actual events.

Daniel in the lions' den

DANIEL:
CHAMPION OF GOD

Is Daniel truly part of the Hebrew Bible?

The official answer is yes. After all, the Book of Daniel is part of the third division of the Bible, called Writings. Daniel himself is someone who lived during the last years of the Kingdom of Judah. But the history covered in this book stretches past the biblical period—which effectively ends in the days of Ezra and Nehemiah (fifth century B.C.E.)—into the time of the Maccabees (second century B.C.E.). Scholars and commentators are divided in their opinions as to whether this book was written during Daniel's lifetime, whereby Daniel is predicting future events, or centuries later, after those events—the rise of Alexander the Great, the splitting of his kingdom, and the time of Antiochus Epiphanes, whom the Maccabees fought—took place.

But this conundrum is only one part of the question whether this book is truly part of the Bible. The other part is the ideas, the style, and even the language, all of which are a clear departure from the classic biblical text. Let us examine these issues one at a time.

Who is Daniel?

When Nebuchadnezzar, the Babylonian king, first attacks Judah, he takes with him back to Babylonia several young boys of the

royal seed of Israel. Among them is Daniel, a very young teen-
ager. The Babylonians pursue a policy of cultural integration,
designed to eliminate the cultures and religions of the conquered
nations and replace them with their own state culture and religion. As part of this policy, Daniel is put in a Babylonian school,
where his name is changed to Belteshazzar, and he is taught
Chaldean, the local language. He is expected to follow the state
religion, but something curious happens. Daniel insists on adher-
ing to his native religion. He refuses to eat the local food and
drink the local wine, and restricts himself to legumes and water.

When the king is having a dream no one can interpret, Daniel
is called upon, finds the answer, and becomes advisor to the king.
Subsequently, the king erects a great statue to his god, and
Daniel's companions, who also adhere to their Jewish faith, refuse
to bow down to it. The king orders them thrown into a fiery fur-
nace, which they escape unscathed, whereupon the king acknowl-
edges the supremacy of the God of Israel.

Daniel goes on living in exile for many years, under several
kings and kingdoms. On another occasion he is denounced by
jealous courtiers and is thrown into a lions' den, which he sur-
vives. He has many visions, foresees the rise and fall of several
empires, and the return of the Jews to Jerusalem, and concludes
with visions of the messianic age and the resurrection.

Was Daniel a prophet?

By not including his book in the prophetic section of the Bible, the
rabbis made it clear that they did not consider Daniel a prophet.
God does not talk to him nor does he transmit divine messages.
He is a clairvoyant who is able to interpret his visions. In Christian Bibles, on the other hand, the Book of Daniel is placed in the
prophetic section of the Old Testament, between Ezekiel and
Hosea. As we shall see below, this was done for a reason.

Why are parts of the book in Hebrew and parts in Aramaic?

The book opens in Hebrew, then changes to Aramaic, and then
concludes again in Hebrew.

There is no apparent reason for this. One theory has it that originally there were two versions of this book, one in Hebrew and one in Aramaic, and only parts were preserved of each version. This seems a little doubtful. It could be that during this time of transition in Jewish history and faith, there was an ambivalence between using classical Hebrew, which is the language of revelation and the Torah, and the everyday language of the ancient world, namely, Aramaic, which closely resembles Hebrew. This ambivalence will continue for several centuries, well past biblical times. Thus, the Mishnah, which is the core of the Jewish Oral Law (as opposed to the Bible, which is the Written Law), is in Hebrew. The Gemarah, which together with the Mishnah constitutes the complete Oral Law, or the Talmud, is primarily in Aramaic. The same is true of Jewish liturgy, which is mostly in Hebrew but partially in Aramaic (including such a key prayer as the Kaddish).

Furthermore, at the end of the biblical period many Jews spoke Aramaic more readily than Hebrew. Outside the Land of Israel, Aramaic became the first language for most Jews, while their knowledge of Hebrew declined. As the Jewish Diaspora grew, the Pentateuch was translated into Aramaic (the Onkelos translation), and on market days, namely, Monday and Thursday, the Torah was read in public in both Hebrew and Aramaic translation, to ensure that everybody understood it.

What is the similarity between Daniel and Joseph?

With Daniel, the stories of Joseph in the Book of Genesis come a full circle. Here again is a young man taken away from his people in the Land of Israel, finding himself in the royal house of a mighty empire, and becoming part of a different culture. Like Joseph, Daniel is endowed with a gift of interpreting dreams, as well as great wisdom and piety. Joseph, by saving Egypt from famine, also saves his own family who comes down to Egypt, and thus plays a pivotal role in Jewish history. Daniel also plays such a role at a new critical juncture. He is, in effect, the first Jew in the Bible who has to assert his faith in Israel's God and traditions while living in exile. He maintains his faith through fervent prayer, and articulates new beliefs that are in effect post-biblical, such as the resurrection of the dead and the messianic age.

Why don't Nebuchadnezzar and Belshazzar, the two kings whose fall Daniel predicts, punish him?

Daniel's captor, King Nebuchadnezzar, has a dream about a colossus with a golden head and other body parts made of less precious metals. Daniel interprets the dream to mean that Babylonia is the head, while the other body parts are new empires that would replace it. Belshazzar, a subsequent king (not confirmed by history), sees a writing appear on the wall (hence the expression "to see the writing on the wall") during one of his banquets, making the statement "*Mene mene tekel u'farsin,*" which Daniel interprets to mean: *Mene*—yours days are numbered; *tekel*—your actions are being weighed by God and you are found wanting; *peres*—you kingdom will be divided and given to the Persians and the Medes.

Both kings, instead of punishing the foreigner for predicting their fall, praise him and promote him. It seems that they themselves realize that the days of their own empire are numbered, and that unlike their own wise men, who always flatter them, this man of faith does not lie. So, at least, it seems.are in effect post-biblical, such as the resurrection of the dead and the messianic age.

Daniel's visions—where do they come from?

Daniel has visions of his own, in one of which he sees fan-tastic animals with body parts of different species, such as a lion with eagle's wings, engaged in a colossal struggle. In another vision he sees gigantic rams and goats also engaged in a struggle, with horns broken and replaced with more horns. He takes all those visions to mean the rise and fall of empires.

When one looks at pictures of Babylonian, Assyrian and other Mesopotamian antiquities, those fantastic animals, such as winged lions, are depicted, usually much larger than life-size, either as bas-reliefs or as monuments (some can be found in the British Museum). No doubt, the boy from Jerusalem, where there were no graven images, who first arrived in the Babylonian empire and saw those gigantic images, was deeply impressed, and in his mind they became emblematic of those powerful empires which, despite their power and splendor, were transitory. Moreover, their gods were also transitory. The only enduring power in the world, Daniel concluded, is that of the one true God of his ancestors.

How does Daniel remind us of Ezekiel?

Daniel's visions of the composite animals, angels, and other visions of a panoramic nature are similar to the visions of Ezekiel, who also belongs to the time of the Babylonian Exile. Ezekiel, however, is still part of the classical biblical prophetic era, while Daniel is the child of a new era. They may not be that far apart in time, but their ideas are not the same. The next two questions explain why.

How do Daniel's visions of angels differ from the rest of the Bible?

Daniel is the first person in the Bible who refer to angels by names. He introduces into the Bible two archangels, namely, Gabriel and Michael. As we have seen earlier, angels do not appear too often in the Bible, and most of the time it is not even clear if they are angels, or actual persons, or just an inner vision of a person in a moment of emotional upheaval. Here, however, we have the beginning of a formal treatment of angels, which will become part of the post-biblical Jewish tradition, and even more so Christian tradition.

Gabriel helps Daniel interpret his visions, while Michael, the archangel who watches over Israel, tells him about the resurrection of the dead and the redemption of his people. One could argue that Daniel is only talking about national resurrection, not personal, but this would mean stretching his actual words.

Does Daniel actually talk about individual resurrection?

The text in Chapter 12 reads:

> *And many of them that sleep in the dust*
> *of the earth shall awake, some to everlasting*
> *life, and some to reproaches and everlasting*
> *abhorrence. And they that are wise shall*

> *shine as the brightness of the heaven; and*
> *they that bring many to righteousness as the*
> *stars forever and ever.*
>
> (Daniel 12:2-3)

These words are quite explicit, and clearly foreshadow the belief in a messianic age when the dead will come back to life. According to the great Medieval Jewish philosopher Maimonides, this is one of the key beliefs of Judaism (see his Thirteen Principles of Faith). But when Maimonides gets down to discussing this belief philosophically, he seems to have difficulties explaining it.

What is the place of Daniel in the development of the Jewish faith?

The Book of Daniel provides the bridge between biblical Judaism and post-biblical, or rabbinical Judaism, whose teaching are embodies in the Talmud. As such, Daniel is neither truly biblical nor yet truly rabbinical. With its apocalyptic visions, it belongs in a transitional phase of the Jewish faith which gave rise to Christianity and later on to Islam. It also provides inspiration to later schools of Jewish mysticism, with such terms as *atik yomin*, or Ancient of Days, a new name for God. In addition, some of Daniel's prayers have been incorporated in Jewish liturgy, specifically in the High Holy Day prayers.

EZRA:
THE RETURN TO ZION

What is the place of the Book of Ezra in biblical history?

The Book of Ezra resumes the historical narrative which stopped at the end of the Second Book of Kings, with an interruption of seventy years between the two. II Kings ends with the fall of Jerusalem in 586 B.C.E., while the key event in Ezra is the rebuilding of the Jerusalem Temple in 516 B.C.E. Between Ezra and Kings we have all the books of the Prophets, as well as the Psalms, the Wisdom Literature, and other books included the Writings.

After seventy years in Babylonian Exile, during which time the nature of Jewish faith and culture began to change significantly, King Cyrus of Persia overruns the ancient world and reverses the Babylonian policy of uprooting and exile. Exiled people are allowed to go back to their land of origin and practice their ancestral faith. The Jews seize upon the opportunity, and as we read in the prophetic books of Haggai and Zechariah, the rebuilding of the Holy Temple commences.

Some sixty years later, around 458 B.C.E., Ezra, a priest and a scribe, is given permission by King Darius of Persia to go to Jerusalem and assume religious leadership over the returned Jews. During those sixty years, Jewish life in Jerusalem began to decline. The Jewish faith had weakened, most Jews had intermarried, and the future of Judaism was in jeopardy. Ezra's mission is to reverse this tide, and ensure the survival of Judaism.

Who is Ezra?

Although Ezra is a key figure in Jewish history, credited with saving Judaism, little is known about his origins and career. There is little doubt about the fact that there was a person named Ezra who performed the religious reforms in Jerusalem at that critical time. Nor is there a reason to doubt that Ezra wrote this book, or at least most of it.

What were Ezra's main activities once he arrived in Jerusalem?

Some of the information about Ezra's career is found in the next book of the Bible, the Book of Nehemiah. The two were contemporaries. Ezra was the religious leader at the time, while Nehemiah was the secular leader, as we shall see in the next section. Ezra, in effect, laid the foundation for a new nation ruled by priests, or a theocracy, which was all the Persian emperor, who ruled the entire Middle East at the time, would allow.

Ezra's task was to create a new framework for religion-based national life, drawing upon the Torah, the teachings of the prophets, and the traditions that were beginning to emerge at the time. The process begun by Ezra would continue for the next nine centuries, until the end of the Talmudic era (500 C.E.), during which time the Jewish religion evolved through the development of the Oral Law of Judaism.

When Ezra arrives in Jerusalem, he finds out that many of the returned exiles, including the priests and the Levites, have intermarried with the surrounding people, such as the Ammonites, the Moabites, the Emorites, and others. People were no longer observing the biblical festivals and the Sabbath, the laws of Moses were forgotten, and the future of the Jewish faith was in jeopardy. Ezra, as well as Nehemiah, prevail upon the people to give up their non-Jewish wives, and rededicate themselves to the faith of their ancestors.

At the same time, Ezra proceeds to reintroduce the observances of Judaism. He gathers the people for the celebration of the Festival of Tabernacles, or Sukkot. He teaches them how to observe the holiday, and in the process he reads the Torah to the assembled crowd. The reading makes a deep impression on the people, many of whom must have lost touch with the stories of God's covenant with Abraham, Moses' crossing of the Red Sea, and the words and activities of the great prophets. The impact seems to be immediate and overwhelming. The listeners realize that they must rededicate themselves to the God of Israel and to the law of Moses. Ezra and Nehemiah call for the renewal of the old covenant, which is done in a solemn ceremony in which the heads of the households of Israel take part. A new, post-biblical Judaism begins to emerge, which will shape the character and beliefs of the Jewish people to this day.

Why doesn't Ezra seek to convert the non-Jewish wives to Judaism?

Throughout the Bible we hear of Jews marrying non-Jewish women. One may wonder why, instead of issuing the harsh order to send away non-Jewish wives, Ezra does not make an attempt to covert them to Judaism.

Prior to the destruction of the Temple, the Jews were an established nation with its own long established religion. It was only natural for them to welcome other people to join them and become part of their religion. When Ezra arrives in Jerusalem a few decades after Jewish exiles began to settle in the city, the situation is entirely different. The Jews themselves have forgotten their traditions, and many no longer speak Hebrew. Ezra has to bring his own people back to their own faith and culture. Quite possibly, in pursuing this task he had to compete with non-Jewish wives and mothers who may have begun to draw their Jewish husbands to their own religion.

Why did the Jewish leaders refuse to include the Samaritans in the renewed community of Israel?

When the exiles return to Judea prior and during the time of Ezra, they find other groups living there who had been brought over by the Babylonians as part of their policy of relocating populations to reduce the prospect of national resurgence. Among the people who now live in Judea are the Samaritans, a Semitic people

Ezra reads the Law

related to the Jews, who were left in the Northern Kingdom of Israel after its destruction in 722 B.C.E. When the rebuilding of the Temple starts, they approach the returning exiles and ask to participate in the task. The Jewish leadership rebuffs them, turning down their offer. Here too, as in the case of the non-Jewish wives, one may wonder why Ezra and the other leaders would not accept them.

The Samaritans, who followed the laws of the Torah, did not accept the teachings of the prophets of Israel, or the new Jewish traditions that were beginning to emerge at that time. Given the tenuous state of the returned exiles, they posed a danger to Ezra's and Nehemiah's undertaking. Once they were rebuffed, they turned against the Jews, and tried to have the Persian king stop the building of the Temple. They were able to secure an order from the king to stop the under-taking for a number of years, but thanks to the exhortations of the prophets Haggai and Zechariah the work was resumed.

What are Ezra's contributions to the survival of Judaism?

Ezra is credited with three things that ensured the continuation and survival of Jewish faith and culture:

(A)   He founded the Great Assembly which transmitted the laws and texts of the Bible. The Great Assembly of Elders was the body that linked between the era of the biblical prophets and the later era of the sages of the Mishnah and the Talmud, thus ensuring the continuation of the development of Jewish law.

(B)   He initiated the tradition of reading the law in public and teaching it to every Jew. This was a revolutionary step, as it took the control over the law from the hands of the priests and gave it to everyone. This was, in effect, the great democratization of the Jewish religion, which no longer depended on a priestly class or a cultic center, but became study and prayer oriented, whereby every individual Jew could study and practice his or her own religion on their own, whether in the Land of Israel or anywhere else in the world.

(C) He reversed the spreading practice of marrying outside the community, a process which began to threaten the survival of Judaism. While Judaism prior to the destruction of the Temple had depended on the priestly class for the teaching and the preservation of the law, now it depended on the individual and the family. Ezra understood the importance of the family unit in preserving the tradition, and acted to strengthen it.

NEHEMIAH:
REBUILDING JERUSALEM

What kind of a leader is Nehemiah?

Nehemiah was born in exile in the Persian Empire, and rose to a prominent position in the king's court. Word came to him about the condition of the returned exiles in Jerusalem. He learned that the new community was not faring well. The surrounding enemies were harassing the city, which had become vulnerable to attacks because of poor fortifications and a low morale.

Nehemiah secures a commission from the king as the new governor of Jerusalem. He goes back to his ancestral land, and takes charge of the construction of the walls of Jerusalem. The task is daunting, but Nehemiah is a man of great energy and determination, and a good strategist. He organizes construction and defense teams. He puts each household in charge of a different section and tower of the city walls, and builds fortifications all around the city at the same time, through continuous shifts. Thus, he is able to complete the task, despite the repeated attempts by enemies such as the Samaritans and the Arabs to disrupt and stop the endeavor.

But Nehemiah, who is a devout Jew, realizes that an even more urgent task than the rebuilding of the walls is the re-building of the spiritual heritage of Israel, which was on the decline. For this task he turns to Ezra the Scribe, a direct descendant of Moses'

Nehemiah rebuilding the Temple

brother, Aaron. Working as a team, they ensure the survival and development of the faith of Israel.

Why do Ezra and Nehemiah provide such detailed lists of the names of the Jewish households of their time?

In both books, which in early Talmudic times formed one book under the heading of "Ezra" and were both attributed to Ezra, we have long lists of names of Jewish households who returned from exile, and those who participated in the rebuilding of Jerusalem. In the next and last book of the Bible, The Chronicles, which is also attributed to Ezra, we also have long genealogies. What is the reason for all this?

One could think of several reasons. Once Jerusalem was destroyed and the people exiled, the generational continuity of the Jewish people was disrupted. One of the tasks of Ezra the Scribe was to reestablish the genealogical identity of the returning exiles. This could have served several purposes. It redefined the social status of each household; it identified the priestly families, the Levites, and the Israelites (every Jew to this day fits into one of those three categories). And It gave families back their credentials as former residents of Jerusalem and landowners in Judea.

What is Nehemiah's historical role in the Bible and beyond?

Nehemiah is the last Jewish leader in the Bible. When Moses, the first national Jewish leader in the Bible gives the people the Ten Commandments, the people are told that the purpose of their becoming a nation is that they will evolve into "a kingdom of priests and a holy nation." Nehemiah, not a priest but rather a political leader, plays a critical part in putting the Jewish people back on the map of history, by enabling them to dwell in safety in their holy city during the coming centuries, until the Roman conquest. His actions also enable his contemporary, Ezra, to reintroduce the teachings of Moses to the people, and to lay the groundwork for the new religion of Israel.

CHRONICLES:
RECOUNTING PAST GLORY

Are the Chronicles a summary of the entire Bible?

The two Books of Chronicles, which conclude the biblical canon, begin with Adam and end with King Cyrus of Persia issuing an order to rebuild the Temple in Jerusalem. As such, they would appear to provide a summary of the entire Bible. But this is not exactly the case. The Chronicles focus on one subject: the Holy Temple in Jerusalem. Everything else is secondary. If the Bible is the biography of God, the Chronicles are a biography of God's house.

Who wrote the Chronicles?

The author of these two books is not mentioned here. The rabbis of the Talmud attributed the book to Ezra. Recent scholars dated it two hundred years later, in the third century B.C.E. It has been speculated that the author was a Levite who sought to preserve the history of the Temple and the various persons and households who served in the Temple, particularly the Levites.

All this remains in the realm of speculation. Regardless of who the author is, it is quite fitting that the last book of the Bible focuses on the Holy Temple. Biblical history is a long saga that culminates with the building of Solomon's Temple in Jerusalem. The destruction of the Temple by the Babylonians about 300 years later effectively ends the era of the Bible and marks the beginning of the new phase of Judaism which, notwithstanding the rebuilding of the Temple less than a century later, marks the beginning of the rise of the synagogue as the center of the Jewish religion.

Why do the Chronicles focus on the House of David?

The main narrative in both I and II Chronicles focuses on David and Solomon, and then primarily on those kings of the House of David who were righteous and followed God's law. The trend here is clear. The author seems to imply that God chose David and his descendants to establish the Temple, and indeed they built it and maintained it for as long as they could. When it was eventually destroyed, God did not forget the promise to Abraham and to David, and once the Babylonians, who destroyed the Temple, were defeated by the Persians, the exiled people of Judah were able to return to Jerusalem and rebuild the Temple.

What new light does the book shed on David's career?

Overall, the long narration of David's career matches the earlier biblical account. Emphasis, however, is placed here on David's great desire to build the Temple, and God's refusal to let a man of war build a temple of peace. The task, David is told, is left to his son. David, however, we are told here, gives Solomon, who is still a young boy, a blueprint of the Temple, and then begins to collect a great deal of gold and building materials for the future construction project. Thus, while David himself does not build the Temple, he certainly has a major part in the preparatory stages.

The other aspect of David's reign related to the Temple which is greatly emphasized in this book is the appointment of Levites and others as Temple officiants, musicians, singers, and so on. The impression one gets is that while David did not erect the actual physical structure of the Temple itself, he certainly had everything ready for both the construction work and for the services and rituals that were to take place in it once his son, Solomon, finished building it.

What do we learn here about Solomon?

Solomon is presented here as the wise ruler who achieves an era of peace, prosperity, and great power. But unlike his father, who was able to ensure a successor who would build the Temple and establish a time of peace and unity, Solomon is not able to secure the continued strength and unity of his kingdom after his death. What becomes clear here, although the author does not emphasize it, is that the splendor of Solomon's kingdom did not come without a price. The far provinces of the kingdom, especially in the central region and in the north, paid high taxes to fund Solomon's Temple, his palaces, horse stables, army, and navy. As soon as the great king died, the northern tribes of Israel broke away from the kingdom and established the separate Northern Kingdom of Israel.

Why did Solomon fail? The answer may be found in the Book of Deuteronomy, where Moses tells the people what the ideal king should do and not do. The two things Moses warns the future king not to do is have too many horses and too many wives. Solomon had both. Great and wise king that he was, he could not escape the trappings of royal greatness, namely, a show of force and splendor. In the end, his greatness was his undoing. Once again we are reminded that the Jews were not meant to be an imperial power, but rather "a kingdom of priests and a holy nation."

What role do the great prophets play in this book?

The great prophets who are the Bible's central characters during the entire period of the monarchy hardly appear in this book. Although we hear about King Saul, we do not hear about Samuel. While Ahab appears here, Elijah does not. Both Isaiah and Jeremiah are only mentioned in passing.

What may be the reason for this? Clearly, the author was not able not to mention the prophets at all, since they did play a central role during the time of the kings. But the emphasis of the book is not on God's spokespersons, but on the Temple and its functionaries.

Why do we have such long genealogies in Chronicles?

The question has, for the most part, been answered in the previous section (see p. 307).

Clearly, the purpose of the chronicler was to preserve the genealogy of those involved in the building and the services of the Holy Temple. The Bible, as we may recall, begins with genealogies related to the beginnings of the human race and of the Jewish people. Other genealogies appear throughout the Bible, whenever there is a census, as in the Book of Numbers, or an event which requires the mentioning of someone's ancestry. According to one rabbi in the Talmud, the genealogies are the most important part of the Bible, since they give us the names of real flesh and blood people, without whom there would have been no history.

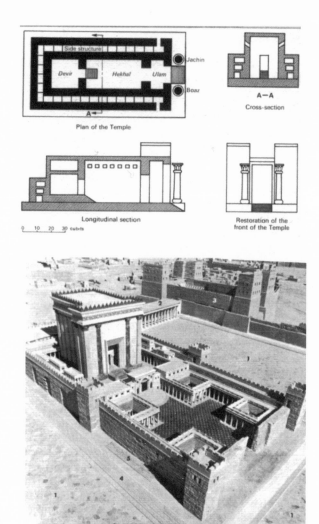

Above: Plan of First (Solomon's) Temple.
Below: Artist concept of Second Temple at
the time of King Herod.

CONCLUDING QUESTIONS

Do people see in the Bible what they choose to see?

It has been often said that one can find support in the Bible to almost anything. Indeed, much of biblical interpretation, or exegesis, is, in fact, eisegesis, or reading things into the text. To Jews, the key figure in the Bible is Moses. To Muslims, Abraham and his son Ishmael. To Christians, Abraham and David, who set the stage for Jesus. And so on.

When all is said and done, however, the Hebrew Bible is the first text in the history of the world that makes the One True Universal God known to the world. It is also the record of the covenant between God and Israel. Everything else is interpretation, be it exegetic or eisegetic.

Can we form an objective idea of God by reading the Bible?

An objective idea of God is a contradiction in terms. It is not given to mortals like ourselves to become acquainted with God as an objective reality, either by reading the Bible or in any other way. Although philosophers like Maimonides, or Nachmanides, or, more recently, Rosenzweig or Buber, have attempted to define God and God's attributes, people experience God on an emotional, rather than a rational level. One may talk about the "idea" of God, but one can only experience God in the realm of feelings rather than ideas. Exepriencing God is a purely personal event, ineffable, incommunicable.

Was the pagan world as evil as the Bible makes it out to be?

The Bible, particularly the biblical prophets, keeps talking about pagan abominations. It is made clear that the pagan religions of the biblical era were preceived by the biblical authors not only as false, but as downright evil. How objective is this view?

We know from general experience that there are always good people and bad people everywhere. Believing that the sun or the moon were deities did not automatically mean one did not treat others well. Witness Ruth the Moabite, perhaps the most unselfish woman in the entire Bible.

What people like the prophets found abominable was not the pagan world per se, but the fact that the descendants of Abraham who were centuries ahead of their contemporaries in their religious and ethical development, would, in the words of Jeremiah, give up the fountain of living water for the brackish water of paganism.

Is the Bible a blueprint for a future world of peace and justice?

If the whole world followed the ethical teachings of the Bible, peace and justice would reign throughout the world. The Bible is indeed a blueprint for such a world. But as we learn early on in the stories of creation, the human race is endowed with free will to do either good or evil. In over 10,000 years of human civilization (harkening back to ancient China, Egypt, Babylonia and so on), organized society is yet to come close to achieving a just and peaceful world. Whether such a world is possible, the future will tell.

Can one benefit from studying the Bible without believing in God?

One does not have to believe in God to benefit from reading and studying the Bible. To begin with, the Bible is great literature, if not the greatest. Its object lessons about life are second to none. One can find comfort and inspiration in the Book of Psalms regardless of what one believes or disbelieves. To many Jews who do not consider themselves believers, the Bible is their national history, literature, language, and collective wisdom.

The ancient Mediterranean world produced two great cultures—The Hebraic and the Hellenistic. Both have shaped our present world. No one can call her or himself a cultured person without a good knowledge of both. The only difference between the two, however, is that no one today believes any longer in Zeus, not even the Greeks, while many millions believe in the God of the Bible (including the Greeks).

Is the phrase "God helps those who help themselves" confirmed by the Bible?

The Bible makes it perfectly clear from the moment the first human couple is created to the moment Ezra and Nehemiah return from the Babylonian Exile that God helps those who help themselves. After Eve is led astray by the snake and, in turn, leads Adam astray, the first human couple is punished for failing to follow the path set for it and letting itself be seduced by someone who does not have their best interest in mind.

Thereafter, human actions continue to determine whether one is given a helping hand from above, so to speak, or not. Nowhere is it made clearer than in Deuteronomy 30:

> Behold, I give you today
> life and good and death and evil. . .
> Therefore, choose life.

Did the Jews, according to the Bible, become "a light unto the nations"?

Looking back on biblical history, it is hard to make a case for the Jews of that time becoming a "light unto the nations," as they were expected to become (Isaiah 42:6). Most of the time, they anger God. In the end, they are destroyed, and when they are forgiven and allowed to go back to the Promised Land, their days of glory are long gone. What's more, the nations at the time of the end of the biblical period do not seem to be any more enlightened than they were in the beginning.

Golda Meir used to say: "People say we Jews are smart. How can we be smart if we picked the only country in the Middle East that does not have oil?"

So what are we to make of all this? Perhaps this: While the

Jews themselves may not have become a "light unto the nations," their story, namely, the Bible, did. If there is one book in this world that can be called "a light unto the nations," it is certainly the Bible.

Did the Jews preserve the Bible, or did the Bible preserve the Jews?

The Bible was preserved as much by non-Jews as by the Jews. To this day, Jewish biblical scholars need to consult non-Jewish versions of the Bible, such as the Greek Septuagint, or the Latin Vulgate, or the Aramaic Onkelos, to shed light on difficult biblical words and texts. Furthermore, the Jewish Bible excluded some important Jewish books such as the Books of Maccabees, which contain important Jewish history. Here Jews must thank the Church for preserving those and other Jewish books of the biblical era.

Conversely, it would be fair to say that the Bible preserved the Jews. Without the Bible, Jews scattered all over the world for many centuries would have lost their common bond. Without the Bible, modern Jewish culture and literature would not exist. Without the Bible, Jews would lose their identity. Without the Bible, the Hebrew language would not exist. In the Declaration of Independence of the State of Israel, the Bible is mentioned as the Jews' most important contribution to humankind. It is also the most important contribution the Jews made to themselves.

Is the Bible strictly a Jewish book?

No. Not any more than God is strictly a Jewish God. The message of the Bible is the brotherhood and sisterhood of all men and women under the parenthood of God. God did not take the Hebrew slaves out of Egypt, gave them the Law, and brought them to the Promised Land for their own personal gain and well-being. Rather, God made an example of the Jews. God made godliness known to humankind through the story told in the Bible. Without that story, humankind would still be worshiping idols.

Does the Bible still hold any secrets?

The Bible still holds many secrets. The greatest secret is who is God. This is beyond human comprehension. The next greatest secret is universal justice, and how does it work. Here we may have some insights, but not enough. We can continue with the meaning of life, the soul, the historicity of biblical events and personalities, and much more. No book can exhaust the questions raised by the Bible, let alone provide all the answers. One can only try.

BIBLIOGRAPHY

Primary sources

Tanakh (Jerusalem: Koren, 1996). The official Hebrew Bible of the State of Israel.

Mikraot gedolot [*Tanakh* with commentaries, including Rashi, Ibn Ezra, RASHBAM, RAMBAN, Sforno and others, as well as the Onkelos Aramaic translation] (Tel Aviv: Schocken, 1959). Includes the greatest traditional Jewish commentators of the Bible.

The Soncino Books of the Bible (London: The Soncino Press,1979). Hebrew text with the King James (1611) English translation and commentaries in English culled from the great traditional Jewish commentators as well as Christian commentators.

The Holy Scriptures (Philadelphia: Jewish Publication Society, 1955). For many years, the English version commonly used by American Jewry, basically following the text of the King James (1611).

The Holy Scriptures, A new translation of (Philadelphia: Jewish Publication Society, 1982). The modernized American-English translation of the Bible.

The Torah, Plaut, W. Gunther, Editor (New York: UAHC, 1981). The Pentateuch commentary of Reform Judaism.

320

The Holy Bible, Containing the Old and New Testaments Translated out of the Original Tongues and with the former Translations diligently compared and revised by His Majesty's special Command, A.D. 1611 (London: Cambridge University Press, 1958). Still the best English translation of the Bible.

The Jerusalem Bible, Jones, Alexander, General Editor (New York: Doubleday, 1966). New Catholic translation of the Bible.

The Koran, Dawood, N. J., Translator (New York: Penguin, 1990).

Concordance for the Bible, Mandelkern, Solomon, Editor Jerusalem: Schocken, 1969). A perfect tool for finding any word in the Hebrew Bible.

Mishnayoth, Blackman, Philip, Editor (New York: Judaica Press, 1964). The original Hebrew text of the first major work of the Jewish Oral Law, with annotated English translation.

Talmud bavli (Jerusalem: Torah La'am, 1961). The traditional text of the Babylonian Talmud with all the commentators.

Talmud Yerushalmi (New York: Otzar Sefarim, 1968). The traditional text of the Palestinian Talmud with commentators.

The Zohar, Sperling, Harry and Simon, Maurice, Translators (London: The Soncino Press, 1970). The main work of Jewish mysticism in English translation.

Mishnat ha'zohar [The Wisdom of the Zohar], Lachover, F. and Thisby, I., Translators and Editors (Jerusalem: Mosad Bialik, 1957). A thematic approach to the Zohar in Hebrew.

Midrash Rabba, Halevi, A. A., Editor (Tel Aviv: Machbaroth lesifrut, 1956). The main Midrashic (Jewish legends and lore) work.

Sefer Ha'agadah, Bialik, Ch. N. and Ravnitzky, Y. Ch., Editors

(Tel Aviv: Devir, 1960). Thematic compendium of Midrash and Talmudic Aggadah.

Sefer Yalkut sipurim, Grinwald, Zeev, Editor (Jerusalem: Eshkol, no date). An extensive Midrashic compendium.

Mishneh Torah, Maimonides, Moses (Mosad Ha'rav Kook, 1957). The great medieval exposition of Jewish law.

Secondary sources

Albright, William F., *The Archeology of Palestine* (Baltimore, MD: Penguin, 1960). The seminal by the father of biblical archeology.

Bezalel, Bar-Kokhba, *Tanakh* (Tel Aviv: Otpaz, 1970).Contemporary Israeli commentary.

Blank, Sheldon, *Prophetic Faith in Isaiah* (New York: Harper & Brothers, 1958).
— *Understanding the Prophets* (New York: UAHC Press, 1969).

Driver, S. R., *An Introduction to the Literature of the Old Testament* (New York: Meridian Books, 1960). A book-by-book analysis by a leading English scholar.

Eldad, Israel, *Hegionot mikrah* (Jerusalem: Carta, 1972). A cultural Zionist commentary on the Torah.

Glueck, Nelson, *The River Jordan* (New York: McGraw-Hill, 1968). The history of "the most storied river in the world" by a biblical archeologist who explored the area.

Herzog, Chaim, and Gichon, Mordechai, *Battles of the Bible* (New York: Random House, 1978). An illustrated analysis of biblical wars.

Heschel, Abraham Joshua, *The Prophets* (New York: Harper-Collins, 1977). An eloquent book on biblical prophecy.

Kaufmann, Yehezkel, *Toldot ha'emunah ha'yisreelit* [The Religion of Israel] (Tel Aviv: Mosad Bialik, 1967). A major work on many aspects of biblical events, concepts, and personalities.

Keller, Werner, *The Bible as History* (New York: Morrow, 1990). Shows how archeology and the new biblical scholarship have corroborated much of the biblical account.

Leibowitz, Nehama, *Studies in Genesis, Studies in Exodus* (Jerusalem: World Zionist Organization, 1978). A highly perceptive contemporary Bible commentary.

Orlinsky, Harry M., *Ancient Israel* (Ithaca: Cornell University Press, 1973). A short lucid history of the biblical period.
—*Understanding the Bible through History and Archeology* (New York: Ktav, 1972). An illustrated version of *Ancient Israel.*
— *Essays in Biblical Culture and Bible Translation* (New York: Ktav, 1974). Insights from the chief editor of the New Bible Translation.

Pfeiffer, Robert H., *Introduction to the Old Testament* (New York: Harper & Row, 1948). A comprehensive analysis of the Hebrew Bible by a leading American scholar.

Sandmel, Samuel, *The Enjoyment of Scripture* (New York: Oxford University Press, 1972). The Bible as literature.

Shalev, Meir, *Tanakh achshav* (Tel Aviv: Schocken, 1985). An attempt by a leading Israeli novelist and humorist to tell key Bible stories in a contemporary vein.

Weber, Max, *Ancient Judaism* (New York: The Free Press, 1990). Social and culture study of biblical Judaism.

Yadin, Yigael, *Hazor* (New York: Random House, 1975).One of the major discoveries of Israel's leading archeologist.

Index